JEWISH SITES AND SYNAGOGUES OF GREECE

Jewish Sites and Synagogues of Greece

Nicholas P. Stavroulakis

Timothy J. DeVinney

Talos Press
Athens

Research for this book was supported by a grant from the Memorial Foundation for Jewish Culture, New York.

Published in Greece by Talos Press
10 Kifisias Ave.
GR-115 26 Athens
Greece

Typeset by Fotron S.A.

Cover photo: The *tevah* of the Scuola Greca Synagogue, Corfu 17th century (Photo: Timothy DeVinney/Jewish Museum of Greece)

ISBN 960-7459-01-6

To Ari Joshua Sherman

Contents

Preface

This guide is designed to fill an egregious gap in the information available to visitors to Greece. Until now, visitors have found themselves awash with information on classical, Roman, and Byzantine aspects of Greek history, but with no ready means to learn about the part played by Jews, Muslims, Catholics, Vlachs, and others. Salonika, for example, was virtually a Jewish city for four hundred years with as many as 32 synagogues, and yet several of the most popular guides to Greece do not even mention that fact, nor do they list the one remaining synagogue still there to be seen. It is hoped that this guide will help begin to fill that gap.

In 1979, not long after the founding of the Jewish Museum of Greece, the staff of the museum began work on photographing and documenting the Jewish sites of Greece. This was understood to be the beginning of an ongoing project, possibly extending far into the future, and we were fortunate from the onset to have the support and financial assistance of the Memorial Foundation for Jewish Culture in New York. Not long after that, Mr. Morrie Camhi came to Greece from the U.S. to begin a personal journey through its Jewries, photographing survivors and whatever active or lingering communities remained. In helping to facilitate his visit, the staff found an opportunity to extend that survey into areas that had not been covered before.

This book would not have been possible without the time and assistance of many people over the years. We wish in particular to thank the representatives and members of the Jewish communities in Athens, Halkis, Corfu, Ioannina, Larissa, Trikkala, Rhodes, and Volos. We are especially grateful for the generous assistance of the following individuals: the late Mr. Isaac Ashkenazi (Didimoticho), Mr. Elias Atoun (Trikkala), Mr. Solomon Behar (Didimoticho), Ms. Victoria Benouziglio (Salonika), Mr. Raphael Frizis (Volos), Mr. Elias Kone (Volos), Mr. Marios Maisis (Halkis), the late Mr. Joseph Matsas (Ioannina), Mr. Jacito Pardo (Salonika), the late Mr. Moise Pesah (Kavala), Mr. Ovadias Sabas (Trikkala), Mr. Maurice Sorianos (Rhodes), and Mrs. Lucia Sulam (Rhodes). We owe special thanks as well to the Central Board of Jewish Communities in Greece.

Thanks to fax we were able to make immediate demands for sources, references and help in finding material that unfortunately does not exist in the libraries of Greece. We especially owe thanks to Prof. Steven Bowman (Cincinnati), Ms. Judith Humphreys (Cambridge), Mrs. Leyla Ipeker (Istanbul), Mr. Abraham Kremer (New York), Mr. Sinan Kuneralp (Istanbul), Mr. Michel Menache (Kos), Mr. Albertos Nar (Thessaloniki), and Prof. Stanford Shaw (Los Angeles).

The work of pulling the final version into order was made possible with the help of docents and staff of the museum:Mrs Victoria Benouziglio, Mr Michael Donnally, Mr Constantinos Gofas, Mrs Maria Issachar, Mrs Annetta Levy, Mr Avi Sharon, and Mrs Jacqueline Simha. We would also like to thank Mr John Chapple of Athens for his help with editorial corrections.

It is hoped that in the future this work will perhaps come out in revised, up–dated and even expanded editions. Criticisms, suggestions, and comments from readers are essential and welcome.

All of this work would perhaps have been delayed indefinitely had it not been for two generous grants from Mr. Joshua Sherman in New York, Mr. Gilbert de Botton in London, and the Rich Foundation in Paris.

Notes on Using This Guide.

1. Total population figures for cities and towns, are from the 1991 Greek census (where available). The Jewish population figures are from the communities themselves. These were not always entirely consistent: sometimes the administrators of a community would give different figures at different times. We've done our best to arrive at a reliable approximation.

Until recently, all Greeks were required to register with a particular religious authority for purposes of birth, marriage, and burial. Thus Jews were automatically "members" of their local Jewish community. This is in contrast to the practice in Europe and the U.S., where membership in a synagogue is voluntary.

2. Distances given in the guide refer to road distances, not line–of–sight, and thus should give a fairly good indication of the times needed to go from one city or town to another.

3. Visitors to sites should be aware that getting someone from the local community to open a synagogue or cemetery will probably involve their closing their shop or leaving their office to do so. Naturally, this is not always possible. Some communities are notoriously unobliging to visitors for basically this reason. Others may have a retired gentleman available who is only too glad to show visitors around. It's best to check with the community. In the guide we've tried to give some indication of which communities are more accessible than others.

4. Regarding directions on reaching a site: some sites are very difficult to find or get to (especially by car), so a detailed verbal description has been offered here. For other sites, the city map should be enough to direct the visitor. It should be kept in mind that some one–way streets, for example, seem to change frequently, and, of course, construction projects may alter the landscape before the visitor arrives.

5. With regard to tipping, it's not normally the practice to tip the person who shows you a site, but some employees or caretakers may make it obvious that a *pour boire* is expected. In general, however, it's more appropriate to make a donation toward the upkeep of the site you have visited. There is often a box or bottle for this purpose, and a small donation will be deeply appreciated by the person who may have given up the better part of a morning to make your visit possible.

6. A note on telephone numbers given in the guide: for long–distance calls within Greece, the area code is preceded by a "0." The area code itself may be one, two, or three digits (for example, Athens is "1", Salonika is "31", and Hania is "821"). Naturally, if you are calling from inside the town itself, only the actual number is needed.

7. Hours given for access to sites: these change all of the time, so it's best to check with the local community or local tourist office (for archeological sites) before you go. Even then, be prepared for surprises: often central authorities will stipulate opening hours for which there is no staff available and which cannot therefore be realized in practice. Also, strikes are very common in Greece, and frequently disrupt normal routines.

8. Kosher food. In general, there are no kosher restaurants in Greece. There is a vegetarian restaurant in Athens in the Plaka. Long–term residents can purchase kosher meat through the local communities in Athens, Salonika, and Larissa.

Historical Introduction

The field of medieval and modern studies on Greek Jews is a comparatively new one. The shared interest in ancient and Hellenistic Judaism on the part of both Christian and Jewish scholars needs no explanation. After all, both Christianity and Rabbinical Judaism were born in the same Hellenistic–Roman world. It is only in recent years, however, that attention has been focused as well on the Jews of Greece as a living link between modern times and antiquity, a study that centers on the Greek–speaking, Hellenized Jewries that Strabo described in the 1st century B.C.E. as present in all of the cities of the Roman Empire. Not to be forgotten, however, is another Jewish presence in Greece with its own quite distinct culture and language: the Sephardi Jews, who arrived much later, in the 15th century. The overall history of the Jews of Greece from the late Middle Ages to modern times is largely the study, then, of the interaction and occasional collision of these two culturally and linguistically distinct traditions within the context of Greek history.

Modern Greece has emerged and evolved out of a very complicated past, which is far too often simplified and presented against the almost theatrical backdrop of the Acropolis and Parthenon. Between the 5th century B.C.E. and 1834, when Athens was made the capital of the modern Greek state, enormous if not horrendous changes occurred that marked the passage from antiquity into medieval and modern Greek history. Inter–urban wars, invasions, conquests, pirate attacks, not to mention natural catastrophes, brought about demographic as well as significant geopolitical changes. It is far too often overlooked that the idea of Greece as a single, unified entity, while not at all modern (it was certainly in the mind of Philip of Macedon) was, nonetheless, never achieved until after the early 19th century. From the 5th century B.C.E. to that time, at least four empires considered Greece an important part of a much larger whole. Throughout that entire period, Jews lived, flourished, declined, re–located, and adapted to a variety of new economic factors and life–styles.

Reliable evidence of a Jewish link with Greece begins during the period immediately following the conquest of Alexander the Great

(356-323 B.C.E.). When Alexander died, he left behind a world changed forever. His brief passage through life marked the end of classical Greece. The boundaries of the narrow world of the city–state had been broken, and a seemingly endless horizon encompassed peoples, cultures, religions, and civilizations that had hitherto only had occasional or remote contacts. It was an exciting, insecure, creative world, and under his successors in Greece, Syria, and Egypt (the last being Cleopatra VII), this fusion of peoples, cultures, and religions resulted in what we call today the Hellenistic world. The crucibles in which this fusion took place were the many cities—all modeled on the constitution of Athens and for which the archetype was Alexandria—founded by the conqueror and embellished by his successors. These Hellenistic cities—from Greece as far east as India—shared a common language (Greek), institutions, schooling and a world view that was virtually universal in its appeal and attraction.

It was in this urban context that Jews and Greeks first encountered each other as two peoples with their own distinct life–styles, literatures, religions, and ideals. Greek values proved to be highly seductive and in Alexandria—where an enormous Jewish community had quickly taken up residence in the new city—we know that it was not long before Hebrew and Aramaic were lost to the Jews entirely. This fusion of cultures produced the Septuagint Scriptures (a Greek translation of the Hebrew Old Testament) and, later, the great Jewish Platonist, Philo, who created the philosophical language through which both Judaism and early Christianity were in a position to make their teachings intelligible to a world that was not Jewish–oriented.

This meeting of Greek and Jew, however, also created problems, beginning with the Macchabean revolt against Hellenizers in Jerusalem, and, later, the constant and troublesome conflicts between Greeks and Jews in cities such as Antioch, Damascus, and others in Asia Minor. By the 1st century B.C.E., Jews were well–settled in mainland Greek cities such as Athens, Corinth, (Salonika), Thessaloniki, Sparta, as well as on the islands of Crete, Rhodes, and Delos. These Diaspora Jewish communities not only attracted Paul of Tarsus, but either gave him hospitality or rejected him.

During the centuries that followed, Rome came to control the Mediteranean and inherited the ideals of Alexander. Under the early Republic (6th century B.C.E.), the villages that constituted "Rome" consolidated and began a period of expansion and conquest that by 270 B.C.E. was realized in subjection of the entire Italian peninsula. Rome had become not only a formidable power but was also put directly in contact with the Greeks in Sicily from whom they inherited the latter's conflict with Carthage. By 146 this violent conflict ended with the destruction of Carthage and, simultaneously, with the absorption of much of Greece. In that very same year, Macedon was annexed to the Roman conquest and Corinth was destroyed. Not long after Rome was willed the kingdom of Pergamon on the Aegean coast of Asia Minor and, after a series of wars in Anatolia and Syro—Palestine, she absorbed Egypt on the death of the last successor of Alexander, Cleopatra in 30 B.C.E.. What is most remarkable about this great world conquest was the fact that Rome was undergoing civil war during most of it and what undoubtedly held the state together was the still quite austere and simple Roman character that had not yet been undermined by urbanism. The Roman was always and ever was to be, a farmer at heart.

The conquest of the world, as it was known to Mediteraneans then, meant the absorption of the inheritance of Alexander the Great as well. Roman imperialism made a fact of what may have been for several centuries only theory. With the coming into power of the Roman Empire, there was one state and one emperor embracing the old Hellenistic cities. The Roman search for unity meant that Greek communities which had found their horizons vastly expanded under Alexander now found their individualism subject to further pressure from a universal authority. The equally individualistic Jews lost Jerusalem in 71 C.E., and by the early part of the 2nd century were forced out into the Roman world at large. Many, if not most, took refuge in the cities of Greece, Syria, Anatolia, North Africa, Spain, and the rest of Europe.

During the first three centuries of the Common Era, both Judaism and Christianity had developed side by side, sharing a common scripture and, to a certain degree, Greek as a common language of thought. New translations of the Scriptures into Greek were made by

Jews, the most famous being that of Aquila, a Greek convert to Judaism. The two sister religions were both quite zealous in proselytizing and, as Christians defined themselves increasingly in Greek modes of thought, the Jews began to distance themselves, and withdrawing further and further into conservativism and their hope of a restoration. Occasionally there was still dialogue: the famous meeting of Justin Martyr and the gentlemanly Jew, Tryphon, in the agora of Antioch may not have been an isolated incident—though such contacts were most likely the exception rather than the rule.

As Hellenized Jews and Judaized–Hellenes (which in fact is what most Christians were) met in intellectual combat, the empire was engaged in its own search for a unified identity. By the 4th century this was achieved to some extent, but only momentarily, before the entire Roman Empire fragmented. In 325, the emperor Constantine the Great indicated his personal favor and Roman approval of Christianity, by calling the Council of Nicaea. All of the bishops of the Roman world were called upon to attend. The purpose of this council was to create a common creed agreeable to all. Not long after, in 331, a new capital for the Roman Empire was re–dedicated on the site of the ancient Greek city of Byzantium. By the end of the century, Christianity had been formally proclaimed the religion of the Roman state and paganism outlawed. The Jews of the empire assumed a rather strange role: on the one hand, they bore witness to the rejection of the Messiah, whose vicar on earth was now defined as the Roman emperor himself, God's reflection on earth; but, on the other hand, the very truth of Christianity rested on God's promises to the Jews. The Jew by his existence was in a sense the very embodiment of God's fidelity to those who follow the Law. At the same time, he was an arch–renegade. As a result of this ambiguous position in Byzantine eyes, the Jews of Byzantium, in contrast to Jews in later western European society, only rarely experienced severe persecution, though one wonders if this would have continued had the empire lasted beyond the 15th century.

Toward the end of the 4th century, the Visigoths, after killing the emperor Valens at the Battle of Adrianople, made their way through Greece, pillaging, and burning. Athens may have been pillaged, Corinth certainly was, and Sparta was totally destroyed. As the

Visigoths terminated the existence of many Greek cities, other Germanic peoples in the West—the Vandals, Franks, Saxons, Burgundians, and others—broke up the unity of the European half of the empire. By 450 the Roman Empire had been reduced to the lower Italian peninsula, Greece proper, Anatolia, Syro– Palestine, and Egypt. Most of these areas were still predominantly Greek–speaking and the Jews of these regions were well–connected amongst themselves by ties of tradition. Constantinople, or "Byzantium" as it was still occasionally referred to, was the capital of this truncated Roman world.

In the early 6th century, the emperor Justinian the Great made an attempt to revive the glories of the Roman Empire. He was only momentarily successful. One of his great tasks was that of codifying Roman Law and modifying it according to Christian ethics and morality. He took a particular interest in the Jews. His peculiar law requiring that Jews read their scriptures in Greek (in the Septuagint, in other words) became a tradition jealously maintained among the Romaniotes (the Greco–Roman Jews) long afterwards.

Late in the 6th century, a new series of invasions began that were to define the nature of the East Roman (or, at this point, more properly called, the Byzantine) Empire until the 9th century. The first invaders were the Slavs, who poured into the very heart of the Peloponnese. They were followed by Avars, Alans, and Bulgars in succession. In the middle of the 7th century, the Islamic invasion began out of Arabia, which by 750 was to completely eclipse Roman–Byzantine power in Syria, Palestine, Egypt, and North Africa. It was not until the late 10th century that the Byzantines responded successfully to this series of invasions, and began a recovery. But even at its greatest extent the empire was reduced to Greece, Anatolia, and Crete, the last only recently re–taken from the Andalusian Moors.

Unfortunately, we know little of the Byzantine (Romaniote) Jews during this period, other than that they continued to inhabit cities of the Empire like Corinth, Thebes, Thessaloniki (Salonika), and Halkis, and were certainly found in good numbers on Crete and perhaps on the islands of the Aegean Sea. Greek–speaking, reliant on the Palestinian Talmud, and already quite distinct and proud of their "Greekness," the Romaniotes lived in a certain isolation, with little if any contact with the Jewries of either Europe or the Near East. That they were in some cases affluent and of considerable economic importance can be seen by the famous raid of George of Antioch into Thebes in 1147, in which, besides looting its warehouses of silk, he also took off large numbers of its Jewish silk workers to introduce silk production into his own kingdom.

Some twenty years later we have our first picture of Jewish life in Greece, through the eyes of a Spanish gem merchant named Benjamin of Tudela. After leaving Otranto, Italy, Benjamin made his way through Greece, up to Constantinople and then along the islands of the Aegean coast before going on to the Holy Land. His observations on the Jewish communities he visited are rather terse, and usually limited to the number of Jews as well as the rabbinical leadership of the communities through which he passed. Occasionally he gives us hints of great wealth and security, as in Thebes. In the case of the Jews of the capital, Constantinople, we are told they bore great humiliations, but apparently did so with patience and pride.

A little over a century later, in 1204, the Byzantine Empire fell to the infamous Fourth Crusade led by the Venetians. After establishing a Latin emperor on the throne, a kingdom was proclaimed at (Salonika) Thessaloniki, and then the Crusaders made their way through Greece, conquering and parceling out fiefs to their leaders in the medieval Frankish manner. Jews apparently did not fare well during this period and several Jewish communities certainly ceased to exist when their members fled elsewhere. The Venetians soon extended their maritime empire by acquiring the island of Crete (with its quite numerous Jewish presence) and the main ports of the Aegean and Ionian Islands. For Jews this meant that many communities were now cut off from each other.

In 1261 Constantinople was retaken by the Byzantines under Michael VIII Palaeologos. Aggressive action was also taken to regain the Peloponnese and other regions held by the Crusaders and Venetians. Michael himself was quite favorable to Jews and it appears that he settled new communities to revive trade.

At the same time, however, to the east in Anatolia, a Turkish tribe was consolidating under its leader Ertogrul, and incorporating other wandering Turkish clans that had survived the break–up of the Seljuq Turkish Sultanate of Rum when it was destroyed by the Mongols. By the early 14th century, the son of Ertogrul, Osman, had seized the Byzantine city of Prusa and established his claim to the sultanate. He became the founder of the Osmanli (or Ottoman) Turkish Dynasty. The last years of the 14th century and early 15th century saw the entrance of the Ottomans into Thrace and their seizure of Constantinople under Mehmet II in 1453. By 1459 almost all of the ancient Byzantine territories in Greece had fallen to the House of Osman.

One of Mehmet's first acts was to revitalize Constantinople, a city that had once had over 1,000,000 inhabitants but had been reduced on the eve of the conquest to some 20,000. From Turkish registers we know that large numbers of Jews were brought from cities such as Thessaloniki, Lamia, and Komotini to settle in abandoned quarters of the capital. Mehmet also attempted to create a centralized Jewish authority by formalizing the Jewish *millet* under a proper "head." According to Ottoman Islamic Law, a *millet* is an officially recognized legal body defined by religous affiliation. Jews and Christians, as People of the Book (having, in other words, received God's revelation) had the right to a *millet*, which guaranteed them the privilege of living under their own law and administration, as well as the obligation to collect and deliver taxes to the proper authorities. The Byzantine Christians were given a similar *millet* status and the Patriarch of Constantinople, Gennadios, was made its leader. The Jews had not had even a semblance of centralized authority since the abolition of the Patriarchate of Gamaliel in the early 5th century by the emperor Theodosios II. It appears that for a short period of time the Jews were placed within the newly made Armenian *millet* until they were given their own. Their first leader was the Cretan rabbi, Moses Kapsalis, who was given the title *hahambaşi* (chief rabbi).

His new position must have been a nightmare for Capsalis. Jews had always been accustomed to a great amount of communal flexibility and the concept of a central rabbinical authority was unknown to them. Added to this was the fact that Jews of a quite "foreign" caste had begun to enter the Ottoman Empire, including immigrants from Hungary, Sicily, Apuleia, and even Provence.

Among European Christians, Jews had for centuries been considered a part of the Christian Church—insofar as they lived according to the Promise and the Law. During that period, the Church was, in a sense, the protector of the Jews —until the fatal discovery in the 13th century that Jews lived the Law through its interpretation by rabbis in the Talmud. At that point the Jews came to be seen as having renounced not only the Messiah, but also the Law of Moses, in favor of the Talmud. Since Christians knew nothing of the Talmud's subtleties, nor of its formation (at times it was even mistakingly thought that *Talmud* referred to a person), Jews were then considered to be heretics and any excuse was used to harass them. The Ottomans were not interested in these theological fine points, and the Jews found a ready refuge in their empire.

In Constantinople there were serious disagreements over practices and traditions even among the Romaniote Jews who had been settled in the city from various parts of the empire. The European Jews brought even further differences. Their rituals, Talmudic usages, and the variety of languages they spoke, caused considerable misunderstanding and friction with the broader Jewish community.

Matters became acute when, after 1492, great numbers of Jews from Spain (perhaps as many as 200,000) began to enter the Ottoman Empire and were given a privileged position. Unlike the Romaniote Jews who had been part of the now conquered Roman Empire, the Spanish Jews (or Sepharadim) were arriving by choice and were allowed to settle with considerable autonomy. Undoubtedly, the great majority of them had been well integrated into Spanish Renaissance life. Still others had been Christians (as Marranos) for a period of time. Most were skilled in professions that made them formidable competitors. All of them spoke either Spanish or Portuguese and had little inclination to learn Greek or to show patience with what appeared to them as less than medieval, Romaniote Jewish practices and customs. It was not long before Romaniote patience and initial hospitality wore thin and minor annoyances became open antagonisms.

For the hahambaşi (chief rabbinate) in Constantinople, settling differences between Romaniotes over differences in custom had been difficult enough. With the Sepharadim, the matter was more complex and involved not only language and minhag (rite) but even two different Talmuds. By 1517, the office of hahambaşli had been abolished, and it was not until late in the 19th century and the last years of the Ottoman Empire that it was re–established, by which time the problems that had prompted the abolition had ceased to exist.

Despite these inner crises, Jewish fortunes in the Ottoman Empire rose, and even the Romaniotes eventually gave in and became "Hispanicized," adopting Castillian Spanish as their language and the ritual of the Sepharadim. The reverse occasionally took place, where the predominant element in a commmunity was Romaniote, but for the most part —imperceptibly in many cases and prompted by the introduction of printing—the Sephardi element came to predominate. A virtually Jewish city evolved in Salonika and there is evidence that even there, among the Sepharadim themselves, there were difficulties in coming to terms with each other. Some 30 congregations were eventually established, each with their own synagogue, and most bearing the names of the regions, or even towns, from which their members had originated.

In the early 17th century, the fortunes of the Ottomans tilted and the empire began the long decline that was to see its demise in the early 20th century. Wars with Venice saw the Jews caught in a vice—especially in the Peloponnese as well as in Crete which fell in 1669. The appearance at roughly the same time of Shabbetai Zvi, a charismatic rabbi from Izmir of a Hungarian–Patran family, who was proclaimed to be the Messiah, shook the entire Jewish world as far as Amsterdam and India. Communities split in discord over whether to reject or accept the claims put forward for Shabbetai Zvi. After his conversion to Islam, many of his followers also converted. These *Donme*, as they were called, became an exclusive and mysterious presence in Salonika. The response of the Jews in Greece and the Near East was to become entrenched in a kind of conservative orthodoxy, though tarnished through shame.

Relations between Christians and Jews also began to disintegrate. They never had had much to do with each other, but the *millet* system of the Ottomans—which equated Jews with Christians—was a pill that Orthodox Christians refused to swallow. As central authority in Constantinople faltered and local government became weaker through the interference of the *yeniçeris* (conscript troops), Jews occasionally suffered from severe antagonisms, even local Chrisitan violence. It was only natural that Jews would turn wherever possible to the Ottoman authorities for protection, which in many cases was given by permitting Jews to live within the fortifications of the Ottoman towns or cities where they were resident.

In 1821 a revolt broke out in the lower Peloponnese that very quickly saw Christian Greeks and Albanians unite against the Ottomans. Within a year, despite the initial reluctance of the patriarch in Constantinople and the quite wealthy Greeks of the city, the revolt became the Greek War of Independence. A long drawn–out conflict ensued, resulting ultimately in the creation of the modern Greek state in 1832 as a monarchy under the auspices of the European powers. The new state was a far cry from that envisaged by many Greeks. It was confined to the Peloponnese, the peninsula of Attica, and the island of Euboea. Many Greek communities remained outside its territory in cities that traced their roots to Greek antiquity. Thus it is understandable that the Greeks were not satisfied with the initial boundaries of their country, and the scene was set for the adjustments and conflicts of the 19th and early 20th centuries.

By the middle of the 19th century, the Ionian Islands had been ceded to Greece by Britain (who had taken them from Venice). By the end of the century, Thessaly had been annexed. Then, after two Balkan Wars, Epirus, Macedonia, and Crete became part of Greece, to be followed by Thrace. After the First World War, an attempt was even made to seize a sizeable portion of Anatolia.

Throughout this period, the Jews were completely at the mercy of circumstances beyond their control and in which they could not participate. Many chose to emigrate. Still others adjusted their lives as much as they could under the new conditions. By 1940 there were signs that Jews were beginning to take an active and significant role in Greek society as co–citizens and highly respected members of the professions. It is estimated that at the outbreak of the Second World War there were some 80,000 Jews in Greece, most concentrated in Salonika, with some 3,000 in Athens.

When the war broke out, Jews served valiantly in the army, but on Axis conquest and division of Greece between Germany, Italy, and Bulgaria, they found themselves once again cut off from one another. The Nazis almost immediately put into effect the machinery of the Final Solution, at the same time putting pressure on both the Bulgarians and the Italians to follow suit. Neither really had any stomach for the racism of the Germans, though the Bulgarians used it to their own ends in an attempt to "Bulgarize" their zone of occupation—Thrace. The Italians did nothing. By August of 1943, over 70,000 Jews had been sent to Polish extermination camps, and after the capitulation of the Italians to the Allies in October of 1943, the Germans began the further arrests that were to destroy communities in Crete, Rhodes, and elsewhere. Today, some 40 years after these horrendous events, the Jews of Greece number approximately 5,000, the majority being in Athens.

A journey through Jewish Greece today can thus be nostalgic, evocative, sad, and exciting. Each community has its own history, and making contact with its members is at times like reaching across the centuries, if not into other lands. Somewhere in the agora of Corinth, Paul of Tarsus argued with the Corinthian Jews, and in Athens he spoke not only with the Jewish community in its synagogue but with the city's archons on the Areopagos. Salonika, as late as 1920, was still a city in which Castillian Spanish was more often heard than Greek, and on Friday evenings the central portion of the old city would grow mysteriously quiet in preparation for Shabbat. Names like as Kalonymos, Abulafia, Alhadeff, Delmedigo, Abravanel, Castro, Constanini, Tarabulus, and Sevillia give some idea of the rich cross-cultural mixture that characterizes the Jews of contemporary Greece. But in many towns there is hardly any evidence at all of the passage of the Jews, as is the case in Thebes, Patras, and Serres. In others, the ruins of a quarter, a synagogue, or a school are all that remain, but even these can evoke images of Jewish life in Greece as it was lived for centuries.

The Synagogues of Greece

A complete, systematic study of the synagogues of Greece may never be possible due to the loss of ancient and medieval examples.

Many of them have been destroyed by fire, as was the case in Salonika in 1917, when over 30 synagogues were burned in the fire that raged through the heart of the city. Other synagogues were destroyed during the Second World War. The most ancient may well still lie buried somewhere in an archeological site that has still to be excavated. The following notes are intended to put what does remain of the synagogues of Greece into some comprehensive pattern.

The most ancient synagogue in Greece is on the island of Delos. It is in fact the oldest synagogue known in the Diaspora, and the oldest of a number of contemporary synagogues throughout the Hellenistic world—including those at Ostia (in Italy), at Miletus, Sardes, and Pirene (in Western Turkey), and others further east in Syria at Dura Europos and, of course, in Israel itself—which all share one common characteristic: while they were synagogues in function there is nothing in their architectural form that marks them off from other buildings. Often they are strongly influenced by local architecture. (This is true as well for the late Roman and early Byzantine synagogues on Aegina and in the Athenian agora, even though these are of a much later date.)

This is not as surprising as it might seem when one considers that the Jewish liturgy during these centuries was still quite fluid and in the process of development. The synagogue had never been envisaged by Jews as a substitute for the Temple in Jerusalem. Until 71 C.E., when the Second Temple was destroyed, the obligation on all Jewish males was to attend the great Pilgrim Holidays by going up to Jerusalem and participating in the sacrifices that marked the Feasts of Pesah, Shavuoth, and Sukkoth. There were the High Holidays as well, which marked the period between the New Year and the awesome Day of Atonement.

Jews who lived in the Diaspora either went to Jerusalem (as is vividly described in the Acts of the Apostles), or sent monetary contributions. The synagogue or, more properly, Beth ha–Knesset (House of Meeting), also known as the Beth ha–Midrash (House of Study), had evolved most probably during, or just after, the Babylonian Captivity, as a place where Jews in exile or at some distance from Jerusalem could meet, study, read the Law, and otherwise honor—by bringing to mind in one way or another—the sacred rituals that were taking place far off in the Temple in Jerusalem. The synagogue was not used for sacrificial liturgies, nor was there any priesthood attached to it. This is still the case today, and even modern Judaism, after some 2,000 years of development, continues without the Temple cult, its sacrifices, offerings, and ceremonial rites, which marked the seasons. As a result, Jews, through force of circumstances, cannot fulfill many of their obligations under the Law of Moses.

There seems to be no doubt that the early development of the synagogue took place in the outlying villages and towns of Judaea and Palestine. After the conquest of Alexander, when Jews began to flock in large numbers to the newly created cities of the empire, or the kingdoms of the successor states, the synagogue became a natural center for each Jewish community. Since it was essentially a house of study in exile, orientation of one's thoughts and intentions was guided by orienting the building in some manner or other toward Jerusalem. Even the manner of orientation varied. Some early synagogues place their entrances to the east, still others place them on the west or south walls and use something else to mark the direction to Jerusalem. But even niches and spaces for aedicules are not always to the east as one might expect. What was required appears to have been that one pray toward Jerusalem, and, unfortunately, we have little if any idea of the form that prayer services took, until well into Talmudic times.

Jewish identity as a whole is determined by adherence to the Law. The synagogue was the natural place to retain the Law in its written form—the Sepher Torah. The Law and the synagogue in which it was kept and studied, thus quite naturally became the heart of a Jewish community. How the Law was retained in the synagogue appears to have been a matter of safety, security, and, of course, honor. How this was accomplished, from evidence drawn from surviving archeological material, appears to have varied from community to community according to local custom. The ark, or *ehal*, as it was also called, a container or contrived space in which the Torah scrolls could be stored, might take the form of a niche or even an aedicule. Even where it was built or placed appears to have been a matter of local custom, and in many of the synagogues which have been excavated there is no indication at all of a space set aside for the Scrolls. This probably means that the container used was portable and made of wood.

The synagogue was also the natural place in which the Law could be read publicly. The early use of a bema (raised platform from which to read the Law) may well have originated in the wooden structure that Ezra had had built in the Temple for this purpose, at the time of its re–dedication after the Babylonian Captivity. The bema, like its descendant in Christian churches, the *ambon* or pulpit, symbolizes Mt. Sinai, from which Moses revealed the Law to Israel and sealed the Covenant. This is the key event in Jewish history and in the synagogue the bema was naturally to assume an important position. Like the *ehal*, however, the position of the bema in these early Hellenistic and Roman– Byzantine synagogues is still a matter of conjecture. At Dura Europos in Syria, a set of steps to the right of a niche in which the Sepher Torah may have been kept is considered by some to have been the bema. But this architectural provision is entirely lacking in examples of synagogues found in Greece. If they were of wood this is no cause for surprise, but their exact location remains problematic.

If we assume that the bema was intended to symbolize Sinai and to commemorate the public reading of the Law as begun by Ezra and Nehemiah, the description of this ceremony is clear in the text. A raised wooden platform was erected facing an open square where the people stood as Ezra raised the Law and read from it. (See Neh. 8:1.) Wooden bemas may well have been part of a conscious symbolism based on the text in Nehemiah. Their location may have been variable, either centrally placed or more oriented to the eastern end of the building—according to convenience and accessibility.

Thus all that can conservatively be said about these early synagogues in the Hellenistic world is that they reflected local architectural styles, were oriented in some manner or other toward Jerusalem, had a niche or aedicule that functioned as an *ehal* (ark), and provision for a raised platform or bema from which the Law was read.

Unfortunately, from the period between the 7th and 16th centuries no surviving examples of Greek (Romaniote) synagogues exist. It is regretable that even after the invention and quite wide use of photography, no efforts were ever taken to record the exteriors, much less the interiors, of even the 30–odd synagogues of Salonika, not to mention those in other cities and towns. One post card exists of the interior of the Italian synagogue of Salonika taken prior to the fire of 1917 and another photograph shows the exterior of another synagogue which is not identified. But we have nothing else. Many of these lost buildings may have held important clues concerning the evolution of the different types of synagogues throughout Greece.

Added to this lack of material evidence is the complexity of the geo– political changes that have taken place in the Balkans during the past 1,500 years. For example, the dispersion of Romaniote Jewish communities some 500 years ago, extended beyond the boundaries of modern Greece to cities such as Bursa (Turkey), Sophia (Bulgaria), and Monastir (Yugoslavia), to mention only a few. The Sephardi dispersion was even wider and more complicated, as it was newer, and initially less homogenous, and without an established local synagogue tradition. The Jews of Rhodes, for example, were closely tied by marriage and rabbinical visits to Izmir, Bodrum, and other Jewish settlements on the coast of Asia Minor. Its synagogue may well represent a tradition that is more local than we can now appreciate.

Despite all of these problems, we can find a pattern to extant synagogues in Greece. These can be placed in three groups according to interior layout, with one exception that will be taken into account separately. The first type is that of the synagogues of Corfu, Patras, Hania, (and what we know of the old synagogues of Herakleion and Zakynthos, both now destroyed). These synagogues were built in strongly Romaniote communities within a zone of influence dominated by Venice, and they all share certain architectural common features. The synagogue proper is built on a first floor, the ground floor having been used for offices or reserved for the *shamash*. The buildings are all quite narrow and stress an axial polarity in which the *ehal* is set at one end, against the east wall, and the bema elevated prominently against the west wall with steps on either side of it. Connecting these two extremities is a relatively wide central aisle along which, on either side and facing across it, benches are arranged.

This layout very clearly indicates the main roles of the synagogue as a place, oriented toward Jerusalem, in which the Law can be retained and honored (the *ehal*), and where it is read in public (from the bema). Further, in these examples the requirements of community prayer are also obvious. The relatively wide aisle permits the performance of processions in which the Sepher Torah is carried to and from the *ehal* and the bema. Within this space there is sufficient room to permit participants either to follow the procession for a few steps or to touch the Sepher Torah with the fringes of their *talleth* or even with their *talleth*–shrouded hands. The arrangement also permits flexibility in facing either east or west according to the place dominated by the Sepher: in the *ehal* or on the bema. During the three main times of prayer, Shahrit,Ma'ariv, and Arvit (which fall at roughly the original times of the daily liturgies in the Temple) this arrangement also allows for flexibility in the movements required for the Amidah and other prayers. All of these examples conform to a type of synagogue found in Venice and northern Italy, and can conveniently be called either Italian or Venetian, though there is good evidence that, in fact, they represent an original Spanish influence which affected Venetian synagogues in the 14th and 15th century.

The second group of synagogues is also found in predominantly Romaniote communities, or where there was an older Romaniote community "swamped" by Sepharadim, such as Ioannina, Halkis, Volos, Larissa and the "old" Naniote (Ioanniotiko) synagogue of Athens. In all of these buildings, the synagogue proper is found on the ground floor. The buildings are almost square structurally and the interior is divided into a number of bays by columns supporting arches. The ceiling can be either cross vaulted or even domed (inscribed domes are the rule). As in the case of the Veneto–Romaniote synagogues, the *ehal* and bema are set axially facing each other at the east–west extremities of the nave aisle. What sets them apart from the first group is the relatively open space between the walls (set with benches) and the benches of the central area. This arrangement is ideally suited for processions in which the Sepher Torah is taken in circuits around the interior of the building. This was a common custom in Ioannina, Arta, and Preveza, and may be a vestige of the now–lost Romaniote rite. (Public processions in which the Sepher Torah was carried through the Jewish quarter were once fairly common. The restriction of these to the interior of buildings made such large areas necessary.)

The third group of synagogues is quite different in the interior arrangement of bema, *ehal*, and even the seating. These synagogues are found in predominantly Sephardi communities. In these the interior is divided by four columns grouped roughly in the center of the room to form a square space, in the center of which is the bema. The *ehal* is to the east and facing the bema. The seats and benches are placed around the bema. From descriptions of the interiors of the synagogues at Kastoria and Serres (now both destroyed), we know that the bema itself was at times fitted with columns supporting a baldequin (canopy). This type of synagogue is very much reminiscent of medieval types found especially in eastern Europe though, oddly enough, these are always found in association with decidedly Sephardi communities in Greece.

The synagogue of Rhodes, built in 1575 and the oldest synagogue now standing in Greece, is unique. It fits into none of the three synagogue types outlined above. It was built by the newly arrived Sephardi community and is divided internally in a transverse manner by four columns supporting wide spanning arches. The building technique is decidedly Ottoman (as is that used in the synagogue of Ioannina), insofar as iron tie beams were set into the joints between the capitals and the stones supporting the initial spring of the arches. The transverse alignment accentuates the considerable width of the building and the east wall is noticeably pierced in the center by a door, with an *ehal* on either side. The bema is located roughly in the center of the room, but slightly to the east to facilitate visibility from the women's section (as at Halkis). The women's section is on an upper balcony running the entire length of the west wall.

Unfortunately, we know nothing of the circumstances that prevailed when this synagogue was built in the late 16th century. It may be that its greater width was determined by a narrow site and the understandable desire to keep the entrance away from the main thoroughfare on which the building is located. Also, a building in this form defies transformation into either mosque or church, and memory may have still been bright of the time when the synagogue of

Rhodes was converted into a church in the 15th century by the Knights of Rhodes (see Rhodes: Historical Background).

The modern synagogue of Athens, the Beth Shalom, deserves a brief mention here because it, also, fits into none of the synagogue groups outlined here, and shows a marked insensitivity to local customs. It is modern and was only completed just before the Second World War, with interior renovations in 1975. Here the *ehal* is built to the southeast with the bema (or, more accurately, the *tevah* or reader's desk) directly in front of it. There is no central aisle and all movement within the building is inhibited as a result. In every respect the interior resembles that of Reform synagogues abroad. Its unsuitable character for a Sephardi or even Orthodox service becomes obvious during the truncated processions with the Sepher Torah and even more noticeably when access to the Sepher Torah is frustrated by the mass of pews in the center. The seating arrangement also inhibits the movements forward and back required in the recitation of the Amidah.

The Romaniote and Sephardi *Minhagim* in Greece

There were once two main *minhagim* (rites) in Greece, corresponding to the Romaniote and Sephardi communities. The *minhag* universally followed in Greece today is that of the Sepharadim. The regrettable disappearance of the ancient Romaniote rite appears to have taken place under the pressure of Sephardi immigration into Greece and their proficiency in printing. Already by 1498, just six years after the expulsion from Spain, a press had been set up in Constantinople, and Sephardi Jews began printing books. An early edition of the *Mahzor Romania* was brought out in the early 16th century, as well as a polyglot bible in Greek, Ladino and Hebrew.

Had Romaniote Jews possessed their own printing presses, they might have produced sufficient numbers of prayer books (with the daily and festival prayers) to keep their *minhag* alive, but for some reason this did not happen. One possible reason lies in the fact that Greek Christians, like Muslim Turks, were forbidden the use of presses until comparatively late. Greeks did establish presses in Jassy (Rumania), which was ruled at various times by Greek princes or

Hospodars under Ottoman suzerainty. They also printed books in Venice (of which many fine examples still exist). But even these presses were not established until the 17th century. Muslims were not allowed to print until the early 18th century! It may well be, then, that the Romaniotes, as Greeks and without many of the privileges of the Sepharadim, also fell under these same restrictions. In any event, the Romaniotes either depended on hand–written texts, or they acquired books from Sephardi printers in Constantinople, Salonika, and Izmir. Attempts were made in the 19th century to correct this, and a press was set up in Ioannina. But, from examples of the type, we know that it was primitive and hardly up to the mass production of books. Mention is made of another press at Halkis and a good press was working in Corfu by the middle of the 19th century. But by this time it was too late.

(Mention should also be made of the fine presses in Livorgno, Vienna, and Amsterdam that produced excellent if not sumptuous printings, some of which made even Salonika texts look shoddy by comparison. But even these produced only Sephardi books.)

One distinctive characteristic of the Romaniote *minhag* is that some parts of it were in Greek, though written in Hebrew characters. We frequently find handwritten directions in Hebrew script for the celebration of Passover glued into Sephardi–rite prayer books used by Romaniotes. Certainly by the end of the 19th century, what remained of the old Romaniote rite were mostly *piyyutim* and other hymns and prayers added to the Sephardi liturgy on holidays. It is still fairly common to hear some of these sung in the synagogue of Athens (the "old" Ioanniotiko synagogue) on the High Holidays and even during the recitation of the Haggadah of Pesah in private homes.

The Sephardi *minhag* was itself not entirely homogenous. Before the last World War, there were minor differences in the various prayer–books used in Salonika itself, though always within the context of the Sephardi rite. Many congregations had their own presses, and certain customary prayers and directions in Ladino for their recitation were often added to the congregation's own editions.

During the Nazi occupation not only did Hebrew printing in Salonika come to an end, but many collections of the books printed there were either destroyed or eventually lost into private or public collections. At the end of the war and during the period of reconstruction of Jewish life in Greece that followed, the Sephardi prayer–book with commentaries by Isaac Luria, the great mystic of Sfad, was introduced. It proved to be either too arcane or kabbalistically oriented to suit the needs of the surviving communities. Further, the loss of Hebrew and Ladino fluency among many of the survivors dictated the need for a Hebrew– Greek prayer–book. A *mahzor* (festival prayer–book) which was Sephardi in *minhag* but translated into Greek appeared first to fill this gap. Ironically, it was put together by a Romaniote. Later a *siddur* (daily prayer–book) appeared, which, if cumbersome in its Greek translation, is apparently sufficient to the needs of Greek Jews and is used today in most communities. The arrangement of prayers and hymns is drawn from the Lurianic prayer book.

Perhaps only in one aspect of contemporary Jewish life can one see a remnant of the old Romaniote rite and this is in the manner of protecting and reading the Sepher Torah. In communities that were traditionally Romaniote, the Sepher Torah was and still is kept within a hinged, wooden or metal case. The case was called a *theke* in Greek and it passed into Hebrew as *tik*. The use of a protective case to store a scroll is very ancient, dating back to classical times when all texts were written on parchment or vellum scrolls. The more important of these would always have been stored upright in order to avoid mould as well as the inevitable migration of letters under the pressure of a rotulus being laid flat on its side. According to old Romaniote custom it was forbidden to allow a Sepher Torah ever to be laid flat. Whether stored in the *ehal*, carried in procession, or read, it had to remain in an upright position. The *tik* served all of these requirements and is used to this day.

The only decorations on the *tik*, apart from those that might be painted, carved or moulded onto its surface, are a veil attached to its surface and *rimonim* (finials of silver, ivory, or other material placed on the supporting spindles of the scroll, which project through holes at the top of the *tik*). In Ioannina, for example, it was the custom to attach to the veil numerous ex votos in silver, which were dedicated by families on important holidays or to commemorate the birth of a son. These occasionally took the form of "belts" of silver ex votos in repeated patterns that were wrapped around the *tik*. Decorated thus, a *tik* was very richly appareled and its passage through a synagogue during a procession was heralded by the sound of the bells of the *rimonim* as well as the tinkling of its silver ex votos.

The Sephardi custom of decorating the Sepher Torah is similar to that of the Ashkenazis. The Sepher Torah is stored in an upright position, but is read lying flat. It is bound by means of a band of cloth that encircles its middle. A veil is dropped over the top of this and fitted onto the spindles of the scroll. In some communities it was common to place a crown on the top of the Sepher Torah and then to insert the *rimonim*. A breast–plate was also placed over the front, usually of silver. If a single breastplate was not used, it was fairly common to have several large metal shields hanging from the front. These invariably were private dedications, and commemorating notable family or even communal events.

Aside from the loss of the Romaniote *minhag*, most of the remaining customs mentioned here are still observed in the communities—both Romaniote and Sephardi—that continue to function to the present day.

Albania
Italy
Greece
Serres
Florina
Salonika
Verroia
Kastoria
Ioannina
Larissa
Corfu
Trikkala
Volos
Parga
Arta
Armylos
Preveza
Lamia
Lefkada
Aphilon
Nafpactos
Krissa
The
Patras
Andravida
Corinth
Zakynthos
Tripolis
Kyparissia
Sparta/Mistra
Corone
0km 50 100 200 300
0Miles 50 100 150

Bulgaria
Didimoticho
Xanthi
Komotini
Lemnos
Turkey
Lesbos
ssa
Chios
Samos
Delos
Naxos
Kos
Rhodes
Rethymnon
Herakleion

Part One: The Synagogues of Greece

Reconstructed mosaic synagogue floor, Aegina, ca. 5th century C.E., *near the entrance to the grounds of the archeological museum, view to the east. (Photo: Timothy DeVinney/ Jewish Museum of Greece)*

Aegina

Aegina, a town on an island of the same name, 25 kilometers (15 miles) southwest of Athens/Piraeus. Total population approximately 6,500 (1981), current Jewish population: 0. Extant sites: an ancient synagogue floor.

Historical Background and Description of the Synagogue

During excavations carried out in 1829, the remains of an ancient synagogue were found not far from the modern harbor. Unlike the synagogues of Delos and the Athenian Agora, the Aegina synagogue was not converted from an earlier building. It conformed to a basilical type common to the 4th century C.E. and later, which was used by both Christians and Jews. For the most part these were rectangular halls, sometimes divided internally by rows of columns, with an atrium (court) outside the entrance and, at the other end of the interior, an apse usually accompanied by a *synthronos* and central throne. Both the *synthronos* and the central throne were usually oriented to the east.

During the rebuilding of the town after the Second World War, the sole important remnant of this synagogue—its mosaic floor—was moved to the entrance of the archeological site. It has recently been carefully restored and is on view. The mosaic floor has two inscriptions with the names of donors and is made of well–cut stone tesserae. It conforms to a style prevalent in the 4th and 5th centuries C.E.. Nothing else is known of the Jews of Aegina and their synagogue.

It is possible that it was built in the 5th century by Athenian Jews who fled to the island in the aftermath of the Gothic invasions and evidence was found to indicate that it was still in use as late as the 7th century C.E..

How to Visit the Synagogue

Turning to your left as you get off the boat, follow the shore road for about 200 meters from where the ferryboats dock. Just past the end of the public beach and before the road starts to go up a hill, turn

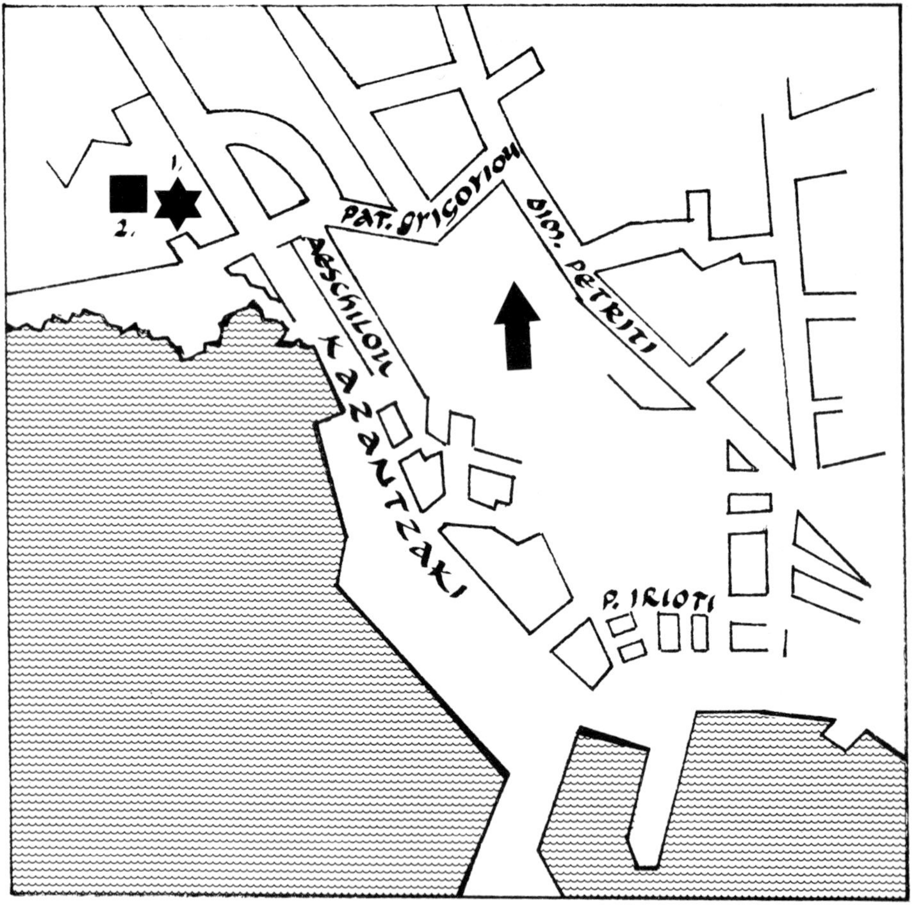

Key to Aegina map: **1.** *Synagogue floor mosaic.* **2.** *Archaeological Museum*

left onto the dirt road (Patriarchou Grigoriou Street) that takes you back toward the sea. After only a few meters you will see the entrance to the archeological site and museum grounds on your right. The archeological site is not marked by any sign until you reach the actual entrance. The floor of the ancient Aegina synagogue is immediately to your right as you enter the archeological grounds.

Contacts for More Information

For current information on the Aegina synagogue floor, contact the Jewish Museum of Greece in Athens (36 Amalias Avenue, Athens 105 58, telephone: 3231-577 or 3225-582).

Dedication inscription in the name of Theodore, one of the archons of the synagogue, Aegina, ca. 5th century C.E. *(Photo: Timothy DeVinney/Jewish Museum of Greece)*

During the office of Theodore the Younger, the mosaic was laid from revenues of the synagogue–blessings be upon the donors.

Theodore, the archysynagogos, who acted for four years built the synagogue from its foundation. The cost included revenues amounting to 85 gold dinars and an offering to God of 105 gold dinars.

Foundation stones to a probable synagogue in the ancient agora of Athens, ca. 3rd century C.E., *view to the west. The Temple of Hephaisteion is in the background, and the remains of the synagogue are among what were once important civic buildings in the ancient agora. (Photo: Timothy DeVinney/Jewish Museum of Greece)*

Athens

Athens, a modern city on the Attic peninsula in central Greece, capital of modern Greece. Total population Athens and suburbs: approximately 3 million (1991), current Jewish population: approximately 3,000. Extant sites: two active synagogues, the Jewish Museum of Greece (with a working reconstruction of the former Patras synagogue inside), and two cemeteries. There is also a Jewish school in the suburb of Psychico, and a club in the center of Athens.

Historical Background

During the period following the conquests of Alexander in the 4th century B.C.E., Hellenism proved to be both attractive and at times repellent. Its influence extended throughout the civilized world and the focal point of that influence was Athens. The great Hellenistic cities of Alexandria, Antioch, and the new Babylon were all modeled on the city plan of Athens, and their institutions followed its example. The old and now quite emasculated institutions that marked the Athenian democracy were little more than antiquated and honorific bodies, and yet the approval of Athens on an undertaking was a sign of its worth, even for Jews.

Athens is mentioned on numerous occasions and in various contexts by Jewish writers in antiquity. In 105 B.C.E., the Athenian assembly voted that a golden crown be sent to Hyrcanus and a bronze statue of him was set up in the Temple of the Demos in Athens. Herod and his family fell under the city's spell; Josephus mentions his close association with it. Considering the enormous dispersion of Jews in Asia Minor, Africa, and elsewhere in the 1st centuries B.C.E. and C.E., it was inevitable that Athens attract a Jewish community. Philo alludes to a letter from Agrippa I to Caligula noting the presence of Jews in Athens, and at roughly the same time Paul of Tarsus not only visited the city but preached in its synagogue and to the Athenians.

Not only were Jews tolerated as a community, but there appear to have been a good number of Athenians who were attracted to Judaism and seem to have kept as close to its pattern of life as they

A probable synagogue in the ancient agora of Athens, ca. 3rd century C.E., *view to the northeast from the absidal area. At the left of the photograph is a piece of the synthronos (see text). The small marble revetment with* lulav *and* menorah *(shown in the next*

raph, on page 34) was found just to the left of the statue of the Emperor Hadrian
the background. (Photo: Timothy DeVinney/Jewish Museum of Greece)

could. But, unfortunately, we know very little else about this early Athenian Jewish community; references to Athens, or Athenians, in both the Babylonian and Palestinian Talmuds, are not very illuminating.

In the 2nd century C.E., Athens was especially honored by Hadrian and almost chosen as an imperial residence. In the 4th century, its schools could still attract intellectuals. We know little of the lives of its citizens, be they Greek or Jewish, but we do know that Athens was slowly losing contact with contemporary life. Christianity assumed an ever greater importance throughout the Roman world,

Marble revetment with menorah *and* lulav, *ca. 3rd century* C.E., *found near the synagogue in the ancient agora of Athens. (Photo: Timothy DeVinney/Jewish Museum of Greece)*

and Athens, in response, became a bastion of conservative paganism, maintaining schools—the Academy, the Stoa, and others—which were no longer creative or productive, but which carried on the traditions of the old pagan world.

An imperial edict in 395 forced almost all of the great pagan religious centers to close, with the possible exception of those in Athens. In the following year much of Attica and a portion of Athens were ravaged by the Visigoths. Still, Athens recovered and it was not until the early 6th century that Emperor Justinian I formally closed the schools and banished the philosophers (who fled to the East). The Temple of Athena (the Parthenon) on the acropolis was converted into the Church of the Theotokos.

How this affected the Jewish community of that time is unknown. Justinian saw the Jews as a problem (as well as the Samaritans, who were numerous in Greece) but his harshness was expressed in legal terms and not harassment. Toward the end of the century, in 580 C.E., Athens was struck by the first great Slavic attack and it is perhaps at this time that what is believed to have been a synagogue in the Agora was destroyed. It is likely that the synagogue on Aegina was built immediately afterwards by Athenian Jews who, like their Christian neighbors, fled to the nearby island for safety. From this date until well into the 11th century, when Byzantine fortunes recovered somewhat, Athens was the target and victim of both land and sea attacks. Slavs and other migrating peoples, plus Cretan Muslim corsairs, took their toll. It may be that there was no Jewish presence in the city as long as it was so vulnerable.

Under the Macedonian Byzantine dynasty, Athens appears to have been especially chosen for the celebration of triumphs and even the construction of several fine churches, but its economic life did not amount to much. The real commercial activity, and in particular the very lucrative production of silk, were carried on in areas north of Athens, around Thebes, or to the south in the Peloponnese. When Benjamin of Tudela made his journey through Greece in the late 12th century, he by-passed Athens entirely, a sure sign that there were no Jews here at that time.

Shortly after the 4th Crusade dismembered the Byzantine Empire in 1204, the new king of Thessaloniki (Salonika) moved south into

Greece with his Franks. As he conquered, he awarded fiefs in the medieval manner. Athens and Thebes were given to the family of Otto de la Roche, a Burgundian, and it is interesting to note that though he proudly bore the title of Duke of Athens, it was Thebes, with its rich silk industry and some 2,000, if not more, Jewish weavers and dyers, that held his interest. During the late 13th and well into the 15th centuries, Athens changed hands a number of times but was never important, other than perhaps for its lingering and evocative atmosphere of paganism.

Oropos (on the coast of Attica) had its Jews, as did the island of Euboea, in general, and the towns of Eritrea and Halkis, in particular. We can only guess about Athens at that time, based on an incident that took place in 1456. In that year Athens was annexed by the Ottoman Empire under Oman Pasha and shortly afterwards Sultan Mehmet II himself arrived to see the famous city. The sultan placed Athens in a quite different category of possessions to guarantee that its monuments were not pillaged and that it was not the subject of excessive and mismanaged taxation. The archons of Athens were summoned to meet with him, and at this or later meetings, he was pressed to guarantee that Jews would not be allowed to take up residence in Athens. Under the Franks, Venetians, and Catalans, native Athenians had been barred from active involvement in trade and commerce and this may have been reflected in their interest now in making it solely a Christian domain of interest.

If Jews were denied residence at that time, it certainly did not last long, for Sephardi Jews began to arrive in the early part of the next century. In 1620 one French visitor noted some 15 to 20 Jewish households, located not in the lower part of Roman Athens but on the acropolis itself. Still dominated by the Parthenon (now converted to a mosque, after having been the Latin Cathedral of Notre Dame for several centuries), the acropolis was the fortified citadel of Athens and it would have been quite normal under the Ottomans for Jews to have been living there. In 1650 Shabbetai Zvi not only visited Athens, but spent some time with its Jewish community.

In 1687 the Venetians attacked Athens and lobbed a shell onto the Acropolis, destroying much of the Parthenon. Subsequent military

Officials leaving a Te Deum service held in Athens Metropolitan Cathedral, on New Year's Day, 1928. In the very center stands Chief Rabbi Joseph de Chavez, next to the Armenian bishop of Athens. (Edmondos Chavez/Jewish Museum of Greece)

action must have destroyed even more. Athens itself never completely recovered. Throughout Greece the Turks fell into a kind of lethargy that saw the sudden success of the Greek revolt of 1821 in the Peloponnese lead to the Greek War of Independence. In that same year, weakly garrisoned Athens was seized and the fate of its Jewish community was undoubtedly the same as that of its Turks. Shortly afterwards, the city was retaken under Rashid Pasha, but was lost again in 1833, and in the following year was designated the capital of the new Greek monarchy.

The first king of Greece was Otto I of Bavaria. The early reign of this romantic, and yet strangely hard–headed, cousin of Leopold (the Swan King), evolved in near isolation from his subjects. He was surrounded by a large entourage of advisors, personal retainers, and bureaucrats brought from Europe. These included a good number of Jews, recently emancipated Ashkenazis, of whom one was Max Rothschild, a member of the famous Rothschild family.

From what is known of this period in the early history of Athen's contemporary Jewish community, it appears that by 1840 or so there may have been as many as 30 Jewish families here. But the first attempt actually to create a community and build a synagogue was instigated by a highly eccentric and quite shrewd non–Jewish woman, Sophie de Marbois, the Duchess of Plaisance. The daughter of a minor French noble and his American (Philadelphia–born) wife, Sophie survived the French Revolution and the Directory, and eventually married one of the newly created Napoleonic nobility, the Duke of Piacenza (Plaisance). On his death, she took her quite considerable fortune and moved to Athens, where she immediately set about creating a circle of local foreigners and invested her money very wisely in real estate.

Children of the Jewish day school in Athens, ca. 1912, with Rabbi Hayyim Castel, who served as rabbi, mohel, and shohet of the Athens community. (Jewish Museum of Greece)

Like several similar, yet highly individualistic, women of the 19th century, Sophie was a romantic, drawn to things exotic and especially to the mysteries of the East. After having settled in Athens she went for a short period to visit Lady Stanhope (a similar character, though

A group of Boy Scouts (predominately Jewish members), in front of the Erectheum on the Acropolis during a visit to Athens in 1938. They were hosted by Mr. Noulis Vital, leader of a Jewish Boy Scout troop in Athens (he appears at upper left). (Noulis Vital/Jewish Museum of Greece)

British and more attracted to things Arab) in Beirut and then to Jerusalem. From there she returned to Athens, abstaining from pork, dressing in white veils, and announcing that she had become a follower of the religion of Moses—which of course did not mean that she had necessarily become Jewish in any formal sense. After constructing an altar to the One God on Mount Penteli (on her estate) she showed interest in assisting Max Rothschild in founding a synagogue. The man put in charge of collecting and managing the funds for this enterprise was a quite dubious entrepreneur by the name of David Pasifico (or Don Pasifico), a Gibraltar–born, Portuguese Jew, who was a British subject and, in fact, the acting British consul in Athens.

In 1840 Sophie set aside a large plot of land for the proposed synagogue on the corner of what is now the junction of Amalias Avenue and Othonos Street, in Syntagma square (the site is now occupied by the offices of British Airways). By 1846 funds were still lacking for the building and Pacifico's reputation was becoming slightly outrageous.

In the following year, matters began to take a peculiar turn when Alfred Rothschild (a wealthy banker from the Neapolitan branch of the family) arrived in Athens to float a loan to the Greek government. At that time it was still the custom (as it is today in Crete) to burn a figure of Judas in effigy during the Christian Orthodox Holy Week. The burning was usually an opportunity to harrass Jews as well, and Prime Minister Colletti was pressed by the Duchess and Don Pacifico, as well as other local Jews, to prohibit the burning—so as not to offend Rothschild. A law was passed and when troops came out to enforce it, the anger of frustrated keepers of the tradition was turned on an already notorious Don Pacifico. His house was stoned and several of his warehouses burnt. In response Don Pacifico filed a suit in which he demanded 28,000 sterling in remuneration for his house, warehouses, their contents, and even the decorations on his wedding bed! The amount demanded was so obviously disproportionate to the loss that the government understandably refused to consider the suit. The case dragged on.

In the meantime, the synagogue still had not been built, so in 1852 the Duchess sued Don Pacifico for the return of her property and won.

Interior of the Ioanniotiki Synagogue, Athens, early 20th century, view to the east. The bema is to the right and the ehal *at the back. (Photo: Timothy DeVinney/Jewish Museum of Greece)*

Shortly afterwards, in 1854, the Crimean War broke out. Greece saw her "friends" Britain and France allied with her enemy Turkey against Christian Russia. Under the British prime minister, Palmerston, the unresolved claim for damages by Don Pacifico was held up as an affront to a British subject. The famous speech he gave in the Commons, beginning with the words of Paul in Jerusalem, "Civis Romanus sum" (I am a Roman citizen), was the opening salvo leading to the blockade of Piraeus in 1857.

In the midst of all of this, the modest Jewish presence in Athens, and elsewhere, suffered considerably. There was still no synagogue in Athens, and fires destroyed synagogues in Halkis, Trikkala, Larissa, and Ioannina between 1847 and 1851.

Finally, in 1857, a settlement was won by Don Pacifico in his case for compensation, and he was awarded what was considered the appropriate sum of 150 sterling.

In 1878 there were some 60 Jews living in Athens. By 1887 the number had risen to 300. The character of the Jewish presence had changed from that of the early part of the century. Many Jews had begun to move to Athens from towns newly incorporated into the growing Greek state; still others came from Asia Minor. Unlike the recently emancipated Ashkenazi Jews who had come in the early part of the century, these were people who had been accustomed to a traditional Jewish formation. To them the need for a proper community was an issue of some importance. In 1890, Charles de Rothschild (a son of the Max who had come to Greece with Otto I), achieved the incorporation of a Jewish community under Greek law and acquired a site for a cemetery. The problem of a synagogue continued to exist and was made more complicated by the differences in rite between Romaniote and Sephardi Jews.

In 1903, under the leadership of the incumbant president of the community, Abraham Konstantini, a Cretan Jew, a site was purchased at 8 Melidoni Street, not far from the Church of the Asomaton. The area had attracted a good number of Jews and provision was made in the construction of the building for a school and community offices. Not long after its completion the differences in rite and custom between Sephardi and Romaniote Jews led to a split in the community and a second synagogue was established down the street

Exterior of the Beth Shalom Synagogue, Athens, original building late 1930's, renovated in 1975, view to the east. (Photo: Timothy DeVinney/Jewish Museum of Greece)

at 2 Melidoni Street. The latter functioned until 1917 when the rift was mended.

The "old" synagogue at 8 Melidoni served the entire community and followed the Sephardi minhag (as the community still does today). After the First World War, new immigrants from Asia Minor swelled the community until it was felt necessary to build a new synagogue. Under the presidency of Zaharias Vital (originally from Patras), a new site at 5 Melidoni was acquired. The new building was completed on the very eve of the Second World War. Due to the relatively large number of Ioannina Jews living in Athens, the "old" synagogue at 8 Melidoni was and still is usually referred to as the *Ioanniotiki* synagogue. (Mention should also be made here that in Piraeus there was apparently a "synagogue" or, more likely, an oratory or *minyan*, that functioned until at least 1920 when it is referred to by R. Hayyim Kastel, the Hebron–born rabbi of Athens of that time).

In 1941, when the Axis Powers (Germany, Italy, and Bulgaria) divided Greece, the Athens community numbered approximately

1,000 Jews, scattered all over the city. They were well integrated, Greek speaking, and generally well regarded. The beginning of the war brought an influx of Jews from all over Greece. Many of them were fleeing from Salonika, still others from Thrace and Epirus. Fortunately, there was no means to inscribe them into the official

Interior of the Beth Shalom Synagogue, Athens, original building late 1930's, renovated in 1975, view to the east. The ehal *and bema are set against each other. (Photo: Timothy DeVinney/Jewish Museum of Greece)*

A commemorative service held in Beth Shalom Synagogue in Athens, shortly after the Second World War. The rabbi in the right foreground is Chief Rabbi E. Barzilai, who served the community during the Nazi occupation and afterwards. (Jewish Museum of Greece)

registers of the community, and in fact no one knew how many of them there were. In any case, Athens was within the Italian zone, in which the Jews were not in any danger, until October, 1943, when the Italians surrendered to the Allies. The Nazis immediately took over and set in motion the machinery of the Final Solution, which had already succeeded in liquidating the 57,000 Jews of Salonika between January and August of that year. They tried to obtain the assistance of Jewish and Christian authorities and individuals to determine how many Jews there were in Athens. But they failed.

In the meantime, the Athens chief of police, Angelos Evert, had his forces issue false ID's to Jews, giving them Christian identities. The archbishop of Athens, Damaskinos, permitted the issuance of false baptismal papers. By the spring of 1944, just before Pesah, when the Nazis made their move, most of the Jews of Athens were either in hiding with Christian neighbors, protected by false papers or, as in the case of Chief Rabbi Barzilai and several others, with the partisans in the mountains. The Nazis were able to arrest only 800 Jews in Athens. They were sent to Auschwitz with convoys that stopped to pick up other Jews in Larissa (who in turn had been collected from several other parts of Greece).

At the termination of the war, the Athens community grew substantually, as a consequence of the resettlement here of Jews from communities that no longer existed or the natural attraction of a growing capital. Today, about 3,000 Jews live in Athens.

Description of the Synagogue: Ancient

In the ancient agora of Athens is a site that may well be that of a synagogue dating back to the 3rd century C.E.. At that time, Athens was ravaged by a somewhat mysterious people known as the Herulians. Large portions of the agora were destroyed, including the Royal Stoa and a number of the council buildings. In rebuilding this area immediately afterwards, the builders chose one site in particular to redesign. A small basilica with an apse was built here. Near the apse a *synthronos* with a central chair (or throne) was set apart from the rest of the interior furniture. This may have been the bema. The Germans excavated this area in the early 1930's, found a small Pentelic marble revetment piece nearby, on which was carved a

Scene from the old Jewish cemetery in Athens, within the confines of the First Cemetery, in the Metz district of Athens. (Photo: Timothy DeVinney/Jewish Museum of Greece)

menorah and part of a *lulav*. The proximity of this revetment fragment to the foundations of a synagogue–like structure supports the view that this may be the ancient synagogue of the city that was destroyed during the 6th century.

Modern Synagogues of Athens

The two surviving modern synagogues of Athens are both on Melidoni Street, facing each other across the street. The oldest of the two is at 8 Melidoni Street and today the same building houses the community offices on the ground floor, in a space originally intended for a school. The synagogue proper bears the title of Etz Hayyim, a name usually used by Romaniote Jews. This building is still referred to among older members of the community as the Ioanniotiko Synagogue. It has an polar–axial layout with the bema at its west end and *ehal* against the east wall. It is used today only during the High Holidays to accomodate those in the community who have either a sentimental or regional attachment to it.

The newer of the two synagogues, called the Beth Shalom, is across the street at 5 Melidoni Street. The exterior is in white Pentelic marble in neo–classic style. The interior conforms to no tradition in Greek synagogue structures. The *ehal* is on the eastern wall but the bema is built directly before it on an elevated platform. The interior decorations, including the bronze–panelled wall of the *ehal* and the windows, were completed in 1975. The *ehal* proper dates from the late 30's.

Other Sites

The Jewish Museum of Greece has a reconstruction of a 19th–century, traditional synagogue (that of Patras). There is a Jewish school housed in a modern building in the Athens suburb of Psychiko. And there are two Jewish cemeteries: one is part of the First Cemetery in the Metz area of Athens (it's no longer in use), and the other is part of the Third Cemetery in Nikaia (outside Athens).

Exhibit in the Jewish Museum of Greece, Athens, showing (at right) instruments, amulets, and clothing used during brith millah (circumcision). To the left are various artifacts used by Jewish women in taking the mikveh *(ritual bath). (Photo: Timothy DeVinney/Jewish Museum of Greece)*

How to Visit the Synagogues

The synagogue site in the ancient Agora can be reached as follows: as you enter from the main entrance to the ancient Athenian agora (from Adrianou Street), you will see the Stoa of Attalos on your left (a long narrow, newly reconstructed building of two stories). Across from the long face of this stoa is a ridge (with the Hephaisteion temple on the top of it). The foundations of what may have been the synagogue are on the side of that ridge facing back toward the stoa. (See map.) The ancient Agora is open daily from 8:30 A.M. to 3:00 P.M., except Mondays.

To reach the Beth Shalom Synagogue, starting from Constitution Square (Syntagma Square), follow Ermou Street past Monasteraki Square. Continue on down Ermou Street to Asomaton Square (the Thesseion electric train station is on the far left corner of that square), past the Thesseion train station to the first right turn beyond the square (there is a Texaco gas station here). This street runs one

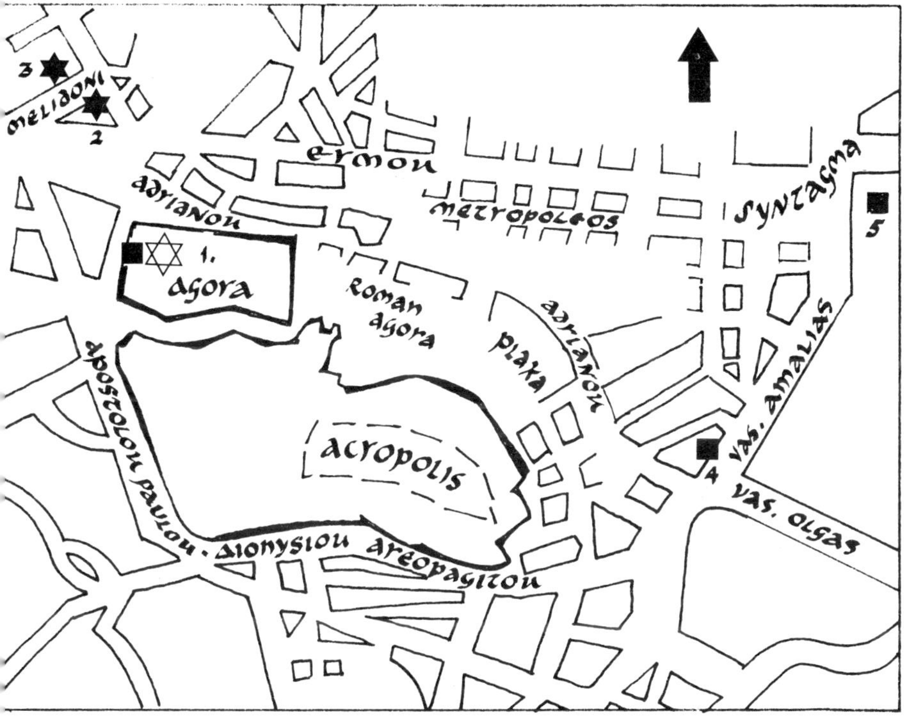

Key to Athens map: **1.** *Ancient Synagogue* **2.** *K'K' Beth Shalom* **3.** *K'K' Etz Hayyim* **4.** *Jewish Museum* **5.** *Parliament*

block and stops at Melidoni Street. Turn right onto Melidoni Street and you will see the Beth Shalom Synagogue on your right after about 30 meters at 5 Melidoni St.

The Beth Shalom Synagogue is open daily from 9:00 A.M. to 1:00 P.M.. Services are held every Friday night (time varies), every Saturday morning, and on all holidays or festivals. Seats for Yom Kippur must be reserved in advance.

The Ioanniotiki synagogue (directly across the street at 8 Melidoni Street) is open only for the High Holidays, but may be viewed by special request to the secretary of the Athens community (the offices of which are in the ground floor of the Ioanniotiki synagogue).

The Jewish Museum of Greece is at 36 Amalias Avenue, and is open daily from 9:00 A.M. to 1:00 P.M., except Saturdays.

Contacts for More Information

For more information on services and other matters contact the Athens community (8 Melidoni St., Athens 105 53, telephone (01) 3252-823 and 3252-875, rabbi's office 3252-773), or the Jewish Museum of Greece (telephone 3231-577 and 3225-582). English is spoken at both the Athens community office and the museum.

Left:
Entrance to the costume collection in the Jewish Museum of Greece, Athens. (Photo: Timothy DeVinney/Jewish Museum of Greece)

Right:
Reconstruction of the interior of an 18th–century Jewish house in the Jewish Museum of Greece. The costumes originate from various communities in Greece. (Photo: Timothy DeVinney/Jewish Museum of Greece)

Corfu

Corfu, a modern city on an island of the same name, 550 kilometers (330 miles) northwest of Athens. Total population: approximately 37,000 (1991), current Jewish population: 65. Extant sites: functioning synagogue and some remains from a second synagogue.

Historical Background

Prior to the 12th century there is neither documentary nor archeological evidence regarding the existence of a Jewish community on Corfu. While in antiquity the island was an important center of commercial activity, its fortunes fell, especially after the late 4th century, when the Adriatic Sea was plagued by corsairs and piracy was commonplace. It may be that Jews came and went depending on the circumstances that prevailed but, considering the ubiquitous presence of Jews elsewhere in Greece, it is unlikely that Corfu did not have a Jewish presence.

In 1160, Benjamin of Tudela mentions that he found one lone Jew living on the island. Not far away in Arta or Lefkada (we're not sure which), he found a community of "100." If that refers to families, the unidentified community would have been quite large, and may well have included Jews from Corfu. It is not until the following century, however, that a Jewish presence of importance is recorded for Corfu. That community seems to have been made up of Romaniote Jews from the mainland and from Anatolia.

Corfu was taken by Charles I of Anjou in 1272. Shortly afterwards, he gave it to his son, Philip I of Taranto, who carried on a lenient and somewhat protective policy towards the Jews. Shabbat was to be respected, Jews were no longer required to act as public executioners, the gallows located in the Jewish cemetery was removed, and forced labor on galleys no longer required. It is obvious from the character of these laws that Jews had been living under harsh conditions prior to the Angevin conquest of the island. These laws protecting the Jews remained in force until 1386, when the island was seized by Venice. We know that a certain David ben Sina

Ehal *of the Apoulia Synagogue, Corfu, ca. 1930, showing an unidentified rabbi and, possibly, the shamash of the community. This synagogue was destroyed during the Second World War.*

was one of six Corfiote Jews who then presented a petition of renewal regarding the legal status of the Jews to the new authorities.

Venetian policy towards its Jews, however, was less lenient than that of the Angevins. By 1406 a ghetto was established after the Venetian custom and Jews were required to wear the yellow badge on all of their outer garments. Nonetheless, by the end of that century, there was a large influx of Jews to the island in the wake of their expulsion from Spain. Sephardi Jews settled here, as did a significant number of Italian–speaking Jews from Apuleia. These new arrivals formed a distinct congregation and obtained permission to build their own synagogue, named the "Pouliezi."

By 1524 the Sephardi–Italian community had become quite large and, when the Venetians decided to enlarge the fortifications of the city, the ghetto was moved to the site it now occupies. The rule regarding the wearing of the badge was re–enforced; the reason given being that it served as a "substitute for the custom of stoning, which does so much damage to houses." Sizeable monetary contributions in the form of voluntary taxes could remove the obligation of wearing the badge, though its removal did not lessen the possibility of personal harassment by Christian Corfiotes. Even the law prohibiting public Jewish processions of any sort did not stop occasional acts of violence, especially during important Christian holidays. A local Corfiote legend claiming that the island was the birthplace of Judas Iscariot, plus the custom of burning him in effigy during Easter Holy Week, did little to improve conditions for the Jews. They were especially maligned during this time of the year. Jews were further required not only to donate a Sepher Torah (the scroll of the Law of Moses) at each consecration of a new Latin archbishop, but on occasion were forced, as in the ghetto of Rome, to listen to a public sermon remonstrating them on their perfidious character.

One might expect that in the face of such aggressive and, in part, united Christian behaviour (as the Orthodox Christians took every advantage to make Jewish life uncomfortable), the Jews themselves would have responded with a united front. In fact the opposite was true. The Romaniotes never came to terms with the new arrivals from Spain and Italy. Traditional rights and privileges (which seem to hint again at a pre–Angevin Romaniote community) were jealous-

Exterior of the Scuola Greca, Corfu, dating from the 17th century, view to the southwest. In accordance with the Venetian custom, the ground floor is set aside for

offices and community functions, while the synagogue proper is on the first floor. (Photo: Timothy DeVinney/Jewish Museum of Greece)

ly protected, and it was not until 1662 that these were extended—with great Romaniote resistance—to their Sephardi brethern. Even after this date, the two congregations remained distinct, with their own officers as well as ritual slaughterer. Even today, in a community reduced to almost nothing, some of this dissension remains.

Despite both inner and outer pressures, the comumunity continued to grow. It is estimated that by 1522 there were over 1,000 Jews here, and by 1663 a reliable census put their numbers at 2,500. By this time, according to the Italian traveller Elijah of Pisaro, the majority of the Corfiote Jews were Italian, and an Apuleian dialect heavily laced with Greek was the common language.

The Luah ha Brith (Tables of the Law) at the apex of the ehal *of the Scuola Greca, Corfu. This is a silver votive plaque inscribed with the name of Iehoshua Hayyim Mathathia and dated 1896. Because of the name, it is likely that this was made in Ioannina. (Compare with that which appears over the* ehal *in Ioannina's Yashan Synagogue.) The text below the representation of the Ten Commandments reads "Know before whom you stand." (Photo: Timothy DeVinney/Jewish Museum of Greece)*

The ehal *of the Scuola Greca, Corfu, 17th century, view to the south. (Photo: Timothy DeVinney/Jewish Museum of Greece)*

The concern of Corfiote Jews for their suffering brethern elsewhere was especially evident after the fall of Modon and Corone to the Venetians in 1685. Some 200 Jews of those towns were divided according to age and sex, with the young and able men being sent to serve on galleys, and the women, girls, and aged to army encampments where they labored as slaves. The Jews of Corfu and Zante (Zakynthos) raised funds to ransom 76 Jews, as well as a number of Sepher Torah Scrolls which had been taken to Malta. In the years that followed, all of the other captives were released.

The Messianic movement precipitated by the revelations of Shabbetai Zvi in 1666, was roughly contemporary to the revelations of the young daughter of a Venetian Jewish resident of Corfu by the name of Hayyim ben Aaron. We don't know her name, only that her ecstasies and occasional hysterics were performed while clad in white garments and surrounded by attendants. Whatever her initial impact on the local community, it fell considerably with the conversion of Shabbetai Zvi to Islam in 1666. In 1668, Nathan of Gaza, the chief apologist of the prophet, visited Corfu twice: once via Ioannina, and a second time on his return from Venice. Several of his letters written on the island have survived in which he explains the apostasy, and the deeper mystical significance of what had transpired in Izmir and Constantinople. Despite his presence, Shabbatianism never did acquire much appeal for the Corfiote Jews.

During the 18th century, Jewish fortunes improved and many rights of considerable importance were achieved. Jews were especially active in both the medical and legal professions. Students from Corfu studied in the famous law school of Padua, and Jewish lawyers appeared in Venetian courts defending not only Jewish but also Christian clients with impunity. Much of this change of attitude on the part of the Venetians was the consequence of the active role played by the Corfiote Jews in the defence of the island against a Turkish attack in 1716, after which they received special honors and commendations.

In 1797, following the dissolution of the Venetian Republic, Corfu was taken by the French. With a small break, their occupation of the island lasted until 1815. During this period the Jews enjoyed the rights of complete emancipation that were part of the ideological

The bema of the Scuola Greca, Corfu, 17th century, view to the north. A portion of the cramped women's section can be seen above to the left. (Photo: Timothy DeVinney/ Jewish Museum of Greece)

Interior of the Scuola Greca, Corfu, 17th century, view to the southeast, showing the strong polar–axial allignment and seating arrangement along it. (Photo: Timothy DeVinney/Jewish Museum of Greece)

framework of the French Revolution. Christians, both Greek and Italian, considered it a humiliation that Jews were on an equal footing with them, and this gave rise to many serious anti–Jewish incidents. Greek Christians even went so far as to refuse to sit on a newly formed administrative council because of the presence of Jewish representatives. Nonetheless, Jews in fact furthered Greek interests. Lazare de Shabbetai de Mordo was active in promoting the use of Greek as the common language of the island. Another Mordo was not only a close friend and supporter of the first president of Greece, Capodistrias, but an avid botanist. He wrote the first Greek botanical lexicon and also was co—founder of the first medical association in Greece.

In 1815, after the fall of Napoleon, Corfu was ceded to Great Britain and almost immediately Jewish fortunes declined. For reasons that are unclear, the British took a very severe position against the Jews, supporting the Greek Christians in their antipathy toward them. Jews were forbidden to serve at the bar and neither allowed to run for, nor hold, public office of any sort. Further restrictions curtailed their public appearance in cafes and clubs. The pent–up frustrations of Greek Christians were unleashed once again during the holidays in the form of riots and public humiliations.

By 1831 Corfu had some 4,000 Jews. Regardless of the restrictions put upon them by the British, the community maintained its schools and produced a number of prominent individuals. In that same year, R. Judah Bibas, a Gibralter–born British subject, was appointed Chief Rabbi. Bibas was quite an extraordinary figure and even managed to bridge the extreme differences between the two Jewish congregations. He was also intensely interested in pre– Zionist aspirations for a return to Eretz Israel, although he was against what he thought was a simplistic approach on the part of people like Montefiore, who sought to purchase land there. Bibas was of the opinion that education was needed to prepare a generation capable of establishing a homeland, and that perhaps even force might be necessary to found it. In 1853 Bibas was succeeded by R. Israel Moshe Hazzan whose views were not appreciably different.

Great Britain ceded Corfu to Greece in 1863, on the accession to the Greek throne of King George I. Pro–Greek feelings were high among many Corfiote Jews, but others prefered to emigrate, either to Trieste or Italy. The Olivetti family was among those who did emigrate. (They were later to become famous for the manufacture of typewriters and computers.) Other families, such as the Mavrogana-to (which gave a wizard of a financial minister to Venice), as well as the Rietti and Bessos, followed suit. But the departure of these leading families did not hinder the community. Joseph Nahmulli established a printing house in Corfu at about this time and began the publication of the *Chronika Israelitika*. He brought out a good number of bi—lingual books in Greek and Hebrew, as well as a *siddur*.

A commemorative photograph of a member of the Corfiote Besso family, Corfu, 1916. (Jewish Museum of Greece)

Corfu was not saved from the pernicious blood libel attacks that broke out throughout Greece from the mid–part of the 19th century onwards. In 1891 an incident occurred that took on quite unaccountable proportions, when a Jewish girl named Rebecca Sarda was found murdered. It was almost immediately claimed that she was a Christian kidnapped by the Jews for the purposes of ritual murder.

Within a matter of days, violence against the Jews broke out and, even after proof was given in court (the trial was held in Patras to avoid local riots) that the girl had in fact been Jewish, the violence continued unabated. In a matter of days, over 1,500 Jews left Corfu for good. The most adventurous fled to Italy or Alexandria. Others stayed closer to home and fled to Ioannina (still outside Greece, but within the safer confines of the Ottoman Empire). Most of those who emigrated were members of the professional and wealthy classes. Those Jews who had neither the means nor the initiative to leave were left behind.

The community was struck by a serious economic blow at almost the same time as the blood libel of 1891. For centuries the Jews of Corfu had exported especially fine *etrogim* (citron) to both European and Near Eastern Jewish communities. These were not grown on the island but in groves near Parga (on the Greek mainland) and nearby Ayas and Rapeza. Annually, just before the High Holidays, the *etrogim* were harvested in preparation for their use in the rites of Sukkot. For unknown reasons, several eastern European Ashkenazi rabbis began to cast doubt on the "purity" of Corfiote *etrogim* by suggesting that their famed beauty, aroma, and especially their size were the consequence of cross–breeding, not to mention being raised by non–Jews. There may have been some element of influence from the competition in the importing of *etrogim* into Europe, as one of the rabbis who was especially active in raising doubts, R. Elazar Ziskind Mintz of Brody, was himself an importer of non–Corfiote *etrogim*. To no avail the Corfiotes defended the purity of their *etrogim*, citing the fact that since most came from the groves of Ayas and Rapeza which belonged to the sultan, they were certainly not cross–bred. In the end, however, through the efforts of Mintz and other Ashkenazi rabbis in eastern Europe, a boycott was put in force against the importation and use of Corfiote *etrogim*. This brought economic disaster to Corfu's Jews and, following as it did in the wake of the blood libel of 1891, resulted in further emigration.

It is not surprising that Zionism now became very popular. Moses Caimi and Joseph Battino were especially active in founding the first organization aimed at furthering settlement in Eretz Israel. Caimi was a journalist of some repute and a school teacher. He was supported by one of Corfu's leading Jewish intellectuals, Professor Lazare Menahem Billeli, and was in close contact with the newly founded Zionist organization in Larissa. The Caimi family produced a number of outstanding rabbis as well as an eccentric and highly prolific author, Julio Caimi, who survived the Second World War and became a figure of some note in Greek literary circles in Athens.

In 1915, a new blood libel was leveled against the Jews and this time the Greek authorities took immediate action to suppress it. Following so closely on the previous libel it still encouraged further emigration at the termination of the First World War. In 1918, strong differences of opinion over common communal questions caused a new rift between the Romaniote and Italo–Sephardi Jews of Corfu and prompted most of the leading families that remained to leave

One of the narrow streets in the Corfu Jewish ghetto. (Photo: Timothy DeVinney/Jewish Museum of Greece)

Corfu for the US, Alexandria, Trieste, and even Athens. Those who were left behind were ill equiped by training or ability to assume leadership of the community, and inner frustrations ran high until the appointment of R. Abraham (Schrieber) Sofer in 1926 as Chief Rabbi. Schrieber was a Hungarian by birth and training from an Ashkenazi background. He found himself immediately embroiled in a community quite divided within itself. Not long after his appointment he put a *herem* (excommunication) on 28 leaders of the Italo–Sephardi congregation and, with the support of Greek civil authorities, organized a new centralized administrative organization.

In 1941, with the Axis occupation, Corfu was put under Italian jurisdiction and the Jews fared neither better nor worse than the Greek Christians. It was not until 1943 that the Germans assumed control and immediately began to enact their racial laws. The community itself was still rampant with discord, its 2,000 members for the most part living within the confines of the old ghetto. In June of 1943 the community was arrested suddenly and all but about 200 of its members (who managed to find refuge among Christians in surrounding villages) were sent by boat to Patras. From there they were sent on to Athens and transferred to cattle cars for the trip north. Almost all of them ended their lives in Auschwitz. Those who did survive returned to re– establish some sort of community after the war. But it has functioned without a resident rabbi since that time.

Of the three main synagogues, the Tempio Maggio, the Tempio Nuovo, and the Scuola Greca (also called the Tempio Greco), and an oratory (*midrash*), which existed before the war, all but the Scuola Greca were destroyed in the Allied bombing of Corfu. The old cemetery of Corfu was destroyed only a few years ago to provide room for a building site. Today only 65 Jews remain in Corfu. These are of Italian or Romaniote descent.

Description of the Synagogue

The surviving synagogue of Corfu, the Scuola Greca (or Tempio Greco,) is one of the finest in Greece and remains substantially as it was prior to the Second World War. It can be dated to the 17th century, and is built in the Venetian manner with the main (ground) floor reserved for community offices, common rooms and, behind them, facilities for a communal *sukkah* (for the celebration of Sukkot), as well as a room for preparing bodies for burial. The synagogue proper is on the first floor. Its interior is open, undivided by columns, and is laid out in an axial–polar plan with the *ehal* on the east wall and the bema projecting from the west wall. Both *ehal* and bema are in wood and decorated in pseudo–Corinthian style. Seating for men is provided by rows of benchs that run the length of the nave along the axis.

We know that the now–destroyed synagogue on Zakynthos was built in a similar style, while the synagogue of Patras (razed in 1984) was, with the exception of the *mehitza* (women's section), directly modeled on that of the Scuola Greca. The Patras synagogue was built in 1921, Carpenters were brought from Corfu to construct the interior furnishings, which are a simplified version of those in Corfu. Fortunately, the interior of the Patras synagogue was saved and has been restored in the Jewish Museum of Greece in Athens.

Other Sites

Today the Jewish ghetto shows the effects of the heavy bombing of the Second World War, but some sense of the narrow streets and tall residences can still be gained in walking through it.

Recently, in August, 1991, the columns of the *ehal* fromof the Apoulia synagogue (burned during the Second World War) were found at 74 Palaiologou Street. (Whether the Apoulia synagogue corresponds to the Tempis Nuovo or the Tempio Maggio is not known.) These are soon to be used as the heart of a monument to the Jews of Corfu.

How to Visit the Synagogue

The Scuola Greca is at 4 Velissariou Street, in the old quarter of Corfu. It is open for Jewish holidays and Saturday morning services or by special arrangement with the community. The Corfu community does not have a rabbi, but a *hazan* holds services on high holidays and on Saturday mornings.

Contacts for More Information

The community offices for Corfu are in the home of the president, Mr. Raphael Sousis, at telephone number (0661) 30591. Visitors may also try Mr. Aaron at (0661) 38802.

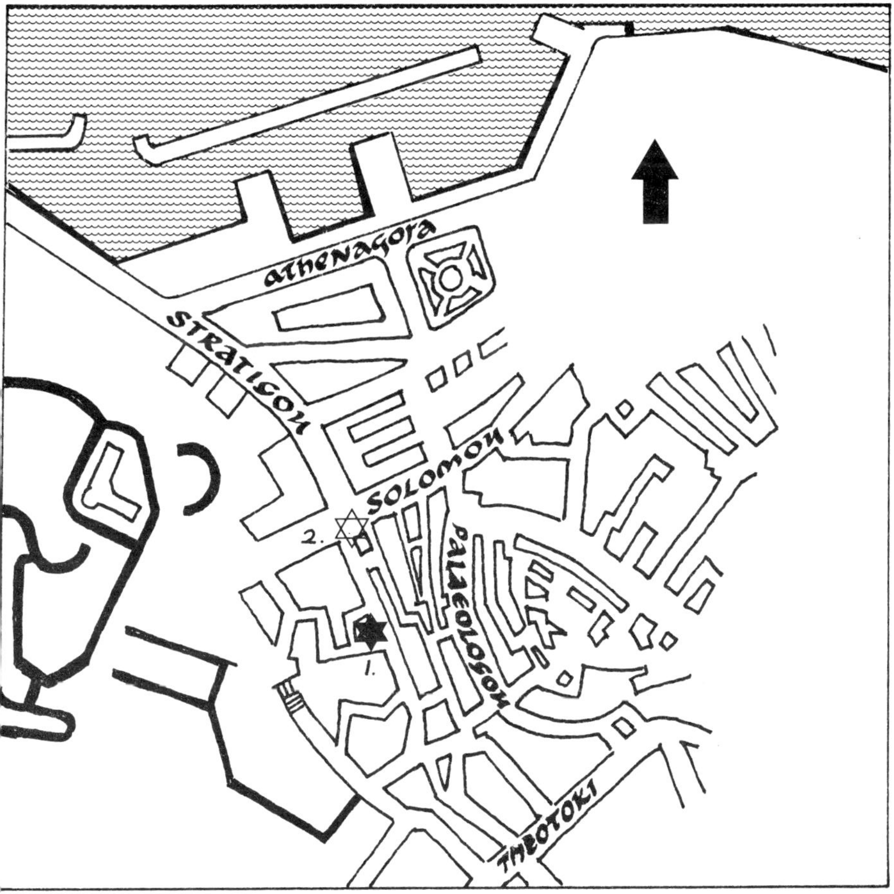

Key to Corfu map: **1.** *Scuola Greca* **2.** *Site of Former Apoulia Synagogue*

The "Throne of Moses" in the remains of the Delos synagogue, ca. 1st century B.C.E.*, view to the west. (Photo: Timothy DeVinney/Jewish Museum of Greece)*

Delos

Delos, an archeological site on an island of the same name in the central Cyclades, 2 kilometers (1 1/4 miles) from the island of Mykonos. Total population: approximately 16 (1981), current Jewish population: 0. Extant sites: remains of two synagogues.

Historical Background and Description of the Synagogue

The existence of a Jewish community on Delos is mentioned in 1 Macc. 15:6, and has been archeologically confirmed by the discovery of five inscriptions dating from the late 2nd or early 1st century B.C.E.. Josephus also mentions the community as existing in the 1st century C.E..

In the course of excavations carried out in 1913 in the area between the ancient stadium and the shoreline, a set of rooms adapted from an earlier house was identified as a synagogue. Within the site, four inscriptions in Greek were unearthed with the expressions "Theos Hypsistos" and "Hypsistos" (the Greek equivalent of the Hebrew "Shadai," the Highest). These discoveries set off a scholarly debate that has—for the most part—now cooled. The original attribution is generally accepted, making the converted house with the four inscriptions the oldest synagogue in the Diaspora.

The site of this oldest synagogue in the Diaspora, is about 60 meters east of the southern end of the ancient stadium, near the shoreline. The structure originally consisted of two rooms set against a portico, which ran along the east wall of the two rooms. When it was converted into a synagogue, the northernmost room was divided in half by a wall and benches were set along the northern half of the west wall. Dominating this arrangement was a fine marble throne and footstool, which still exists and is now referred to as the "Throne of Moses." There are no indications of either a Torah shrine or bema. Associated with this same site is a cistern that may very well have been a *mikveh* (ritual bath). One of the inscriptions can still be seen on a stone just east of the synagogue remains. The others are in storage in the museum.

General view of the remains of the Delos synagogue, ca. 1st century B.C.E., *view to the southwest, with the "Throne of Moses" at center right, and the arch over the entrance to*

the cistern just visible to the left. (Photo: Timothy DeVinney/Jewish Museum of Greece)

The second converted house is about 60 meters northwest of the first synagogue, built along the east wall of the stadium. It is sometimes referred to as the "House of Agathocles and Lysimachos." It was near this site that a stele in honor of Serapion, an Israelite from Knossos, was found (now in storage in the museum). This converted building has a cistern directly underneath it, reached by descending a set of stairs (now covered by a stone slab).

It has been suggested that the Jewish and Samaritan (Israelite) communities were located in roughly the same area and that this second synagogue was that of the Samaritans. (This attribution is based on the discovery of the inscription mentioned above, plus the fact that these are the only two "houses" in ancient Delos with cisterns of this sort.)

Unfortunately, we know nothing of the fortunes of either community. In the fourth century B.C.E., Delos had been granted self-government under Ptolemy I of Egypt, and that may well have been when the Jews (and later the Samaritans) settled here. By the 1st century B.C.E., Delos had passed its days of glory as the center of the Delian League. Under the Romans, Delos became an important slave market, in which Jews may well have taken an active role. In 88 B.C.E., King Mithridates of Pontus defeated the Romans on Delos

General view of the ruins of the Samaritan (or Israelite) synagogue, Delos, ca. 1st century B.C.E., view to the northeast. At left is the top of the wall of the stadium. (Photo: Timothy DeVinney/Jewish Museum of Greece)

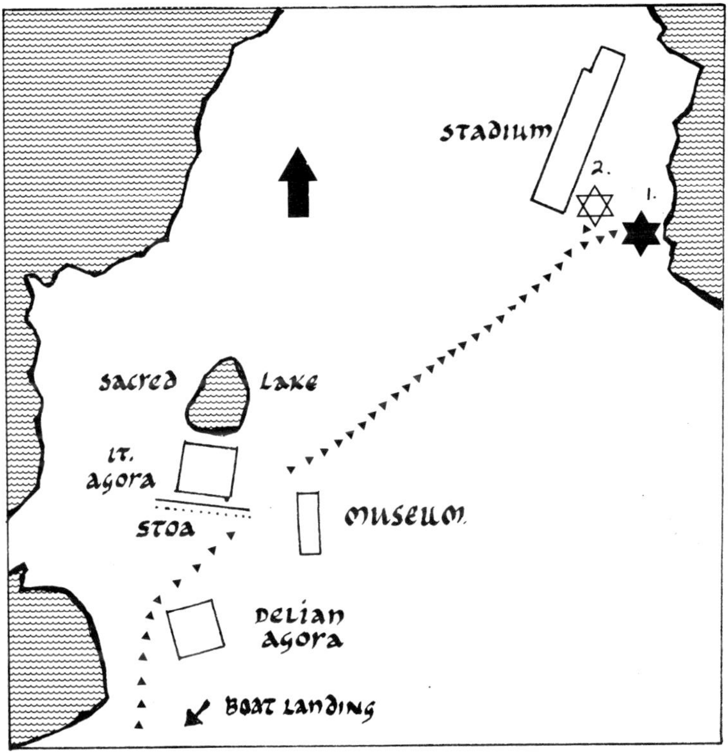

Key to Delos map: **1.** *Synagogue* **2.** *Samaritain Synagogue*

and, after taking a large number of slaves, destroyed most of the town, leaving some 20,000 dead. It is most likely that the two synagogues were destroyed at that time.

How to Visit the Synagogue

The synagogue remains are accessible whenever the archeological site is open. The island can be reached only by boat from Mykonos. In the summer boats leave every hour or so, weather permitting.

The synagogues themselves are in the northeastern corner of the island between the ancient stadium and the shore (see map).

Contacts for More Information

For current information on the status of the Delos synagogues, contact the Jewish Museum of Greece in Athens (36 Amalias Avenue, Athens 10558, tel. 3231-577 or 3225-582).

Interior of the synagogue of Halkis, built in 1854, view to the east from the mehitza. *(Photo: Timothy DeVinney/Jewish Museum of Greece)*

Halkis

(Halkis also *Negroponte*, and *Egripon*), a modern town on the island of Euboea, and about 75 kilometers (45 miles) northeast of Athens. Total population: approximately 51,000 (1991), current Jewish population: approximately 100. Extant sites: a functioning synagogue and cemetery.

Historical Background

Claims have been made that the Jewish community of Halkis dates back to the early Hellenistic period. One of these accounts goes on to assert that Antiochus had large numbers of Jews brought to the island of Euboea from Palestine, and that later, as freemen, they were involved in trade with Tyre and Sidon, exporting Murex shells used in the making of red dyes. Both Philo and Josephus mention the Jews of Halkis in the 1st century C.E., but from the 1st to the 12th century there is no other record of any community here. It is unlikely, however, that a city dominating the Euboean Gulf would have failed to attract a continued Jewish presence, at least until the 5th century. From that time on, Greece became the scene of numerous foreign incursions, beginning with the Goths, and followed by the Slavs and Bulgarians. During the 9th and 10th centuries, the Aegean Sea was dominated by the Andalusian Arab emirate, which controled Crete and many coastal cities, especially those lacking natural defenses. The paucity of Byzantine remains in Halkis suggests a hiatus of some duration and it is very likely that the Halkis Jews moved elsewhere quite early on, as was the case in Athens.

The Byzantine recovery began toward the end of the 10th century, at which time Halkis and other port cities assumed an important economic role. Benjamin of Tudela, in 1168, noted 200 Jews living in Halkis (which may be a reference just to heads of households), who were involved in the production and dying of silk. Thus community appears to have been well established at the time of his visit.

Shortly after the Fourth Crusade dismembered the Byzantine Empire in 1204, Halkis and the island of Euboea were acquired by

Exterior of the synagogue of Halkis, built in 1854, view to the north. Offices and community center are to the right. (Photo: Timothy DeVinney/Jewish Museum of Greece)

Venice. Renamed "Negroponte," the city became an important port for Thebes, as well as a connecting link with other Venetian–held territories in the Aegean and Ionian Seas. Not long after this, the Jewish community was restricted to a ghetto, following the Venetian custom, and subjected to heavy taxation which was periodically increased. The Jewish ghetto was outside the area enclosed by fortifications but the community was still required to contribute to their erection in 1304. At that time a special tax was also levied on the community to pay for the salaries of two new Venetian councilors.

By 1355, Venice began to experience difficulty in managing her large colonial empire. This followed a rebellion in Crete and the beginning of Ottoman Turkish intrusions into the lower Balkans. As a result, policy toward the Jews was changed, prompted mainly by the fact that an active Jewish community provided a lucrative source of taxation, not to mention trade. In 1355, the community was allowed to move the ghetto—but not the synagogue—to a designated area within the fortifications, and by 1440 it had begun to expand into the neighboring Christian quarter, prompting a series of restrictions and threats.

We also have references at this time to ghettos in Karystos (on the island of Euboea) and Oropos (on the Attic coast), both of which were probably within the commercial orbit of the Jews of Halkis. In the face of Ottoman raids and the general commercial insecurity of the 15th century, the fortunes of the Jews began to decline. By 1470, when the town fell to the Ottomans, the community appears to have become quite poor.

Under Ottoman rule, Halkis and the island of Euboea were not developed for the most part, and the Jews of the island had little to offer when the first Sephardi Jews began to enter the Ottoman Empire in 1492. The Jews of Halkis remained Romaniote, speaking Greek and maintaining the ancient Romaniote *minhag*.

Immediately after a Jewish wedding in Halkis, ca. 1929. The bride, Mary Cohen, the groom (to her left), Albertos Cohen, and their guests, are shown in front of the entrance of the Halkis synagogue. Haham Sallis appears at the far right. (Alexandra Cohen/ Jewish Museum of Greece)

When the Greek revolt of 1821 exploded into a full revolution, those Jews from the Peloponnese who survived sought refuge in Halkis and other communities outside the zone of hostilities. There may also have been an influx of Jews from the island of Chios after the massacre there, as a number of Halkiot Jews have Sephardi names to this day.

Halkis and the island of Euboea were incorporated into the new Greek state in 1833 and from this date more stable conditions appear to have allowed the community to maintain a quiet and conservative existence. A press was set up and a good number of Hebrew books were printed, though none are known to have survived.

In 1847 a series of events, very disquieting for Jews, began in Athens and were soon repeated in other Jewish communities. In that year, the Duchess of Plaisance and Don Pacifico persuaded the Greek authorities to forbid an annual event of some discomfort to Jews. It was customary (and still is, in certain parts of Greece) to construct a "Judas," a large straw–stuffed effigy, that was subjected to various forms of public abuse and then burned on Good Friday evening. This was also a means of expressing adverse feelings toward the local Jewish population. In Athens the legislation prohibiting the burning of the Judas effigy prompted a mob to storm the house of a well–known, and quite possibly unscrupulous, Gibralter–born Jew with British papers, Don David Pacifico.

In Halkis, as well, the community felt the consequences. The custom here was to drag the Judas through the Jewish quarter, past the synagogue, and then on to the small square in front of the Emir Zade mosque, where it was burned. On this occasion, however, the mob set fire to the synagogue and it was totally destroyed. According to a tradition still referred to within the community, the synagogue at that time had an archive of manuscripts, books, and memorabilia dating back to antiquity, all of which went up in flames. In 1854 the synagogue was rebuilt by Sophie de Marbois, the Duchess of Plaisance, whose empathy with Jews was well known. (For a more detailed account of this very interesting event see the section on Athens.) Toward the end of the century the synagogue was also given a new protective wall by Baron Ferdinand de Rothschild.

Between the First and Second World Wars, the Jews of Halkis

Jewish students dressed in costumes for a performance of a Purim play, Halkis, ca. 1928. The man seated in the center wearing glasses is their teacher, Mr. Psaltof, and to his right is Mrs. Alexandra Cohen dressed as Queen Esther, and to his left, Mr. Isaac Levy, as King Ahasuerus. (Alexandra Cohen/Jewish Museum of Greece)

became more and more integrated into Greek life, while maintaining close relations with other Romaniote communities in Ioannina, Preveza, Arta, and Patras. Greek–speaking and intensely proud of their Halkiot character, they easily identified with local and national interests despite being known for their orthodoxy in religious matters.

By 1941, Jews and Greek Christians both faced the horrors of the Nazi occupation as co–citizens. At the first sign of restrictions being applied to the Jews of Halkis, Archbishop Gregorios gave refuge to the religious artifacts from the synagogue in the crypt of the local cathedral. Shortly afterwards, the Jews of Halkis went into hiding in the mountains, leaving the keys to their property in the hands of their Christian neighbors. Gregorios infuriated the Germans by calling on the Christians to protect and feed the now destitute Jews in hiding. As a consequence of this daring action the Jews of Halkis, with very few exceptions, were saved.

Today the community, though small, is quite energetic and well

One of the graves in the Halkis cemetery, 16th century. This one shows the typical slanting upper portion, with a recess at the front for the dedication stone. (Photo: Timothy DeVinney/Jewish Museum of Greece)

integrated in the commercial and urban life of Halkis. It numbers about 100 people, most of whom are Romaniote.

Description of the Synagogue

The synagogue is at 27 Koutsou Street, most likely on the same site where it was erected after the Jews were allowed to move their ghetto into the town. There are indications that it was rebuilt after the fire of 1847, in the same proportions and using some of the surviving sections of the older synagogue. It is, thus, an important example of the traditional Romaniote type of Greek synagogue. As is common with most Romaniote communities, the synagogue is referred to by the local community simply as "the synagogue."

The exterior is low and modest. Adjacent to the synagogue is a small garden with an *etrog* tree, as well as other plants for the necessary fruits for the celebration of Sukkoth. There is also a frame for a communal *sukkah* along the outside of the north wall. The *mikveh* was once located in the garden, but recently it has been filled in and closed.

There are two entrances to the synagogue. The main one is on the south wall and facing it is a second entrance in the center of the north wall. Both of these were used by the men of the community. The interior is laid out as a small basilica with three aisles divided by antique columns that were part of the old synagogue. The center aisle is slightly wider than the side aisles. The *ehal* is post– Second World War, as is the bema, which protrudes prominently into the central aisle. Nonetheless, the axial polarity of *ehal* to the east and bema to the west, characteristic of Romaniote synagogues, is clear. The present–day *mehitza* (women's section) seems to be of greater depth than the original wooden one from the 19th century. The bema was probably moved out into the central aisle so that it could be seen from the women's balcony above.

Other Sites

The cemetery of Halkis is on Mesapion Street (see map). The graves in the cemetery date from the Ottoman period. The earliest are of considerable interest as they have gabled superstructures that are slanted and with an opening at the head to permit the insertion of a commemoration stone. Most of the 16th century graves have disintegrated and the headstones have been incorporated into the arches above the windows of the synagogue. A number of other headstones in the synagogue were found during the razing of the old Venetian fortifications of Halkis. It is recorded that the Jews were forced to assist in constructing those fortifications in the 14th century, using materials from their own cemetery.

There is a monument here to Colonel Mordechai Frizis, a native Jew of Halkis. He was the first Jew to graduate from the Greek officer's school, and was killed in the Albanian campaign of the Second World War. He was well known as a brave and popular leader to his troops. Just after crossing the bridge from the mainland to Halkis, you will see a public park on your right. Facing the water are a row of commemorative statues—that of Frizis is the third one down.

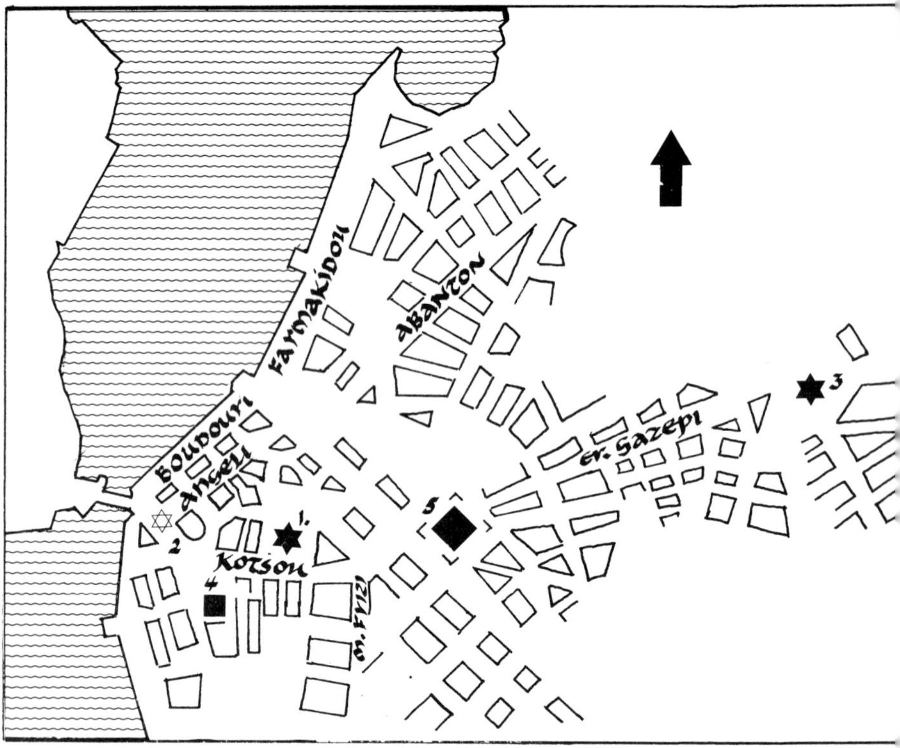

Key to Halkis map: **1.** *Synagogue* **2.** *Frizis Memorial* **3.** *Cemetery* **4.** *Emir Zaade Mosque*

How to Visit the Synagogue

The synagogue is at 27 Koutsou Street and can be reached by walking for several blocks up Koutsou Street from the bridge that crosses over from Attica. It is on the left side of the street just as it goes up an incline. (See map)

Visitors wishing to see the synagogue should first contact the community to gain admittance. Services are normally held on Friday evenings and all High Holidays.

Contacts for More Information

Further information regarding access to the synagogue and other sites can be obtained from the community at telephone number (0221) 27297.

Hania

Hania (also *Canea, Hanya*, and *Khania*), a city on the island of Crete, 265 kilometers (160 miles) south of Pireaus/Athens. Total population: approximately 50,000 (1991), current Jewish population: 0. Extant sites: an abandoned synagogue.

Historical Background (including Crete as a whole)

The island of Crete has had a history quite distinctly its own, due to its relative isolation from the mainland of Greece and its proximity to North Africa, Egypt, and the coast of Palestine. Depending on the dominant power in the eastern Mediterranean, Crete has thus been drawn into a variety of orbits at different times. It is not surprising, then, that Jews have been associated with the island from antique times.

The Jews of Crete are first mentioned in 2 Maccabees and appear to have had a community at Gortys. This city came into prominence during Hellenistic times and attracted artisans and technicians from Alexandria. It is likely that the members of this early Jewish community were originally from Egypt. Inscriptions found on the island of Delos indicating the existence of a Samaritan community at Knossos/Herakleion in the 1st century B.C.E., make it likely that a Jewish community also existed there.

With the Roman conquest of Crete in 67 B.C.E., it was linked administratively with Cyrenacia (Libya). Cretans, certainly Cretan Jews, are referred to in the Acts of the Apostles as having been present at Pentecost when Peter spoke in tongues. Philo and Josephus, both writing in the 1st century C.E., allude to the Jews of Crete. Moreover, Josephus was married to a Cretan Jewess from the western end of the island, which indicates that the Jews were present in areas other than the administrative centers of eastern Crete.

Tacitus, in his *History* written in the 1st century C.E., has an interesting theory regarding the origin of the name "Judaean." He claims that the Jews were in fact Cretans and that their original name was "Idaeans" (in other words "from Mt. Ida"). Beyond the obvious etymological similarity, this may also be based on some strand of the

Chief Rabbi Abraham Evlagon, the last chief rabbi of Crete. Hania, late 1920's. (Judith Humphreys/Jewish Museum of Greece)

tradition that links the Palestinians to Eteo–Cretans fleeing the island with the arrival of the Greeks.

Unfortunately, none of the Roman sites on Crete have been systematically excavated and inscriptions from this period are at times ambiguous. A few have been identified as possibly alluding to Jews. They come from sites near Herakleion and as far west as Kisamo–Kasteli. Other inscriptions have been found at Agioi Deka near Gortys and in Gortys itself. At Kassanoi (Arkades), about 43 kilometers (25 miles) southeast of Herakleion, there is an area known as the *Evraioi* ("Hebrews") which has been designated by archeologists as possibly the site of a cemetery.

During the reign of the Emperor Theodosios II (408-650) Cretan Jews were singled out for prohibitive legislation. Under Theodosios, the Jews of Egypt and Palestine especially, bore the brunt of a wave of anti–Jewish sentiment that, among other things, led to restrictions on the erection of synagogues as well as the abolition of the office of Nasi when Gamaliel II was deposed.

It may well be that the difficulties they were facing in adjusting to the new Christian Roman Empire led to the appearance of a Cretan Jewish Messiah in about 430. In that year a rabbi named Moses appeared in Crete and spent a year traveling about the island announcing that he was the same Moses who had led the Israelites through the Red Sea and into Sinai. He promised that in the following year he would lead Crete's Jews to the Holy Land. Commercial and economic interests were abandoned in anticipation of the miracle and on a specified day the Jews of Crete met together at some point unknown to us and, to the horror and amazement of Christians watching the event, threw themselves off the cliffs and into the sea. Many were drowned, still others were saved by fishermen who had assembled in boats to watch. In the account of the historian Socrates, special mention is made of the fact that there was a general conversion to Christianity on the part of the survivors. What happened to R. Moses is not known. Whether or not the Jews of Crete actually did convert through shame or despair at this point in their history is unknown, but for several centuries afterwards they are not mentioned in histories dealing with the island.

In 825, Crete was seized by Andalusian Moors who established an

Interior of the former Beth Shalom Synagogue of Hania, December, 1913. This synagogue, built in 1880, once stood at the south end of Kondylaki Street. The throne

shown here to the right has been set up for Prince George of Greece, on the occasion of his visit just after Crete's annexation by Greece earlier in 1913. (Judith Humphreys/ Jewish Museum of Greece)

emirate and centralized their authority over the island at what is now the city of Herakleion. Out of its port sailed corsairs that became the scourge of the Aegean. Athens appears to have been attacked, if not occupied for a period of time, and Thessaloniki was seized and sacked during one of these raids. Though Jews are not mentioned in accounts dealing with this period it is probable that they were active in urban areas. They were well established in Herakleion in the llth century not long after the reconquest of the island by the Byzantines in 961. At that time the walls of Herakleion were enlarged, and the Jewish quarter was not excluded, but incorporated within its new limits. Its inclusion hints at a sizeable quarter which, following a Byzantine custom, had hitherto been outside the walls.

Venice acquired Crete by purchase in 1207 as part of her share in the partition of the Byzantine Empire, following the sack of Constantinople by the participants in the Fourth Crusade of 1204. Not long after the incorporation of the island into the Venetian maritime empire, Cretan Jews began to enjoy at least some of the positive aspects of the resulting expansion of trade. They were placed for the

A Jewish family, Hania, 21 June, ca. 1900. (Victoria Minervo/Jewish Museum of Greece)

first time on an equal footing with Greek Orthodox Christians, because the Venetians, being Latin, looked upon the latter as schismatics, if not heretics. Jews were restricted in their public appearances by the use of the badge and also forced to live in a ghetto, but they still took an active part in trade. Greek– speaking and Romaniote in their traditions, they were also, it appears, quite lax in some aspects of their religion. In 1228, the Herakleion community was visited by a Palestinian rabbi named R. Baruh ben Isaac, who was sufficiently horrified to enact a special set of regulations for the community. The *Takkanoth Kandya* as these are known, are one of our main sources of information about the Herakleion Jews of this time.

Life under the Venetians was not without difficulties and Jews found themselves caught in the middle of the intense animosity that existed initially between Cretans and Venetians. By 1250, not only was the badge required on external garments, but signs were also required on the doors of their houses. These are an indication that Jews did do business outside the ghetto. Cretan Christians were also discriminiated against by the Venetians who exploited the island in colonial fashion. In 1364 a massive uprising took place that almost succeeded in breaking the Venetian hold on the island. At Kastel Nuovo the entire community of Jews was killed. It was after the uprising of 1364 that Venice began to play a more committed role in Cretan life and Crete became almost a separate republic with its own *signoria* and *rector*.

According to Venetian accounts, the community in Herakleion swelled appreciably toward the year 1395 when they were reassessed for tax purposes and given certain trade privileges. The cause for this expansion of the community may well have been the influx of Jews from the Iberian peninsula following the exodus of 1391.

A century later, in 1481, there were 400 families in Herakleion with four synagogues. We have no information on the communities in either Rethymnon or Hania during this time. Apart from the urban Jews, there appear to have been agrarian Jews as well who produced kosher cheeses and wines for both export and local use. In order to restrict Jewish competition in rural commerce and agriculture, laws were enacted to inhibit the Jews from making further

Exterior of the Etz Hayyim (or Zakynthiniote) Synagogue of Hania, built in the late 17th century, view toward the north. (Photo: Timothy DeVinney/Jewish Museum of Greece)

purchases of land. This forced the Jews into moneylending, and into trade in silk, metals, dyes, and leather.

The fall of Constantinople to the Ottomans in 1453 certainly saw the arrival of many emigre Jews and Christians to Crete. At least in Herakleion, tensions between Christians and Jews raged at times into riots and violent attacks. In the same year as the fall of Constantinople, Herakleion's Jews were accused of showing contempt for Christians by crucifying lambs and, in a separate incident, of blaspheming the Host. The former attack was certainly made by Orthodox Christians, while the latter reflects accusations common to Latins in the West.

Gradually, in the course of the late 15th and early 16th centuries, the Catholic and Orthodox Christian churches in Crete began not only to reach a modus vivendi with each other, but to create a hybrid Creto—Venetian culture. Some Jews took advantage of these broadened horizons to travel to Italy for schooling in places like Padua and Mantova. Contacts were maintained with other Jewish communites with strong Italian influences, including Corfu, Zankynthos, and Livorgno, and a number of prominent secularly oriented intellectuals were active at this time, including members of the Del Medigo family.

At the same time, however, Jews found themselves facing a united Christian front against them. News reaching Crete of the relatively peaceful and prosperous life of Jews in the Ottoman Empire created sympathies which occasionally led to acts of treason. In 1538, they were accused of hiding Turks in Herakleion and the community was saved from being massacred only at the very last moment by the intervention of Venetian troops. A special Purim was inaugurated to celebrate the miracle of that salvation.

The Ottoman conquest of Crete took the better part of the 17th century to accomplish. Hania and the western end of the island fell quickly, but it was not until 1669, after a twenty—year seige, that Herakleion fell and the Venetians departed.

The lot of the Jews on Crete changed dramatically under the Ottomans. In the towns the ghettos were opened and Jews were allowed to settle in neighboring quarters abandoned by the Venetians. Crete was also drawn into a quite different economic orbit and ports such as those of Hania, Ierapetra, and Rethymnon were now in close contact with Izmir, Alexandria, and Bengazi. Judaeo—Cretan family names reflect these contacts, such as Constantini (from Constantin in North Africa), Minervo (from Alexandria), Mizrahi (Izmir), and other names that appear to belong to Ashkenazi Jews from Europe. Unfortunately, the Ottoman Empire had passed its zenith by this time, and Crete did not fare well. Jews continued to have contacts with Venice and the Ionian Islands and many emigrated. In general, we know little if anything about individual communities during this time.

During the 19th century, there were a number of increasingly violent revolts on Crete against the Ottomans. Conditions for Jews deteriorated, leading to further emigration. It is estimated that in 1817 there were 150 families, divided between Herakleion and Hania. In 1858 there were 907 Jews on the island as a whole, and in 1881 only 647, most of them in Hania. Accusations of blood libel were common. In 1887, for example, the Sultan himself was called upon to intervene in an especially violent incidence of blood libel.

Toward the end of the 19th century, Crete was made into an independent republic under a Greek prince regent. A parliament was established, with several Jewish representatives, who managed to claim their seats with some difficulty. After Crete was formally annexed to Greece in 1913, Jewish emigration continued until, by 1941, there were only 364 Jews in Hania, 1 in Rethymnon, and 7 in Herakleion.

Crete was taken by the Germans in 1941. They were met by fierce resistance from the local population and the three main towns, Hania, Rethmynon and Herakleion, were badly bombed. It was not until June of 1944, and almost as an afterthought, that the Jews of Crete were arrested and sent to Herakleion, where they were put on the ship *Danae*, together with some 600 Greek and Italian prisoners. The *Danae* sank off the island of Melos on the night of the 6th of June with no survivors. To this day the sinking of the *Danae* poses an open question as to whether it was scuttled by the Germans themselves or hit by Allied bombing at night.

Street facade of Etz Hayyim Synagogue, Hania, late 17th century, view to the southwest.

The door to the right leads to the main (north) courtyard. (Photo: Timothy DeVinney/ Jewish Museum of Greece)

Description of the Synagogue (see also Herakleion and Rethymnon)

There were two synagogues in Hania. The oldest of these still stands. Over the street gate to the front courtyard is an inscription reading: "Blessed are the Just Who Enter Herein." The synagogue proper is a fine Venetian building. It appears to have been originally the old church of St. Catherine. This was probably ceded to the Jewish community in the 17th century, at the time of the Ottoman takeover, when the ghetto was opened and the old Venetian quarter abandoned. The old entrance to the church can still be seen in the east wall under a very finely carved ocullus. The round arched windows with iron grills and magen David insets date from the late 17th century when the building was made into a synagogue.

Inside the north courtyard is an inscription set in the outside wall of a small room adjoining the synagogue. It has not been deciphered due to its poor condition. A stair leads up the outer wall to a small room that at one time had an opening permitting one to look into the synagogue. This was part of the *mehitza* (women's section).

The main entrance into the synagogue itself is in the north wall. On its lintel is an inscription that reads: "For you shall light my lamp. O Blessed God, my Lord shall dispell my darkness." It bears the name of Moshe ben Michael Yaniti and the date "1521" (in the Jewish calendar, this is equivalent to 1761).

The synagogue interior has been stripped to its stone walls. After the bombing of Hania in 1941 the synagogue was not used again. At the termination of the war it was occupied for several years by squatters who blocked in the windows with rubble. In the east wall, one can still make out the support for the *ehal* as well as brackets along its sides. Facing this, on the west wall, can be seen the holes for the sockets supporting the bema. The low flat arch over this wall divided this part of the building from what must have been the apse (now completely swallowed up by an adjacent house) of the old church. In the north wall is a rubble–filled arch in which two fragments of an inscription (both upside down) can be seen. Rabbi Abraham Evlagon, the last Chief Rabbi of Crete (d.1927), mentions it as having been over a gate. It reads: "7 Adar 1487 (1727 C.E.). This

North courtyard of the Etz Hayyim Synagogue, Hania, view to the southwest. The stairs to the right lead up to a small room used as a mehitza. *(Photo: Timothy DeVinney/ Jewish Museum of Greece)*

opening was built and dedicated by me Eliahu Kurtish. May it be His Will to forgive my soul and those of my children and grandchildren. May they be granted many years."

The south wall of the synagogue has an additional door and leads to what was once a domed building with an upper story. The upper section was the *mehitza* (which can also be reached, as mentioned above, from an outside stair), and the arched windows over the interior of the synagogue proper were set with lattices allowing the women to see but not be seen during services. On the ground floor was a toilet and also the mikveh (ritual bath). This has been filled in, because of periodic overflows into the neighborhood.

At the very southern end of Kondylaki street, on the right hand corner, on a site now occupied by a house, was a second synagogue, built in 1880. This was completely destroyed in the bombing of 1941. Known as Kal Shalom, it was probably used by Spanish–speaking Haniotes, because the older synagogue was known as Etz Hayyim, a title normally used by Romaniotes. Chief Rabbi Evlagon was quite severe in remarking that it was wrong for the Jews to still be speaking Spanish, the language of those who had caused the Sepharadim such

Interior of the Etz Hayyim Synagogue, Hania, late 17th century, view to the east. The outline of where the ehal *once was can be seen at center. (Photo: Timothy DeVinney/ Jewish Museum of Greece)*

misery. Fortunately, a photograph exists of the interior of the Shalom Synagogue taken at the time of the arrival of Prince George in 1897. This shows a quite different layout from that of the Etz Hayyim Synagogue, with the *ehal* facing the bema and a ballustrade separating them both from the congregation.

Other Sites

The Jewish quarter in Hania is still known locally as the *Ovraiki* (that is "Hebrew," a word used in Greek for the Jewish quarter) and can be found off the harborfront in the old town. This *zudeccha* (ghetto) was outside the walls until the 16th century. Only after a particularly savage attack by Barbarossa were the walls enlarged and the ghetto brought within the town. It had one central street, known today as Kondylaki Street, which runs parallel to Halidon street (on which is located the archeological museum).

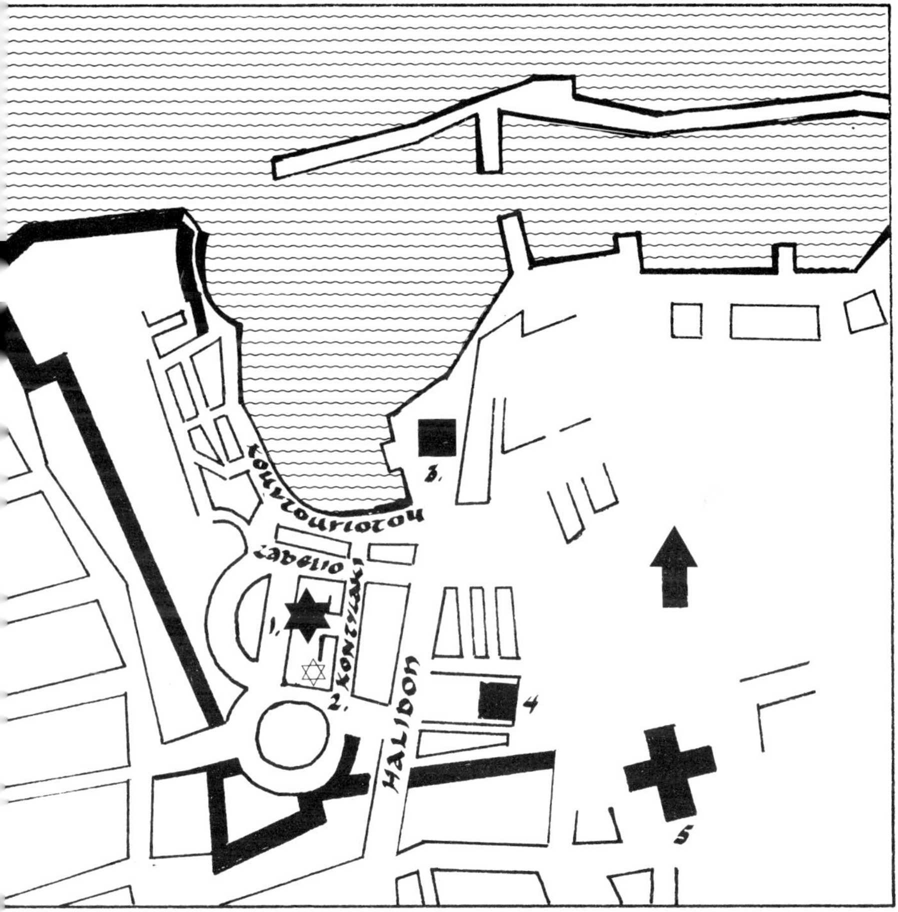

Key to Hania map:**1.** *K'K' Etz Hayyim* **2.** *Site of K'K' Shalom* **3.** *Hassan Pasha Mosque* **4.** *Cathedral* **5.** *Market*

A few inscriptions from the old cemetery are in private hands, and one quite fine tombstone can be seen in the courtyard in front of the Domo Hotel. The Jewish cemetery was destroyed during the war.

How to Visit the Synagogue

The synagogue can be reached by walking up Kondylaki Street from the harbor and taking the second turn to the right. This street is only about 25 meters long and leads to a cross street with no other

General view of the former Jewish quarter of Hania, looking to the north. Kondylaki Street is to the right, and the Etz Hayyim Synagogue is just to the right of center. (Photo: Timothy DeVinney/Jewish Museum of Greece)

exits. On reaching that intersection, the stone wall and entrance to the courtyard of the synagogue are directly in front of you.

The synagogue is not open to visitors as of this writing. There is a chance, however, that it may soon become a municipal cultural center.

Contacts for More Information

For current information regarding the status of the Hania synagogue, contact the Jewish Museum of Greece in Athens (36 Amalias Avenue, Athens 105 58, telephone: 3231-577 or 3225-582).

Ioannina

Ioannina, a modern city about 445 kilometers (280 miles) northwest of Athens. Total population: approximately 56,000 (1991), current Jewish population: 62. Extant sites: functioning synagogue and cemetery.

Historical Background

Local traditions claim that the Jewish community of Ioannina dates back to the time of Alexander the Great or— less extravagantly—to the period just after the destruction of the Second Temple in 71 C.E. In fact, both of these claims are unlikely, because the first documented evidence regarding the town of Ioannina itself dates from the 7th century C.E., when a bishopric and citadel are mentioned. A Hebrew inscription on a now–lost dedication was recorded in 1810 that alluded to the foundation of an early synagogue of the 9th century. It is unlikely that there was an unbroken Jewish presence in the town for any extended period before or after this date. Epirus, in general, and Ioannina, in particular, felt the full brunt of a series of invasions beginning with the Slavs in the 6th century, Bulgarians from the 7th to the 10th centuries, Uzes and Petchenegs in the 11th, and in 1185 the Normans sacked Ioannina and razed it to the ground. Benjamin of Tudela had little if anything to attract him here in the course of his travels through Greece in the mid–12th century, and thus we have no mention of it in his account of the Jewish communities of Greece.

In the aftermath of the 4th Crusade, Epirus was ruled by a Byzantine pretender from the town of Arta in southern Epirus. According to R. Jacob ben Elia (writing in ca. 1270), Jews were persecuted under the Despot Theodore Ducas I (1215-1230) and their holdings were confiscated. Jewish fortunes picked up during a brief Bulgarian occupation and then fell again when the successors of Theodore, Michael II and Theodore II, began to pressure the Jews once again. The Jews were an easy and, at times, profitable target as «strangers» during a time when Greek ethnic identity was asserting itself in the face of centuries of invasion.

Interior of the Yashan Synagogue in Ioannina, built in 1829, view to the east showing the ehal. *(Photo: Timothy DeVinney/Jewish Museum of Greece)*

After the reconquest of Constantinople in 1261 by the Palaeologue dynasty, there followed a brief period of tolerance under Michael I and his son Andronikos II (1281-1328). Several laws regarding the Jews were reconfirmed, whereby they were guaranteed not only freedom to practice their religion but also to carry on business and commerce. This short respite was followed by a period of persecution under Andronikos II and then, in 1348, Stephen Dushan of Serbia seized Epirus and Jewish fortunes suffered again.

It was not until 1430 that this centuries–long period of invasion, conquest, and periodic persecution of the Jews ceased. In that year Murad II lay seige to Ioannina. The town almost immediately surrendered, thus saving itself the horrors of being sacked. Special firmans were issued immediately afterwards, in which the inhabitants of Ioannina —Christian as well as Jewish—were given privileges under Ottoman law, which they retained until 1913 when Ioannina became part of the modern Greek state.

Jews were guaranteed the right to practice their religion as well as to conduct their own law courts and be administered by duly appointed members elected by the community. Within the relatively safe confines of the empire, the Jews of Ioannina were drawn into close association with other Romaniote communities in Greece, especially after 1459 when Mehmet II completed his conquest of the Peloponnese. Both the Jews and the Christians of Ioannina prospered, despite heavy taxation; we find them becoming members of specialized guilds as silversmiths, dyers, textile manufacturers, and merchants. Needless to say, a sporadic but fierce rivalry developed between the Christians and Jews.

Under Sultan Beyazid II (1481-1512), an unknown number of Sephardi (Spanish) and Sicilian Jews were settled in Ioannina. That they were numerically insignificant is reflected by the fact that these newcomers very quickly lost both their native language and their *minhag*, and began to conform to the customs of the Romaniotes. This is a rather rare case of Romaniote survival in the face of the Sephardi immigration of the 16th century. Today all that remains are the Sephardi and Italian names of some Ioannina Jews, as well as a special Purim that was celebrated each year by the Siciliote Jews of Ioannina.

General view of the exterior of the Yashan Synagogue in Ioannina, built in 1829, view to the southeast. The entrance to the synagogue courtyard can be seen to the far right. The

apsidal projection marks the location of the bema. In the foreground can be seen the supports of the communal sukkah. *(Rae Dalven/Jewish Museum of Greece)*

The absorption of the newcomers did not occur without difficulty. Shortly after the arrival of the Spanish Jews a rift occurred between them and the Romaniotes, and they constructed a synagogue of their own outside the kastro. In 1540, not long afterwards, the Sephardi rabbi, disgusted by the inner–communal friction and turmoil, left Ioannina, but not before he'd delivered a *herem* (proscription) on its Romaniote community. This ban remained for some years, until it was lifted by R. Samuel di Medina.

What is especially peculiar about the community during this and the following century is that it is hardly ever mentioned by either Greeks or Turks in documents or even legal actions. At the beginning, the Jews appear to have kept to themselves in a special quarter of the town located outside the citadel. Occasionally, however, the community was involuntarily drawn into conflicts between Greeks and Turks as a scapegoat. One such case occurred in 1611 when the Bishop of Trikkala, Dionysios Skylosophos (the Cynic), led a popular Christian revolt in Ioannina that spread to the surrounding villages. Large numbers of Muslims were massacred. It would appear that Jews were involved in Dionysios's apprehension by the Ottomans. He was flayed alive, and his straw–stuffed skin was sent to the sultan.

Following this incident, the Christians were expelled from their quarter within the citadel, and it was given over to the Jews. The site of the present K'K' Yashan, or Old Synagogue, is probably the same as that of the synagogue erected when the Jews created their new quarter inside the kastro.

The Turkish traveller Evliye Çelebi visited Ioannina in 1670 in the course of his travels through Greece and made some interesting observations regarding its Jews. Admittedly, Çelebi was drawn by temperament to the ebullient character of Greek Christians, with whom he shared a curious mind and a sharp eye for new things. His encounter with the Jews of Ioannina, whatever it was, left him impatient with their insularity and lack of social graces. He noted 160 Jewish households (approximately 800 people), and found the Jews here fanatic, bigoted, and mean. He was especially shocked by their unsociability in refusing to join him at table or even for a drink. Çelebi was a good observer and, on the whole, a reliable judge of the character of the various peoples he met during his journeys.

That the Jews of Ioannina were of a difficult temperment was even commented on in a *responsa* of R. Samuel di Medina (1506-89), in which he mentions that a matter of some importance had been brought for his consideration in Constantinople: the Jews of Ioannina had petitioned for a special rabbinical decision that would forbid Jews from other communities from settling or doing business in Ioannina. Medina curtly refused, making note of the fact that even the Turks did not forbid other peoples from doing business and settling where they wished within the empire!

Relations between the Christians and Jews of Ioannina during the 18th and 19th centuries were not, on the whole, amicable. Even the seclusion of the Jews within their own quarter in the citadel did not prevent incidents of violence. Mutual accusations of sacrilege between these two groups were a constant source of vexation to the Turks. Especially at Easter it was taken for granted that the Jews would be subject to some form of retribution, whether in the form of verbal invective, the throwing of earthenware pots against doors or, as in 1829, the burning of the synagogue.

Jews, for their part, were not beyond heckling and causing peripheral pandemonium during religious processions of Christians. The Turks were always on special guard duty during the holidays of either community.

Throughout the late 18th and early 19th centuries Ioannina found itself the center of the famous revolt led by Ali Pasa. This complex, unpredictable, and exquisitely cruel Albanian managed to create an almost autonomous state that fascinated European visitors, presented a continual source of annoyance to the Ottomans, and led to a virtual renaissance in the town of Ioannina. Muslims, Christians, and Jews all shared alike in a brief moment of broadened horizons, as Epirus, Albania, as well as large sections of Macedonia and the Peleponnese, were united under his despotic and fickle rule. Heavy taxation was universal—Ali claimed that it stimulated more active trade. Laws were severely enforced—Ali claimed to have put to death more than 30,000 people during 40 years of rule. But the ensuing stability was reflected in economic growth. Because Ali's vices included neither ethnic nor religious prejudice, Christians and

Interior of the Yashan Synagogue in Ioannina, built in 1829, view to the southeast,

showing the inscribed dome to the right and the ehal to the left. (Photo: Timothy DeVinney/Jewish Museum of Greece)

Jews, as well as Muslims, served on his councils. Greek studies prospered, schools were endowed, printing presses set up, and Ioannina—although ruled by a cantankerous despot—became a model of progressive life in the Balkans. Threatened by the sultan, Ali raised a general revolt that led to his execution in 1822. The long and short results of Ali's rule were many. While it lasted, it meant a significant period of economic growth for Jews as well as other groups. Its end marked the beginning of the Greek War of Independence in 1821 in the Peloponnese, with significant implications for Jewish life in Ioannina.

By 1840 the Jews of Ioannina had outgrown not only the quarter within the *kastro* but felt the need to construct a new synagogue. The new quarter was inhabited predominantly by the wealthier and more progressive Jews of the town. The New Synagogue, K'K' Hadash, was richly endowed and many of the artifacts we can associate with it indicate close commercial ties with Istanbul, Edirne, and other Ottoman centers of trade in the Balkans.

A street in the Jewish quarter of Ioannina, ca. 1912, showing a rabbi at center. (Rae Dalven/Jewish Museum of Greece)

Interior of the Yashan Synagogue in Ioannina, view to the northeast. The mehitza *be seen running along the upper balcony. To the far right is the* genizeh *(repository for discarded liturgical items). (Photo: Timothy DeVinney/Jewish Museum of Greece)*

Interior of the Yashan Synagogue in Ioannina, view to the northwest showing the bema recessed into the west wall. (Photo: Timothy DeVinney/Jewish Museum of Greece)

Relations between Greek Christians and Jews began to worsen again after 1860 as Greeks tended to identify with the newly established Greek state in the south. Jews, for protection, tended to identify with the Ottomans. In 1869 a great fire destroyed over 107 Jewish shops in the central market area, and in 1872 a major riot broke out against the Jews during Easter Holy Week. Several Jews were severly injured and at least one was murdered. Similar incidents occurred later that year, with the result that the Turks were forced to set up special guards around the Jewish quarter. In 1897, with the renewal of open Greco–Turkish hostilities, many Jews began to emigrate, especially to Arta, Preveza, and even south to Athens (where the Romaniote Jews felt a growing affinity).

By 1905, a Zionist association had been formed and Jews began leaving for Eretz Israel. The establishment of an Alliance School in the previous year provided an important means for those who remained to share in contemporary intellectual life in Europe. 1905

Wedding in the "new" Jewish quarter, outside the ancient walls of Ioannina, 1904. (Errikos Levy/Jewish Museum of Greece)

An outing on the lake of Ioannina with Jewish students from the Alliance School, ca. 1905. (Rae Dalven/Jewish Museum of Greece)

was also, however, witness to an incident that prompted a whole–hearted emigration of Jews from the town. Twelve Jewish merchants from Ioannina traveling to a nearby village were set upon by brigands and murdered. The brigands mutilated their bodies and stole their goods. On the following morning, men entering the Old Synagogue courtyard for Shahrit prayers found the ears of the murdered victims floating in the ablution fountain. By the end of 1905, over 500 Ioannina Jews had emigrated to Constantinople, Athens, Alexandria, Palestine, and New York. They were followed in 1906 by another 1,000.

In 1913, at the end of the First Balkan War, Epirus and Ioannina were annexed to Greece. The Jews of Ioannina, who were Greek speaking and suprisingly enthusiastic about this change, immediately began to adjust their lives to the new circumstances. Avid supporters of Venizelos, they entered politics and the army and, in general, committed themselves wholeheartedly to Greek fortunes during the

First World War and the Smyrna disaster of 1922. Despite this commitment by some Jews, others continued to emigrate. The secular attractions of Athens and the possibilities of economic advancement drew many of the young. The more adventurous chose to leave Greece during the years of the Great Depression. The older generation, conservative in their religious life, were resistant to the many changes that were affecting traditional Romaniote Jewish life. One of the more serious of these was a law passed whereby shops were to remain open on Saturdays and shut on Sundays.

In 1941, on the eve of the Second World War, there were 1,950 Jews left in Ioannina. When hostilities broke out, many of the Ioannina Jews fled to the mountains. Those who remained fell under the Italian Occupation until 1943, when the Italians capitulated to the Allies. With the German takeover, the Jews were almost immediately segregated. In March of 1944, 1,870 Jews were arrested, shipped to Larissa, and from there by cattle car to Auschwitz-Birkenau where nearly all of them perished.

Today there are about 62 Jews still living in Ioannina. They are generally of Romaniote origin.

Description of the Synagogue

The Old Synagogue of Ioannina, called the K'K' Yashan, is at 16 Justinian Street, just inside the *kastro* on the flank of what was the old Jewish quarter. According to the inscription over the entrance it was built in 1829 and apparently occupies the site of an older synagogue which probably dated back to the 17th century when the Jews moved into this area. The wall and gate enclosing the synagogue were built in the late 19th century.

As one enters the courtyard, there is an ablution fountain to the right and to the far left a pergola constructed in part against the wall. Similar pergolas are often found in Romaniote synagogues in Greece for use as a supporting frame for a communal *sukkah* in the celebration of the Feast of Tabernacles. The main entrance to the synagogue is in its west wall. This was used solely by the men of the community. The *mehitza* (women's section) is inside along the north wall in an upper gallery and is reached by an external staircase.

The synagogue proper is architecturally quite simple and its exterior rather stark. As one enters, however, one is struck by its apparent size and space, both of which are accentuated by rather low furnishings and arched ceiling supports. In the center of the interior are four columns linked by arches that in turn connect to the four walls. The two transverse arches that connect the central columns to the north wall are smaller in span as they intercept the women's gallery, which rests on squat piers. Within the area set off by those piers there were once benches for students.

The central bay forms an inscribed dome. This highly centralized plan is broken, however, by the polar–axial alignment of the *ehal* and *bema* built against the east and west walls, respectively. The *ehal* is of marble and is built on a large marble plinth. At its apex is a plaque showing the Luah ha Brith (Tables of the Law). A silver copy (smaller in size) is to be found at the apex of the *ehal* in the Scuola Greca (the "Romaniote Synagogue") of Corfu.

At the other end of the synagogue and opposite the *ehal* is the bema (reader's platform). This, unlike the *ehal*, is accommodated within an apse–like projection and is quite grand. The bema was used only during Shabbat, High Holidays, and other important events. During the week, it was customary to read the Law at a *tevah* (reader's desk) under the inscribed dome. The seating arrangement is such that the male members of the community sat facing each other along the central axis. What is especially striking about the Ioannina synagogue is the amount of space provided for allowing changes in the direction of prayer during the liturgy. Seated or standing participants could face east or west, or follow in procession the movements of the Sepher Torahs (Scrolls of the Law) as they were carried throughout the building.

The centralized architectural plan of the Ioannina synagogue appears to have been in common use throughout central and northern parts of Greece at least during the period after the 16th century. The use of iron tie beams to stabilize the columns supporting the arches are an Ottoman innovation and the square layout is similar to that of neighborhood mosques. This design appears to have been used by both Romaniote as well as Sephardi communities. The polar–axial alignment of the interior, however, is more common to what we know of Romaniote synagogues.

During the German occupation the synagogue was requisitioned as a municipal library. A great number of its silver ex votos, wooden and silver *tikkim* (Torah cases), liturgical books, and textiles were hidden in a crypt. At the termination of the war, these, together with the building itself, were returned to the surviving members of the community. Many of these furnishings are now on display in the Jewish Museum of Greece.

The New Synagogue (K'K' Hadash), which was dedicated in 1841, has unfortunately been razed. It was located on Joseph Eliya Street, roughly at the site of what is now an apartment building that houses almost the entire Ioannina Jewish community. From snapshots taken of the entrance and its dim and ravaged interior just prior to its demolition, it appears to have been built in a style that was more akin to that common to Jewish communities from the Ionian islands. The building was rectangular and thus conformed to the polar–axial layout of *ehal* and bema.

The ehal *of the former Hadash Synagogue, Ioannina, built in 1841, on Joseph Eliya Street, shown here as it was just after the end of the Second World War. In its pre–war state it had been very richly endowed and fitted. (Rae Dalven/Jewish Museum of Greece)*

Other Sites

Mention should be made of the remains of two *minyans* (oratories) that were connected to the two synagogues for the use of members of the community who came early to pray. The foundations of the *minyan* connected to the Old Synagogue can still be seen to the northeast of the building (within the surrounding wall).

The Jewish cemetery is on the western edge of town on Mega Alexandros Street, in an area called Agia Triada, near the tourist pavilion and outdoor theater. It is surrounded by a wall. It contains little of interest as it has been neglected over the years. But some of the stones are peculiar in that they bear no inscriptions and are simply roughly quarried slabs of local limestone. As they are located in the foremost part of the cemetery they are most likely the oldest, but whether they date to the 13th century, as claimed by some local community members, has not been confirmed.

A monument to the Holocaust was recently set up by the municipal authorities at the crossing of Soutsou and Karamanlis Streets. Plans are also afoot to create a special permanent exhibit concerning Jewish life in Ioannina in the municipal museum (the former Aslan Pasha Mosque) in the citadel.

How To Visit the Synagogue

Visitors can try to contact the community to see the synagogue, but the feasibility of this will depend on how busy the local representatives are with their own businesses. Otherwise, the synagogue has no regular visiting hours and is in use only for High Holidays.

Contacts for More Information

The telephone number of the local community offices is (0651) 25195. Great persistence may be required.

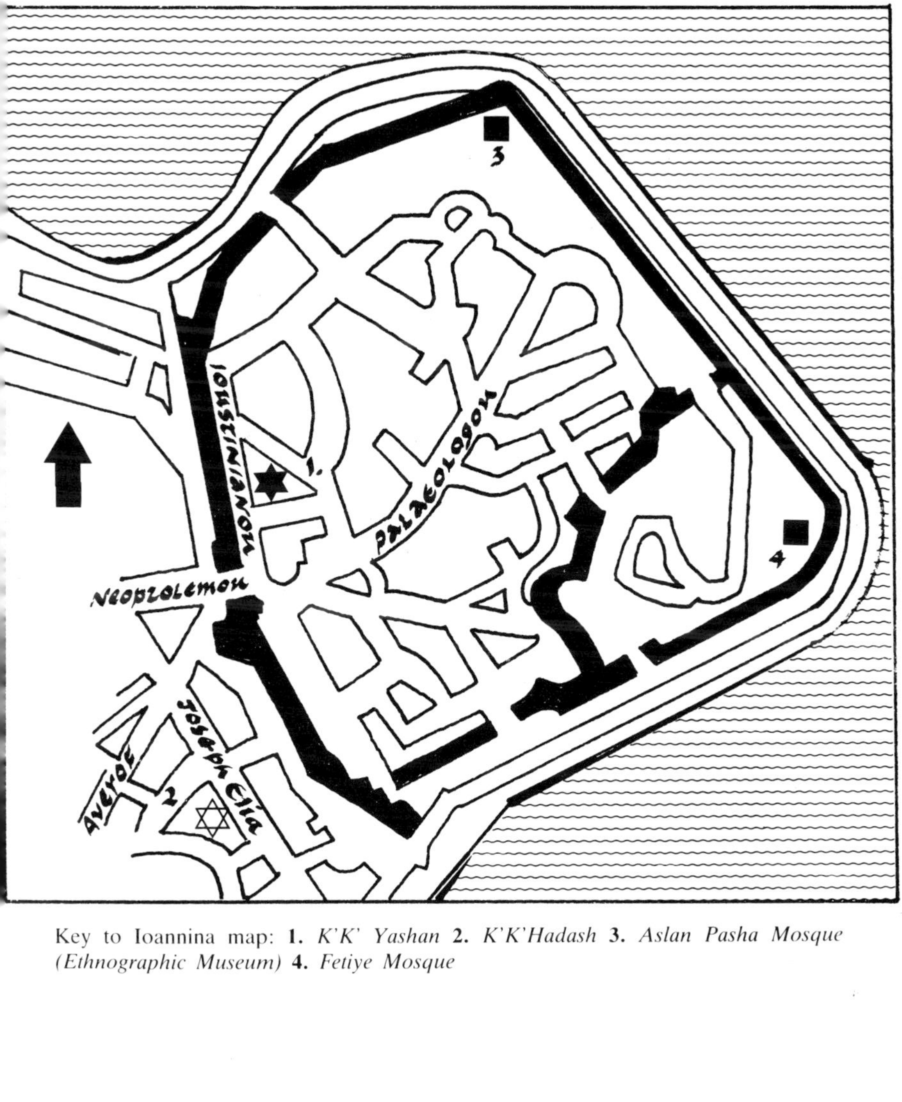

Key to Ioannina map: **1.** *K'K' Yashan* **2.** *K'K'Hadash* **3.** *Aslan Pasha Mosque (Ethnographic Museum)* **4.** *Fetiye Mosque*

Interior of the synagogue of Komotini, in Autokratoros Theodosiou Square, built in the 18th century, view to the east toward the ehal, *photographed in August, 1980. This synagogue has many similarities with the Gerush Synagogue of Bursa (Turkey). (Photo: Timothy DeVinney/Jewish Museum of Greece)*

Komotini

Komotini, a modern town in Thrace, 348 kilometers (215 miles) east of Salonika (Thessaloniki). Total population: approximately 40,000 (1991), current Jewish population: 1. Extant sites: derelict synagogue.

Historical Background

The early history of a Jewish presence in Komotini is unknown. Its proximity to Adrianoupolis (Edirne), Drama, and other towns where there were Romaniote Jews would make it unlikely that Komotini did not have its own community. In the early 16th century, the community was emphatically Sephardi, and it remained such until its destruction during the Second World War. The 16th–century Jewish arrivals appear to have come either from Adrianoupolis or from Salonika, possibly as a consequence of an overflow of immigrants. Close commercial ties were maintained with both of those cities until well into the 18th century, when banditry made communications risky and financially unsound. As a result, Drama appears at that time to have assumed an increasingly important position as both an outlet for goods from Komotini and as a provider of necessities for its markets. Jews were especially active in textiles, both silk and wool. They seem to have switched over to the tobacco industry after it was introduced, as well as to the production and exportation of cannabis, hashish, and opium. Cannabis, hashish, and opium were important commodities in an age that had few if any pain relievers, and involvement in both production and trade of these did not have the connotation of drug trafficking that they do today.

Towards the middle of the 18th century the fortunes of the Jews here began to look up. An interesting incident associated with this revival in fortunes, involved the wife of Hacanio Hayon, one of the leaders of the community. Her name has not come down to us, but we know that she became ill shortly before Passover and that the doctor who treated her prescribed a concoction to be made up from hashish. It was discovered, however, that there was none available in the market, because the entire supply had been exported for sale. At

Exterior of the synagogue of Komotini, built in the 18th century, view to the southwest, as photographed in August, 1980. To the left and extending behind the synagogue are

the ancient city walls of Komotini. The lantern dome of this synagogue is quite exceptional but, unfortunately, has recently collapsed. (Photo: Timothy DeVinney/ Jewish Museum of Greece)

the termination of Passover, a request was made to one of the city's leading citizens (non–Jewish). He agreed to supply the necessary medication on the condition that the entire Jewish community sit at appointed times during the course of one year and hear him speak (about matters that are not recorded). He also promised to provide the Jews with a new site for a synagogue within the fortifications, as well as some 70 houses in the Turkish quarter.

Hidden within this story is the suggestion that the Jews were in fact subject to regular harrassment, and that the community had not, as in many other cities, been given a quarter capable of being officially protected. The new Jewish quarter was located just inside one of the principal gates and the site designated for the synagogue was almost flush against the walls.

By the year 1786, banditry was again rife throughout Thrace, Macedonia, and Epirus. Under Sultan Abdul Hamid I, an attempt was made to initiate reforms in the empire. In a number of towns there were significant revolts, and Komotini was not spared. A certain Ali Effendi from a nearby village who had a considerable following of rebels managed to seize Komotini. Christians as well as Jews within the town were forced to assist the rebels by providing supplies and funds, and the arrival of the Ottoman troops outside the walls created panic within. It was a Turkish woman by the name of Emine Hanim who "saved the day" by circulating a rumor that peace had been concluded between the rebels and the army, so that fighting ceased. After daybreak the gates were opened and the troops entered the city. Large numbers of rebels were killed and the Jewish community placed in mortal terror when its quarter was surrounded. With some difficulty, however, it was made clear that the Jewish community had been forced to comply with rebel demands, and in the end the troops dispersed. In memory of this event, the Jews of Komotini annually celebrated their own Purim with a recitation of the event in the form of a hymn written by R. Daniel de Avila. Unfortunately, the hymn has been lost.

We have little if any information concerning the community during the 19th century other than that it continued to prosper and grow. In the course of the Balkan Wars of 1912-13, Komotini found itself caught in the very center of hostilities involving Greeks,

The back (west) wall of the synagogue of Komotini, with the supports for the mehitza, *photographed in August, 1980. It had both an upper and lower section. As can be seen here, nothing remains of its floorings, railings, or lattice work. (Photo: Timothy DeVinney/Jewish Museum of Greece)*

Bulgarians, Turks and Serbs. Many Jews left and moved to Salonika, or went east to settle in Edirne and Istanbul. It was only after the middle twenties that stability was restored to this area and the Jews of Komotini began actively to modernize their community by creating a French School, as well as youth clubs and Zionist groups.

In 1941 the Bulgarians, as members of the Axis coalition, occupied almost all of Thrace and for their own nationalist motives tried to "Bulgarize" the region by forcing Bulgarian identity on the inhabitants or creating conditions forcing Greeks to flee. At the same time, the Germans were pressuring the Bulgarians to arrest the Jews, which they finally did in March of 1943. The Jewish community at that time numbered 819 persons. Their fate is still not clear, but there is evidence that they were sent to Treblinka. Only 28 persons avoided arrest. Today there is just one Jew left living in Komotini, and he was originally from Drama.

Description of the Synagogue

The synagogue of Komotini is of great interest and importance, being without doubt the original building constructed when the community was allowed to settle within the walls of the city in the 18th century. It is also the only surviving synagogue in Greece that has an externally prominent dome. The building is wedged in a corner of the original city walls and has a simple exterior with a wide–eaved, tiled roof. A lantern dome dominates the center. The building is quite large, and the plot it covers, coupled with the distinctive appearance of its dome, probably give us a clue as to what the now lost synagogue of Serres looked like as well.

The interior, unfortunately, was stripped of its furnishings during the Occupation and then used for a number of years as a stable. Nonetheless, some evidence remains to enable us to reconstruct what it was like. The main entrance to the synagogue was through a central door on its north wall. Even today the interior, broken here and there by columns supporting a proportionately low ceiling, is still impressive. Most of the ceiling panelling, which radiates out from the dome in concentric circles, is intact.

The axis of the building runs from east to west, through the area where the bema was located under the dome. Nothing remains of the bema, but the niche in the east wall which enclosed the *ehal*, is still prominent. The entrance to the *mehitza* (women's section) was through an outside door in the south corner of the east wall. It led directly into a small aisle cut off from the men's section by a ballustrade. At its terminus on the west wall it led to a stair to the now–lost balcony that ran along the south and west walls. This was covered by lattice work as was the side–aisle beneath it. The interior of the synagogue was well lit with rather low–set windows and there are distinctive architectural features pointing to the influence of mosque architecture. A number of synagogues of this type can be found in Istanbul and Bursa. The layout of the interior, with the central bema marked off by columns, is characteristically Sephardi.

How To Visit the Synagogue

The synagogue is in Autokratoros Theodosiou (Emperor Theodosius) Square (see the map). It is an abandoned building (as of this

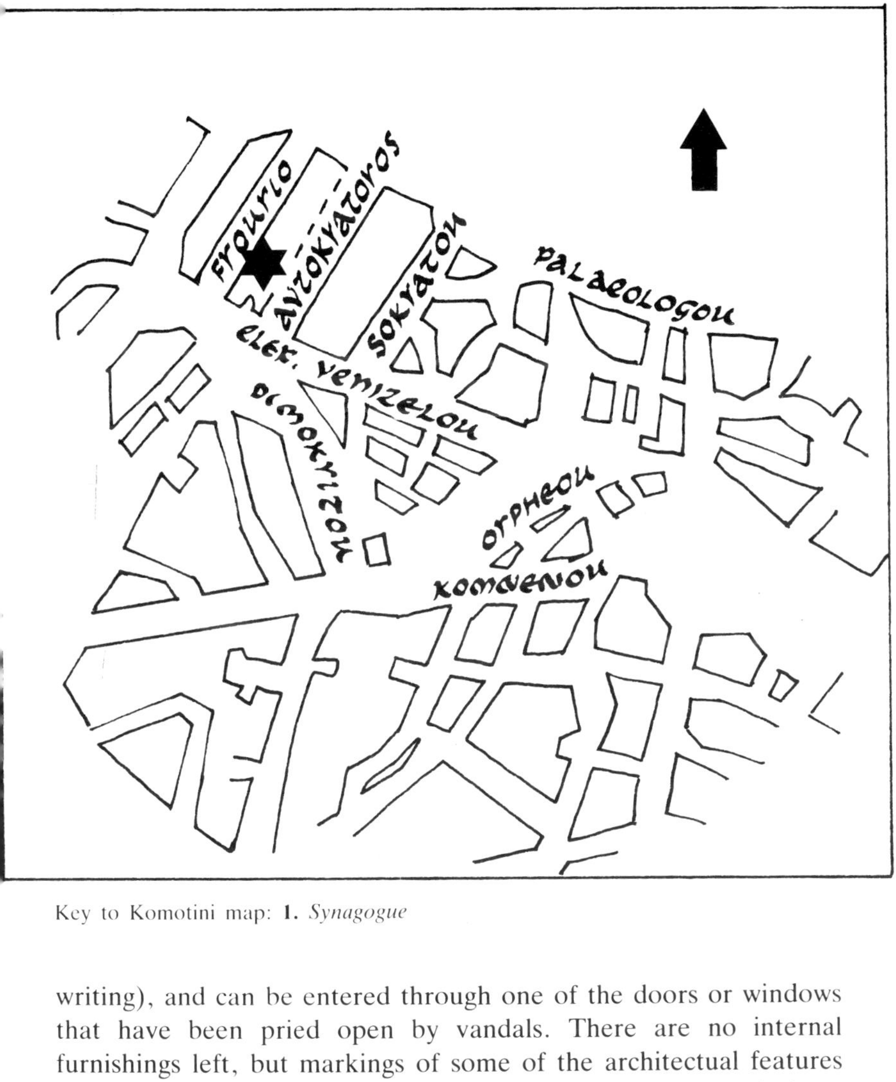

Key to Komotini map: **1.** *Synagogue*

writing), and can be entered through one of the doors or windows that have been pried open by vandals. There are no internal furnishings left, but markings of some of the architectual features mentioned above can still be made out. There have recently been reports that the dome has fallen in.

Contacts for More Information

For current information on the Komotini synagogue, contact the Jewish Museum of Greece in Athens (36 Amalias Avenue, Athens 10558, telephone 3231-577 or 3225-582).

Exterior of the Shalom Synagogue in Kos, built in 1934, view to the east. The street entrance to the synagogue. (Photo: Timothy DeVinney/Jewish Museum of Greece)

Kos

Kos, a modern town on an island of the same name in the Dodecanese islands, 360 kilometers (220 miles) east of Athens/Pireaus. Total population: approx. 15,000 (1991), current Jewish population: 0. Extant sites: a former synagogue now in use as a municipal cultural center, and a cemetery.

Historical Background

A Jewish community existed on Kos in antiquity and is mentioned in 1 Macc. 15:16-23, as well as later by Josephus in the first century of the Common Era (C.E.). During his travels through the Jewries of the Byzantine Empire in the 12th century, Benjamin of Tudela does not mention Kos, though he sailed past it. After the seizure of the island by the Knights of Rhodes in 1306, some 1,500 Jews from Kos were exiled to Nice and never returned. These would undoubtedly have been Romaniotes, and descendants of the medieval community of Byzantine Jews. Not long after the Ottoman conquest of Kos in 1522, large numbers of Spanish Jews settled here and maintained close relations with Rhodian Jews, as well as with communities in Izmir (Smyrna) and Bodrum.

Little is known of the fortunes of the community until the 19th century when it figured prominantly in a blood libel that would indicate that relations with the Christian community on the island were not especially cordial. By 1850 there were only 40 families, a number that fell to 20 by 1880 and 3 in 1910. After the Greco–Turkish War of 1918-22, there was an influx of Jews into Kos from Asia Minor, especially from Izmir. As the Dodecanese Islands had been acquired by the Italians after the First World War, these islands enjoyed a somewhat isolated and almost neutral position and Jews quickly took advantage of the improved conditions. By 1933 there were 160 Jews actively involved in small crafts and in commerce with Alexandria, Izmir, and Italy. In that year, the old synagogue was destroyed and immediately afterwards the community built a new one on a site not far from the harbor.

After the Italian capitulation to the Allies in 1943, Kos, along with all of the other Dodecanese Islands, fell under German control.

General view of the exterior of the Shalom Synagogue in Kos, built in 1934, view to the southeast. The architecture of the Kos synagogue reflects contemporary architectural

styles introduced by the Italians in most of the Dodecanese Islands. (Photo: Timothy DeVinney/Jewish Museum of Greece)

The cemetery of Kos, established in the 17th century. Many of the tombs bear a close resemblance to contemporary 18th–century Ottoman types, and are elevated and set with both headstones as well as footstones. Many were in fact ordered from stone–cutters in Izmir (Turkey). (Photo: Timothy DeVinney/Jewish Museum of Greece)

Many Jews from Kos fled to Turkey. Those who remained—some 120—were finally arrested in the spring of 1944, and transported to Auschwitz–Birkenau where, as far as we know, they all perished. Today there are no Jews on Kos.

Description of the Synagogue

The synagogue, Kal Shalom, which dates from 1934, is at 4 Alexandros Diakou Street, near the harbor. It was recently given to the Kos municipality and functions today as a cultural center and library. Its exterior remains much as it was, but the interior has been completely secularized.

Other Sites

Today there is also a small cemetery on the outskirts of town to the west, which can be reached by following Meg. Alexandros street and then Zaraflou street. It has some quite interesting stones, dating from the 17th century.

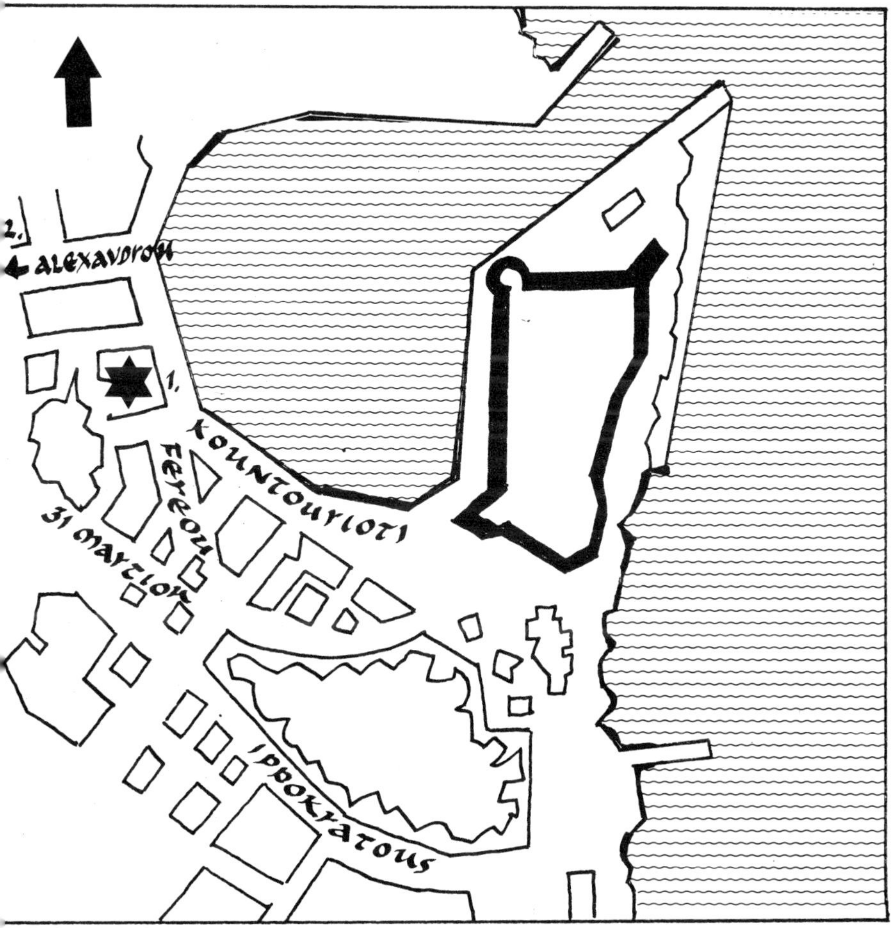

Key to Kos map: **1.** *K'K' Shalom* **2.** *Direction to Cemetery*

How to Visit the Synagogue

The synagogue is at 4 Alexandros Diakou Street (see map). The interior has been entirely reconstructed but the building functions as a municipal cultural center and can be visited during public office hours.

Contacts for More Information

For current information on the Kos synagogue and cemetery, contact the Jewish Museum of Greece in Athens (36 Amalias Avenue, Athens 10558, telephone 3231-577 or 3225-582).

The ehal *of the Etz Hayyim Synagogue of Larissa, 19th century, interior rebuilt after 1945, view to the south. (Photo: Timothy DeVinney/Jewish Museum of Greece)*

Larissa

Larissa, a modern city in central Thessaly, 360 kilometers (220 miles) north of Athens. Total population: approximately 113,000 (1991), current Jewish population: 350. Extant sites: a functioning synagogue, a cemetery, and a modern monument to victims of the Holocaust.

Historical Introduction

Larissa is situated in the very center of the Plain of Thessaly, on the bank of the Pineios river. The city has a history stretching back to Paleolithic times. Pindar, Hippocrates, and Gorgias the Sophist all enjoyed the patronage of its rulers. After the Roman conquest it was made the capital of Thessaly. While not mentioned by Paul of Tarsus, it is known that Larissa had a very early Christian community that claimed to have some Jewish connection. Considering the relatively large Jewish community in Thessaloniki (Salonika) at this time, it would have been natural for Larissa to have attracted Jews.

From the 5th through the 9th centuries, this region of Greece saw the continuous passage of Goths, Slavs, and Bulgarians. It is not until after the Byzantine recovery that we have our first definite mention of a Jewish community. Benjamin of Tudela visited the city in the 12th century, and noted its Jews and their connection with those of Halmyros (Almyros), which served as the port for Thessaly.

During the 13th and 14th centuries, Larissa was plundered a number of times both by Crusaders and the Catalan Company. It is known that Halmyros lost its Jewish community at this time, which raises questions about the survival of the Larissa community. But the existence into modern times of a Romaniote synagogue in Larissa indicates some Jewish presence at the time of the arrival of the Sephardi Jews in the 16th century, which in turn would seem to point to their not having been wiped out in the 13th or 14th century.

Under Ottoman rule, Larissa and the Plain of Thessaly, enjoyed relatively peaceful conditions. With the arrival of Hungarian Jews fleeing pogroms in the north in the 15th century, Larissa's community began to growth significantly. Sicilian Jews and others from Spain

Exterior of the Etz Hayyim Synagogue in Larissa, view to the east. The exterior dates from before the Second World War, though it still retains some hint of the generally austere exteriors of many synagogues in Greece. (Photo: Timothy DeVinney/Jewish Museum of Greece)

arrived soon afterwards, most likely via Salonika. In 1687, there was a considerable influx of Jews from the Peloponnese fleeing the aftermath of the Turko–Venetian War. Some of these were Romaniotes, but the majority were no doubt Sepharadim, because in 1790 there were a number of communal regulations set down in which Romaniote customs regarding bethrothal and marriage were curbed, if not forbidden.

Larissa earned the title "Madre di Israel" ("Mother of Israel"), because of its status as a refugee center. Many of its leading members proudly bore the title *Celebi* ("most honored"), in recognition of their philanthropic activities. Close connections were maintained with other Jewish communities in Salonika, Izmir, Adrianoupolis and even Sarajevo. The Beth Din of Larissa and its learned rabbis were widely respected.

In 1857 a fire destroyed much of the Jewish quarter as well as two of its seven synagogues. The coincidence of this and similar fires in other Jewish communites reflects the tense atmosphere that prevailed during the Crimean War. Great Britain sided with Turkey,

Greece's traditional enemy, and the close association of Turks and Jews brought out a wave of xenophobic responses to the Jews in general throughout Greece, as well as in Turkish–occupied areas.

By 1860 both of the destroyed synagogues had been rebuilt with assistance from European Jews. Shortly afterwards, in 1865, the Alliance Israelite Universelle founded a school here. Both this school and the yeshivah of Larissa played an important role in lifting the intellectual life of the community, as well as in keeping it informed of European life in general. It is not surprising, then, that Larissa had a very early interest in nascent Zionism.

The community in 1882 numbered over 2,800 Jews. Most of these were involved in mercantile activities. After the absorption of Salonika into the Greek state in 1913, many Larissan Jews went there to establish businesses. Others moved to Athens.

By 1940 there were approximately 2,000 Jews in Larissa, with seven synagogues still in use. The oldest synagogue was called the Etz Hayyim, and it appears to have originally been Romaniote. The others had initially been established to accommodate the Ashkenazi and Sephardi rites, as well as those of the congregation of Sicilian Jews. These differences in ritual, however, no longer existed in the 19th century (the Sephardi ritual having displaced the others). Larissa was a cosmopolitan city, with Greek, Ladino, and French widely spoken, and the Jews, on the whole, enjoyed quite good relations with their Christian neighbors.

When the Germans seized this part of Greece, the Larissan Jews had already played a notable role in the resistance and a good number had taken to the mountains as partisans. In 1943, when the Germans began their mass arrests throughout Greece, most of the remaining Jews of Larissa also took flight to the mountains. Only 250 Jews —those who had remained in town—were arrested and sent to Auschwitz, where most perished. At the end of the war, Larissa's Jews returned and reestablished a community that is still quite active. Of only its seven synagogues the Etz Hayyim synagogue remained. It had been severely damaged and practically gutted, but through the assistance of JOINT it was rebuilt, and is in use today. Over the years many Jews have left Larissa and today there are only about 350 Jews living here.

Interior of the Etz Hayyim Synagogue of Larissa, 19th century, interior rebuilt after 1945, view to the south. The central portion is clearly marked off by columns and

accentuated by arches, with the bema underneath.(Photo: Timothy DeVinney/Jewish Museum of Greece)

Esdras Esdra dressed as King Ahasuerus, Larissa, 1935. Larissa was famous for its annual Purim plays, in which actors drawn from the Jewish community were lavishly costumed in Ottoman velvets and embroidered silks. (Jewish Museum of Greece)

Description of the Synagogue

The interior of the Etz Hayyim synagogue dates from after the war. It is similar to that of most Sephardi synagogues in central Greece, with a central bay set apart by four equidistant columns. The bema is under the bay and faces the *ehal* in the east wall.

Cemetary of Larissa, showing 20th–century tombs. (Photo: Timothy DeVinney/Jewish Museum of Greece)

How to Visit the Synagogue

The Etz Hayyim synagogue is at the intersection of Kentauron and Kyprou Streets, at 29 Kentauron Street. By car, it can be reached by following the signs off the main road into town (coming from Athens) to the center and to M. Sapka Square (where the town hall is). From the west side of the square take Papanastasiou Street north, take the second left onto Eleftheriou Venizelou Street, and drive down toward the river. Before reaching the river turn left (virtually a 160 degree turn) onto Manolaki Street, turn right at the second street (Hephestiou Street), go one block, turn left, and after one block you will reach a tiny square formed by the intersection of Kentauron and Kyprou streets. The synagogue is on your left at the southeast corner of the intersection.

The synagogue is normally open for services every Friday evening, Saturday morning, and all High Holidays. For exact times, visitors should contact the community.

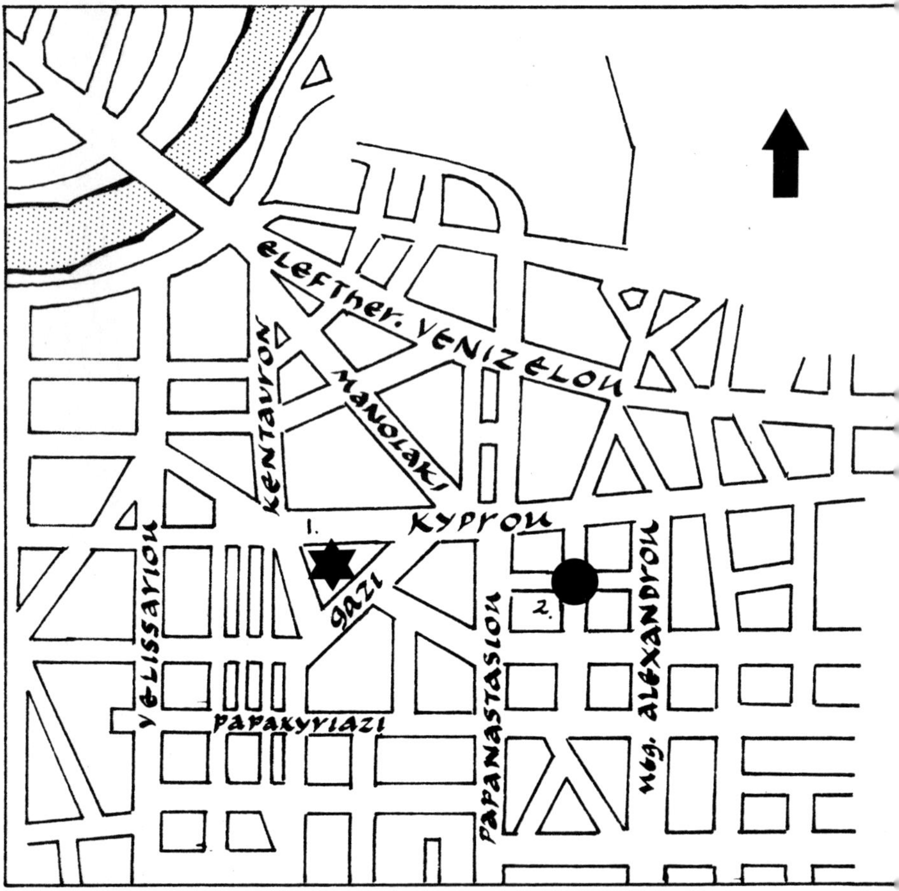

Key to Larissa map: **1.** *K'K' Etz Hayyim* **2.** *Square*

Other Sites

The Jewish cemetery of Larissa is south of town in the Alexandroupoleos district (just on the other side of the railway tracks). It is normally kept locked up, and arrangements to see it should be made through the community.

In the square in front of the synagogue, at the intersection of Kentauron and Kyprou streets, there is now a large monument to the victims of the Holocaust.

Contacts for More Information

Visitors should contact the community at (041) 226-396, between the hours of 11:30 A.M. and 2:00 P.M. (They speak English.)

Rhodes

Rhodes, a modern port city on an island of the same name, 420 kilometers (250 miles) southeast of Athens/Piraeus. Total population: approximately 44,000 (1991), current Jewish population: 35. Extant sites: one functioning synagogue and cemetery.

Historical Background

Rhodes and Rhodians are mentioned a number of times in Scripture, though it's not clear if it is Jews that are being referred to. It is likely, however, that Jews were attracted to the island very early, due to its location on an important sea route between the Judaean coast, Cyprus, and the Aegean islands. We know that Jews had settled on the island by the 2nd century B.C.E., because they are mentioned in the Book of Macabees. At that time Rhodes, Delos, and Crete were linked economically and there were considerable Jewish communities on each of them. Whether or not they came from Judaea is unknown. It is more likely that their roots were in Alexandria.

The first Rhodian Greek to write about Jews was Apollonius Molon. His observations in 87 B.C.E. are usually cited as an example of early anti–Semitism. A student and contemporary of the stoic philosopher Poseidonius, his writings reflect a common complaint against Jews, citing them as anti–social, secretive, and intolerant in their religious views. In all fairness it should be kept in mind that this was a common and quite popular view. Poseidonius himself found the Jews to be exclusive, insular, and incapable of assimilating or respecting the ideology of the Roman Empire. These two invectives do not proof of a Jewish community on Rhodes, since Apollonius and Poseidonius, while writing from Rhodes, were intellectually involved in horizons much wider than those provided by the island.

Tensions between Greeks and Jews erupted at times into serious incidents. In Alexandria and Antioch (and probably Rhodes and elsewhere along the Aegean Coast, as well), Jews were demanding 'isonomia' or equality before the law, while at the same time they refused to enter into full civic life, because, as they claimed, its

Interior of the Shalom Synagogue on Rhodes, originally built in 1575, view to the east. Taken from the mehitza *this photograph gives a clear picture of not only the transverse arches but also the alignment of the bema to the door leading to the courtyard and two* ehals. *(Photo: Timothy DeVinney/Jewish Museum of Greece)*

demands were at odds with their own laws and traditions. Greeks and Romans felt they had good reason to feel offended by Jewish refusal to respect their Gods, their communal socio–religious banquets, and customary laws.

In the next century, Paul of Tarsus more or less skipped both Rhodes and nearby Kos, not stopping at either for more than a day. This would seem to hint that there was no community here, though Paul is said to have been in a great hurry to get to Jerusalem. (We are told in the Acts that he took a "straight" course.)

It is not surprising, either, that we have no documentation or evidence concerning a Jewish presence on Rhodes during late antiquity and up until the 12th century. The island faired badly after the 4th century, when traders tended to avoid sea routes. In addition, there were periodic attacks by pirateers, Goths, and other tribes who took to the sea after invading Romano–Byzantine territories. In the 7th century the feasibility of trade with the Near East was ended, because of the Islamic invasions. By the 9th century, Rhodes was being attacked frequently by Cretan–Muslim corsairs. It was not a propitious time for settlement or for the pursuit of commerce.

The first explicit mention of Jews on Rhodes comes in the 12th century when Benjamin of Tudela visited the island on his way out of the Byzantine Empire. He mentions a community of some 500 members, led by two rabbis. The community's size may reflect the movement of Jews to the Aegean islands following the inroads of Seljuq Turks into Anatolia, especially its southwestern coast. It is interesting that Benjamin's itinerary carefully avoided stopping at any point other than the islands. In the following century a small group of Tarragonese Jews settled on the island after fleeing from Spain.

Our knowledge of Rhodian Jews becomes more detailed after the island was seized by the Hospitalers or Knights of St. John. After being driven from Jerusalem by Salah ad–Din they settled at Acre, and from there they moved on to Cyprus and seized Rhodes in 1309. Rhodes thus became economically linked with a network of ports that had emerged after the dismemberment of the Byzantine Empire in 1204. Modon, Corone, Oropos (on the Attic coast), are all known to have had Jewish communities. Doubtless, the Jews of Rhodes

Interior of the Shalom Synagogue on Rhodes. The present day ehals *are modeled on those of the Sardes synagogue (4th century* C.E.*). There is no description of what they*

looked like prior to 1943. The pebble mosaic floor represents a local Rhodian tradition. (Photo: Timothy DeVinney/Jewish Museum of Greece)

prospered initially through commerce with these towns and took advantage of other opportunities in Crusader–held territories, such as Kos and Bodrum. From what we know of the Rhodes community at this time, its members were Romaniote, Greek speaking and adhered to the Romaniote *Minhag*. Their quarter in Rhodes was enlarged shortly after the Crusader takeover. It extended, as can still be seen today, from the port area up along the southeast fortifications. Because the Knights were a religious community with an international membership (as is the case with their descendants, the contemporary Knights of Malta) and maintained close contacts with its roots in France, England, Germany, and Spain, Rhodes quickly became a center of trade, piracy, and quite aggressive military activity. It became a hornet's nest of activity and its Jews enjoyed a period of great prosperity. They were particularly active in producing silk.

In 1480 Sultan Mehmet II launched a great attack on the island aimed at destroying the Knights and their stronghold. The area chosen for the main assault was against the walls adjacent to the Jewish quarter, and we are informed by contemporary sources that the Jews valliantly defended their sector, filling in breaches in the walls with rubble gathered from their destroyed houses. Jews and Christians fought side by side to drive out the Ottoman troops after the success of their initial attack, and in the end the Turks withdrew. R. Meshullam of Volterra, who visited Rhodes in 1487, describes in detail the ravaged conditions of the Jewish quarter and Rhodes as a whole. The saving of Rhodes was attributed to a miracle by both Jews and Christians. In 1493 R. Ovadia of Bertinovo also visited Rhodes, and mentions the miracle, noting that the Knights had "honored" the site (apparently referring to the synagogue) by converting it into a church. A new synagogue was constructed elsewhere and furnished by the Knights for the Jewish community.

Rhodes never really recovered from that attack of 1480. Felix Fabri describes a city that had been given a death blow, and when he left the island in 1487 he mentions that the boat was filled with fleeing Knights as well as Jews. Only 22 Jewish families remained on the island. Because they were without a ritual slaughterer and the means for producing kosher wine, they were forced to do without either. Despite the horrors of this initial Turkish onslaught, however, though, the Jews of Rhodes recovered quickly and continued to work in silk production. Moreover, the part played by the Jews in the defence of Rhodes raised them in the esteem of the Knights.

Two gentlemen in Rhodes in the early 1930's, holding Sepher Torahs adorned in the typical Sephardi manner with crowns, breast shields, silver finials (rimonim)*, and pointers* (yads)*. (Jewish Museum of Greece)*

Exactly what changed this high regard is unknown, but early in the 16th century, the Grand Master, Pierre d'Aubusson, who had initially been quite amicable to the Jews, suddenly demanded from the Council of the Knights that the Jews be expelled from the island. It may well be that he had been pressured or influenced by the recent expulsion of Jews from Spain in 1492. Severe action was taken against the community. Some Jews were forced to convert. Others were sent to Nice, and still others were thrown into a pit where they eventually died of starvation and exposure.

Ironically, as soon as the community had ceased to exist formally, new Jews were brought to the island. The Knights in continuing their lucrative pirateering, seized several ships among the captives of which were large numbers of Jews. Thus, by 1553 Rhodes could boast of a population of some 3,000 Jews. How and under what

Exterior of the Shalom Synagogue on Rhodes. (Photo: Timothy DeVinney/Jewish Museum of Greece)

conditions they lived is unknown, but it appears that they were not allowed to form an organized community. Jewish sympathies with the Turks understandably rose as a result, and there were several incidents of converted Jews assisting Ottoman intelligence, until a new attack was launched in 1522 under Sultan Suleiman. This time all attempts to defend Rhodes failed and the Jews of Rhodes rejoiced to see an end to the occupation of the Knights. Those who had been forced to convert returned to their faith and a community was formally reestablished.

The size of that new community was quickly depleted, however, because those Jews who had been brought to the island as slaves emigrated. Those who remained formed the core of what was still basically a Romaniote community. Suleiman was active in following the policy of his grandfather, Beyazid II, encouraging Jewish immigration. Large numbers of Sephardi Jews from Salonika, Izmir, and Constantinople began to arrive.

There are signs that the interaction between the Sepharadim and Romaniotes was not cordial. This was not a new phenomenon as the first hahambaşi (chief rabbi) of the Ottoman Empire, a Cretan by the name of Moses Kapsalis, had been outspoken for some time in supporting Romaniote customs in the face of Sephardi pressure. In Rhodes, the two congregations evolved separately, each with its own synagogue. The older synagogue, built in 1480 and known as the Kadosh Gadol, was Romaniote. While the new synagogue, built in 1575 and given the name Kal Kadosh Shalom, was Sephardi. (The latter still stands.) This did not, however, end tensions and it was not until the mid–17th century that the problem was solved by the smothering of Romaniote resistance. By that time the *Gregos* (Greeks), as they were called derogatorily by the Sephardim, had been obliged not only to conform to the Sephardi *minhag*, but to speak Spanish and, in some cases, even adopt Hispanicized names.

Under Sephardi leadership, Rhodes entered into a quite brilliant period of intellectual activity and produced a number of notable rabbis. Many of these wrote *responsa* that were considered authoritative as far afield as Constantinople, Cairo, Safed, and Salonika. The poet Yehuda Zakko, writing in the late 16th century, continued the intense Iberian curiosity in matters other than religion.

Despite all of this, however, Jewish life was quite insular. The Orthodox Christians were, for the most part, hostile and held Jews responsible for the fall of the island to the Turks. There must have been resentment as well against the privileges showered on the new Sephardi arrivals. It may well have been in response to this resentment that a decision was finally taken in 1668 to unite the two congregations under a single chief rabbi. That was not an easy task and the first incumbant, R. Moshe ha–Cohen, a Salonikan by birth, failed entirely and left the island. His successor was R. Moshe de Vushal, who achieved the union by taking advantage of the recent appearance of followers of Shabbetai Zvi and asserting the need for a strong, united community in the face of the challenge posed by the Messiah of Izmir. That challenge must have been quite strong, as we know, for example, that de Vushal's own son, Shlomo, followed Zvi in converting to Islam.

Nonetheless, dissension appears to have been the rule within the newly united community, especially during the 18th century. Rabbinical *responsa* reflect some quite petty issues, involving, for example, the purity of grape–leaves to which infinitesimal insects have adhered (the Rhodian Jews were fond of *yaprakites*, or stuffed vine leaves), or the question of eating swordfish, which has scales only when it is young (see "kosher" in the Glossary). Perhaps more serious questions were those concerning the use of the *hamam* (Turkish bath) for performing the *mikveh* and the legality of taking Shabbat strolls onto visiting ships in the port. A long drawn–out battle ensued under R. Moshe Israel II (d. 1750) over the abilities of a certain *shohet* (ritual slaughterer) whose competence in examining the knife was questioned due to the fact that he was a heavy drinker. In this instance, the matter was taken as far as the Beth Din in Izmir by the *shohet*, whose drinking "on the job" was severely reprimanded.

By 1850 Rhodes could boast of three Jewish schools with a total of 120 boys. Attendance was normally until the age of twelve. They learned to read, write, and do basic arithmetic. Instruction was in Ladino. Further education was not encouraged, mainly due to lack of stimulus and the general poverty of the community. At twelve or thirteen a boy was set to work as a fellow–bread–earner in his family. Silk production was no longer a Jewish occupation and had been

East courtyard of the Shalom Synagogue on Rhodes. The door to the left leads out of the synagogue, while that to the right gives access to the street. This courtyard was used for the communal sukkah *as well as other community gatherings. (Photo: Timothy DeVinney/Jewish Museum of Greece)*

replaced by petty trade in perfumes, spices, cloth, slippers and sweets. A good number earned their livelihood as stevedores. A few individuals traded in wheat, exported wine, and even acted as money–lenders.

These reduced social and economic conditions were the cause for an appeal made to the Alliance in Paris in 1900 for the establishment of a school. The resulting establishment of an Alliance Israelite School only furthered emigration, as those who became exposed to wider horizons took advantage of opportunities to leave the island. By 1910 there was a constant movement of Rhodian Jews into Africa, especially Rhodesia (named of course for Cecil Rhodes, but the similarity in name appears to have attracted some Rhodian Jews who now became *Rhodesians*!), the Congo, and South Africa. Still others left for Brazil, the US, and Mexico. Whatever may have been the cause for inner strife in the Rhodian community itself, it was quickly replaced by a cohesiveness among the expatriots that is still characteristic of the descendants of these early emigrants. There is a very distinctive Rhodian Jewish identity that is still strongly maintained, be it in Pretoria, Rio de Janeiro, Atlanta, Seattle, or Los Angeles.

In 1923 Rhodes was ceded to the Italians after the peace agreements following the First World War. The Italians did much to develop the island but the Jews appear to have lost any sense of initiative. By 1941 there were only 2,000 Jews on Rhodes. Four synagogues were still being maintained, as well as several *midrashim* (oratories). The oldest synagogue was that dating back to the 15th century. After that there was the Kal Shalom which still stands

One of several wall decorations in the Shalom Synagogue on Rhodes, dating from the 19th century. (Photo: Timothy DeVinney/Jewish Museum of Greece)

today, much as it was when it was built. In the 19th century the wealthy Kamondo family of Istanbul founded another synagogue, in their own name, and a fourth and last synagogue was called, derisively, the "Kal de los Ricos" (Synagogue of the Rich).

In 1943 the Italians surrendered to the Allies and the Nazis immediately took control of Rhodes. The racial laws were put in place and in the following year the entire community, along with the Jews of Kos, was arrested and shipped under horrific conditions to Piraeus/Athens, and from there to Auschwitz.

There were 151 survivors after the war, but none of them chose to return to the island. Despite this the international Rhodian identity has been strong enough to maintain both the surviving synagogue as well as a legally incorporated community.

Description of the Synagogue

The Kal Shalom is the only synagogue on Rhodes to have survived the ravages of the Second World War. Not long after the termination of the war it was renovated through the efforts of Rhodian Jews living abroad, and it still functions occasionally—when a *minyan* can be established. The exterior, in keeping with all synagogue architecture in the Balkans, is simple and austere. As one enters the main gate, a pebble–decorated path leads directly to the stairs to the *mehitza* (women's section). The main entrance to the synagogue is to the left.

The interior of the synagogue is divided transversely into three aisles by great arches supported on heavy columns. The windows are very high and provide an even illumination. The bema and its placement in the center of the room are typically Sephardi. But the east wall is exceptional in that it is pierced in the center by a door leading into the east courtyard, which served as a communal *sukkah* during the Feast of Tabernacles. There are two *ehals*, one located on either side of this central door. The walls have several large 19th–century paintings which have been restored. These show various symbols such as the *lulav*, *menorah*, *ner tamid*, harps, and *shofarim*.

Some of the liturgical silver from Kal Shalom as well as a number of 18th century ivory components for decorating the spindles on which the Sepher Torah is rolled, were acquired by the Jewish Museum of Greece as a gift. These were part of a large number of liturgical artifacts were hidden by the Turkish Muslim community from the Nazis after the arrest of the community. They were returned to the Jewish community at the end of the war and are now on display in the Jewish Museum in Athens.

Other Sites

The Jewish cemetery has been reconstructed and many of its stones are of interest as they incorporate symbols of the trades practiced by the deceased. None of them are of exceptionally great antiquity. Some were certainly carved in Izmir with which Rhodes always had specially close associations by marriage and custom.

Interior of the Shalom Synagogue on Rhodes. The synagogue interior looking west with bema in the foreground and mehitza *running along the back wall. (Photo: Timothy DeVinney/Jewish Museum of Greece)*

A woman's tombstone in the Rhodian Jewish cemetery, dated 1885. The scissors and thimble at the bottom indicate that she was seamstress. In general razors, basins, cooking utensils, and so on were symbols also used to indicate the deceased profession. This was a common custom among Sephardi Jews. The small indentations in the foreground were for setting candles. (Photo: Timothy DeVinney/Jewish Museum of Greece)

The Jewish quarter is still identifiable within its ancient limits. It is filled with narrow lanes and small facades that were often described by travelers as "poor and mean," which was usually the case in quarters such as these. People tended to present a low economic profile so as to avoid theft and harassment. Life was lived quite Jewishly within this area and its central street (we are not certain which street this was) was frequently used for processions and public events.

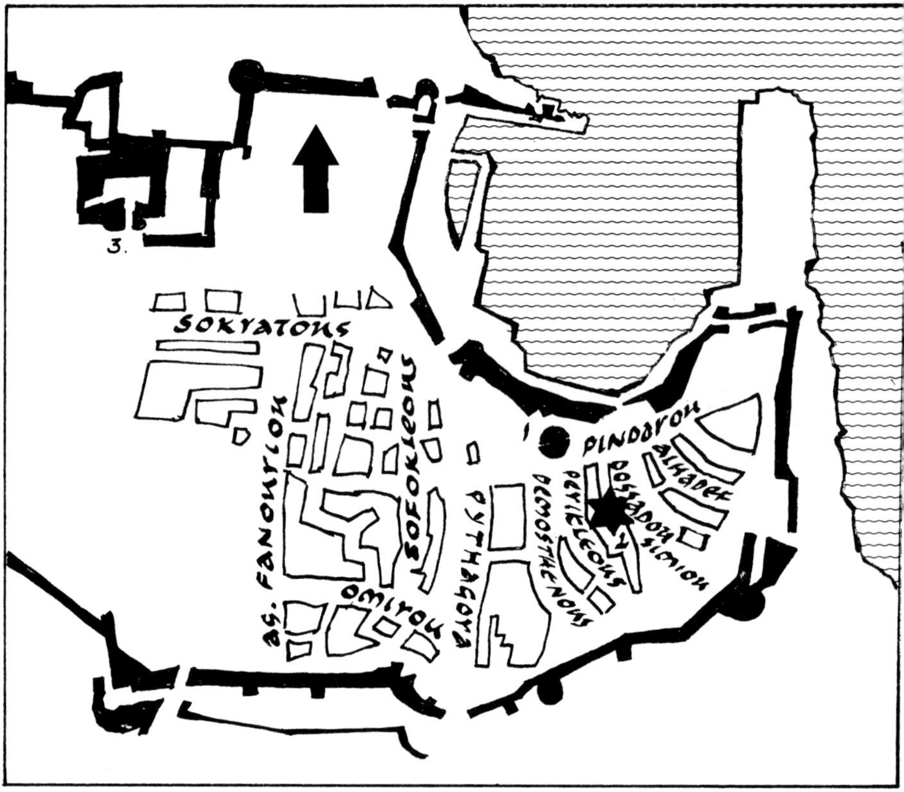

Key to Rhodes map: **1.** *Jewish Martyr's Square* **2.** *K'K' Shalom* **3.** *Palace of the Knights*

How to Visit the Synagogue

The Kal Shalom is at 8 Simmiou Street. To reach it starting from the Calle Ancha (the Square of the Sea Horses), go east along Pindarou Street and turn right at the first opportunity (onto Dossadou Street). This becomes Simmiou Street after a short distance. The synagogue is on your right–hand side.

During the summer, the synagogue is open for visitors daily from 8:00 A.M. to 1:00 P.M. and from 5:00 P.M. to 8:00 P.M. Services are held when enough visitors are present to form a *minyan*.

Contacts for More Information

Visitors should contact the community at (0241) 223-64.

Salonika

Salonika (Thessaloniki) is a modern city about 515 kilometers (310 miles) north of Athens. Total population: approximately 740,000 (1991), current Jewish population: 1,000. Extant sites: three synagogues (only one in its original building), cemetery (postwar), a hospital, many villas once owned by Jewish families, community offices, a modern retirement home.

Note: Salonika has seen many name changes, including Salonika, Salonica, or Saloniko in Ladino, Selanlik in Osmanli, and today Thessaloniki in Greek. In this text Salonika is used, because that was its name throughout the greater part of its Jewish history.

Historical Background

Salonika (or Thessalonika, as it was known then) was founded in 315 B.C.E. by King Cassandros, and Jews began to arrive not long afterwards. It is likely that the earliest arrivals were from Alexandria—quite possibly sailors, who would have been quite Hellenized, internationally oriented, and Greek speaking. Their synagogue was known as the Etz Hayyim and was located near the waterfront. Substantial segments of it were still standing in 1917.

The Salonikan Jews undoubtedly maintained close relations with other Greek Jewish communities at Philippi, Verroia, and elsewhere throughout Macedonia and Thrace. The most vivid picture of these communities is found in the Acts of the Apostles, in which Paul of Tarsus describes his visit to Salonika, where he preached in the Etz Hayyim synagogue and was promptly driven out of the city (Acts 17:1–10). It is also of interest that he journeyed on to nearby Verroia. There he was not only invited to preach several times by its Jews, but also created a small Christian community (Acts 17: 10–13).

During the early Roman period, Jews would have enjoyed the rights of law and the continuation of what privileges they had enjoyed earlier. It was not until the period after Constantine I's commitment to Christianity and its declaration as the state religion of Rome under Theodosios I (between the years 313-395) that Jewish fortunes began to change appreciably. By this time, Salonika was a very great city and figured centrally in imperial policies. Jews and Christians were not on comfortable terms and their religious debates and differences, stemming as they did from a common source, could be violent and quite vindictive. The victory of the Church saw an almost immediate curtailment of earlier Jewish privileges, as well as a restriction of their social and religious activities. Those restrictions continued into the reign of Justinian the Great (527-565 C.E.).

Despite those restrictions, however, the Jews of Salonika appear to have prospered, as did those elsewhere in the Balkans, until the onslaught of the Slavic invasions in the 6th century. After that date, and until the 12th century, we have only occasional—though intriguing—hints at a Jewish presence in the city. The Slavic invaders were followed by Bulgars, Avars, Gepids, Huns, and Kotrigurs in succession, and the economic life of the city was cut off from the hinterland. At the same time Salonika suffered the ill effects of the ascending fortunes of Constantinople and the decline of traffic on the Via Egnatia, which ran through Salonika and had been a principal artery linking ancient Rome to Greece. Its importance as a commerical artery ceased after the late 5th century.

Even under such conditions, however, Salonika still seems to have continued to prosper. We know that in 904, for example, Cretan Muslims joined in a great attack on the city led by Leo of Tripoli (a Greek convert to Islam). Contemporary accounts refer to the enormous wealth both in slaves (some Jewish) and produce that was carried off to Crete and the Syrian coast.

In 1169 Benjamin of Tudela found a community of 500 Jews in Salonika. If this number refers only to householders, then the total community was comparatively large, perhaps numbering as many as 2,000. He notes that they were governed by what appears to have been a rabbinical family, headed by R. Samuel and his sons Elijah and R. Michael. As in most cities in the Greek peninsula, the Jews of Salonika were involved in the very lucrative silk industry through which they prospered, even though—and this may well reflect the impact of their commercial rivalry due to the size of their community—they were often oppressed. (Later, when Benjamin visited Constantinople, he also mentions "oppression" there, which took the form of public beatings, as well as heavy labor. He is honest enough, however, to point out that the Jews did not make themselves very popular with their custom of emptying out sewage from tanning vats into the gutters of the Christian quarter of Pera.)

Shortly after the Fourth Crusade in 1204, Salonika became the capital of the newly created Latin kingdom that emerged from the breakup of the Byzantine Empire. How the Jews fared is unknown, though it is unlikely that they did well. In 1223 the city was seized by Theodore Angelos and Byzantine rule was reestablished. The fortunes of Salonika were still, however, by no means stable and it was not until 1376 that the Jews appear to have enjoyed more settled circumstances. In that year a considerable number of Hungarian

Etching from Stuart and Reeves' Antiquites de la Grece *(17th century), showing a Jewish house and courtyard in Salonika in the 17th century. The Roman statues on the entablature were known in Ladino as* Las Inkantadas, *and in Turkish as* Surelter *(the sorceresses or idols). The four statues were taken to Paris in 1875. The Jewish man at left of center is shown talking with an Armenian. (Jewish Museum of Greece)*

Jews were settled here with imperial approval. As "foreign" Jews they maintained their own congregation (Ashkenazi) and built their own synagogue which was located at the present junction of Aristotelous and Herakleiou Streets (see map). (It was destroyed during the Great Fire of 1917.) In 1394 additional Jews arrived from Provence in France, and founded their own synagogue which was known as the "Provenzia" and was located in the vicinity of Othonos Square.

Jewish life was already becoming quite complicated in Salonika at this point, and these quite different congregations were not always on good terms. Greek Jews, for the most part, followed traditions based on the Palestinian Talmud, while the European Jews generally followed the Babylonian Talmud. Added to this divergence of traditions, there was a problem in communication and culture. The Ashkenazi Jews spoke German, the Provence Jews French, and the Romaniotes Greek. Mention should also be made of the existence of a large Karaite community, which may have afforded some point of unity for Rabbinical Jews. The Karaites and Rabbinical Jews were always at each other's throats. This was true not only in Salonika, but in Constantinople as well, where a wall had to be built to separate their respective quarters.

In the early 15th century, Salonika was drawn into the chaos that preceded the formal end of the Byzantine Empire. By 1423, when Venice acquired the city by purchase, it was all but an island in an Ottoman sea, though still attractive enough to draw Jews from Sicily and Venice. These Jews followed what appears to have become a tradition in Salonika: they founded their own synagogues. In their case, they founded the Sicilian and the Italian synagogues, respectively. They also added a new linguistic factor to this growing Babel by maintaining Italian as their common language. Nothing is known of the Sicilian synagogue, but the "Old" Italian synagogue, as it was called, was located near the present crossing of Aristotelous and Tsimiskis Streets. These "Latin" Jews had less difficulty in integrating, because of the pre–existing Provence congregation with which they felt some affinity. They saw both the Romaniote and the Ashkenazi Jews as strange, because the former had been influenced by centuries of living in Byzantium, and the latter by living in central and eastern Europe. But with the Romaniote Jews they also had serious differences stemming from the use of a different Talmudic tradition.

The end of this long period of invasions came in 1430, conquests, seiges, and internal turmoil, when the city fell to the Ottomans. Not much was done in terms of a re–organization of the life of the city, however, until after the fall of Constantinople to Fatih Mehmet II in 1453. Almost immediately, the sultan set about bringing back life to cities that had seen devastation and inner turmoil for centuries. A systematic program of conscription was set up whereby designated towns were required to provide Jews, Greeks, and Armenians to be resettled and thus revitalize the inner life of cities such as Salonika, Izmir (Smyrna), Constantinople (Istanbul), and many others.

In 1470 large numbers of Bavarian Jews were settled in Salonika, adding considerably to the Ashkenazi presence. It was not until after 1492, however, that the very character of Salonika began to change. Then, under the continuation of the policy of his father, Sultan Beyazit II opened the Empire itself to Jews fleeing Spain and, later, Portugal. Between 1493 and 1536, over 20,000 Jews and Marranos (Jews who had converted to Christianity) poured into the city.

The orthodox Sephardi Jews had little if any difficulty in adjusting to the Italian, Provencal, and Siciliote Jews of the city. Their languages were related. They shared many common customs, and a substantially similar *minhag* (ritual).

With the Romaniote and Ashkenazi Jews, however, it was another matter. The new arrivals quickly adopted the term *Grego* as a decidedly derogatory characterization of the Romaniote Jews, while the synagogue of the Ashkenazis became known colloquially in Ladino as the "Kal de los Lokos" ("the Congregation of the Crazies"). To make things worse, there was serious friction, as everywhere, with the Marranos, who, despite reembracing Judaism, had difficulty adjusting to orthodox Jewish custom as determined by rabbinical laws.

Mention must also be made of the fact that the Jews who arrived from the Iberian Peninsula were not from one area but many, scattered from the Pyranees down to the Straits of Gibraltar. In reorganizing themselves in Salonika they tended to band together

SALONIQUE. — Synagogue des Italiens.

The interior of the Italian Synagogue, Salonika, as it stood prior to the great fire of 1917. (Jewish Museum of Greece)

according to their towns, cities, or areas of origin, and within a short period of time Salonika was dotted with synagogues that bore names such as Castillian, Aragon, Catalan, Lisbon, and Portugal. The Marranos stuck together and even emphasized their differences from the orthodox communities. Eventually, all told, some 30 semi–independant congregations were established in Salonika, each with its Talmud Torah, Beth Din, and community services such as hostel, hospital, school, charity center, and burial society. These, in turn, were brought together in a kind of federation based on common interests and obligations to the Ottoman authorities. Taxes were paid by the community as a whole. Inheritance and marriage laws were also considered to be a common concern.

Castillian Spanish (or "Ladino," as it became known) quite rapidly became the common language of the Jews of the city. Romaniotes as well as Ashkenazis were forced to adopt a new language. Rabbinical schools flourished and produced quite fascinating musings and commentaries as well as a number of great hymns. R. Solomon Alkabetz gave to the Jews of the Diaspora the beautiful hymn "Lehah Dodi." The mystics of Safed were in close contact with those of Salonika and even Joseph Caro was an occasional resident. R. Isaac Luria matured under the influence of Salonika's kabbalists. Legalists such as Almosninos and R. Samuel di Medina took great pains through their *responsa* to standardize Jewish practice in the Balkans.

In the early 16th century, the old Jewish quarter was expanded into three main areas: one directly on the port near where the city walls reached the water (we don't know who settled here); a second adjacent to this and extending behind it, where mainly Spanish Jews settled; and a third, more ancient one near the Roman hippodrome, which was Romaniote. So quickly and extensively did Jews settle Salonika that it was given the title of "Madre de Israel" ("Mother of Israel") by Samuel Usque. By the early 16th century, books were being printed, a silk and wool–weaving and dyeing industry had begun, and trade was extended into surrounding areas.

We know, as well, that Jews from Salonika soon began to settle elsewhere in Thrace and Macedonia, extending the influence of their city and culture to places such as Komotini, Sophia, Monastir, and

Page from a calendar for 1911 found in a prayer book from Salonika. Published and distributed by an Austrian firm out of Constantinople its entries are in Ottoman Turkish, Arabic, Greek, Armenian, Bulgarian, Hebrew, Ladino, and French—a silent comment on the incredible plurality that Salonika once knew. (Jewish Museum of Greece)

even Constantinople (Istanbul) itself, and as far away as Rhodes. Though rarely recorded and usually discernable only through inference, it appears that the impact of the Sephardi Jews of Salonika on pre–existing Byzantine (Romaniote) communities, was not always amicable. Differences in language, custom, ritual, and even marriage customs inevitably led to inner–community tension and strife. Even the Sephardi Jews within their own ranks had great difficulties in absorbing the Marranos, many of whom, perhaps like Spinoza in Amsterdam, found themselves at odds with rabbinical conservatism.

Other crises evolved in 16th–century Salonika as well. Plague broke out on several occasions and a number of great fires destroyed sections of the different Jewish quarters. Despite this, the community as a whole grew and by the mid–17th century Jews represented well over half of the population of the city, numbering some 30,000. Linked intimately with Ottoman interests in trade and commerce, it was inevitable that the fortunes of the Jews closely reflected general economic circumstances. By the 17th century, the Ottoman Empire had begun to decline. The discovery of the New World had drawn the attention of Europe to the west, and the Atlantic Ocean now provided an alternate route to Africa and to India and China further east.

The response of both Jews and Ottomans was an entrenchment that led the Jews to become more conservative, and to take up an interest in mystical musings on the meaning of Exile—twice experienced by Spanish Jews. It was in this context that a rabbi from Izmir, Shabbetai Zvi, was proclaimed the Messiah. The declaration took place in Salonika in the year 1669 and almost immediately his following grew enormously—though he was driven from Salonika itself by general rabbinical agreement. There was not a Jewish community, either in the Ottoman Empire or in Europe, that did not feel the impact of Shabbetai Zvi's teaching, until he was finally brought before the sultan and, in the presence of the court, he converted to Islam. His conversion drew many of his followers into Islam as well. After his death some 300 families in Salonika converted, to become known as the *Dönme* or, less offensively, the *Ma'min*.

This sect, not quite accurately called "crypto–Jewish" (since there were no attempts to be rabbinically Jewish even under the guise of Islam), became very important in Salonika. It is of interest that most of the original followers of Shabbetai Zvi were from Marrano families and the exclusive, hidden character of Ma'min life and institutions reflected what was perhaps a more natural form of life for Jews who had at one time been Christians. By 1923, the Ma'min numbered some 20,000 persons. The last mosque erected in Salonika, in 1904, known as the Yeni Cami (New Mosque), was theirs. The richest sect of Ma'min, the Kapanci , were active in every aspect of Ottoman economic and even political and military life.

The response of the rabbis of Salonika to the Ma'min crisis was, as elsewhere in Europe, an assertion of orthodoxy, reorganization, and most significantly, a deep suspicion of mysticism in any form. In Salonika a new council was established to exert closer control over the 30 some congregations. The council was made up of three rabbis: R. Abraham di Botton, R. Elia Kovo, and R. Moses Hayyim Shabbetai. Under their direction, the rabbinical courts were reorganized and given greater jurisdictional definition and authority.

Toward the end of the 18th century and the beginning of the 19th, the problems of the empire became bifurcated. On the one hand, there were attempts from within to reform the empire, its institutions and army, while, on the other, there were a number of severe crises with minority groups— especially the Greeks, Armenians, Bulgarians, and Serbs.

In the face of these nascent nationalistic movements, the Jews of the empire, and those of Salonika especially, tended to become more and more conservative in their habits, language and thought. Lacking a national homeland, they asserted their Spanish roots more and more. It was only toward the end of the 19th century, with the reforms of Sabri Pasha, the foundation of an Alliance Israelite School, and the beginnings of Zionism, that the Salonika Jews began to enter contemporary life.

By 1900 there were 80,000 Jews in Salonika, almost half of a total population of 173,000. 60,000 of its inhabitants were Muslims and the remaining 30,000 or so were a mixture of Greeks, Armenians, Bulgarians, Serbs, and even some Arabs. (The Ma'min were counted as part of the Muslim population.) New *yeshivoth* were founded and the council was reorganized so that there was only one hahambashi (chief rabbi) who represented the community as a whole to the Ottoman authorities. The first incumbant was R. Jacob Kovo.

In 1904 the Young Turk Revolt was proclaimed in Freedom Square in Salonika. Some of its leaders and many of its supporters were Ma'min or Jews. Its proclamation of "Freedom, Equality and Brotherhood" for all in the empire was but a short–lived idealism. The revolt degenerated very quickly and Jews as well as Greek Christian supporters felt the weight of universal conscription into the Ottoman army. Because of this, a major emigration from Salonika began, especially of young men. Zionism became more attractive as well, because it offered an alternative identity to that of being a Sepharad. Jews began to leave for Eretz Israel, Paris, London, and even New York and South America. For the young who remained, various socialist movements were founded.

Between 1912 and 1923, Salonika found itself a bone of conten-

Yeni Cami (New Mosque), built in 1904, view to the south. This was the last mosque built in Salonika. It was used by the Ma'min (Donme) and once had a quite elegant minaret. Designed by an Italian architect, it gives some idea of the mixed traditions at work in Salonika. (Photo: Timothy DeVinney/Jewish Museum of Greece)

A Ma'min (Dönme) woman with her son, Salonika, early 20th century. She is wearing a carsaf (headscarf) typical to many young Muslim women of the period just before the First World War. (Jewish Museum of Greece)

tion between Greece, Bulgaria, Turkey, and Serbia, in the First and Second Balkan Wars. When the wars ended, Salonika (now once again referred to as "Thessaloniki"), was absorbed into Greece and an aggressive policy of Hellenization began. At that point, it was still largely a Jewish city. Its harbor all but closed on Saturdays. A marked silence hung over the commercial heart of the city from late Friday afternoon until Sunday mornings, when life began again.

The great fire of Salonika in 1917. This photograph shows the night–time horizen of the

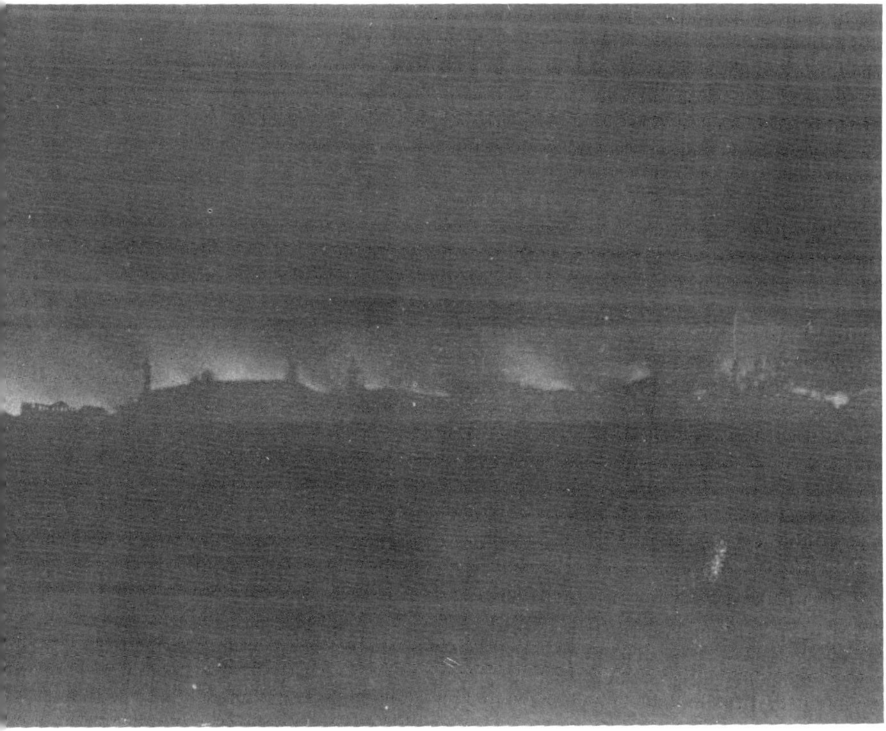

city in flames. Almost all of the Jewish quarter was destroyed, as well as its 32 synagogues. (Modiano family/Jewish Museum of Greece)

Inauguration of a maternity wing in the Baron Hirsch Hospital, established by Rachel and Elias Benousiglio, Salonika, 1936. (Jewish Museum of Greece)

Spanish was heard everywhere and newspaper vendors peddled any number of monthlies, weeklies, and dailies, all in Ladino.

There was bound to be resistance to the changes that were coming, and it would do violence to history to say that there was none. When Greece entered the First World War in 1917, many Jews left because of the pressures of Hellenization and Greece's forced entry into the war. Then, in August of 1917, an enormous and inexplicable fire broke out in the Jewish quarter. Fanned by an unfortunate wind, the flames spread through the heart of the city leaving it in ashes and over 50,000 Jews homeless. All of the 32 major synagogues of the city were destroyed, countless libraries burned, and the accumulated wisdom and occasional foolishness of centuries of secure and settled Jewish life were destroyed.

It is to the credit of the hahambaşi, who at that time was Jacob Meir (later to be appointed chief rabbi of Eretz Israel by the sultan),

The Baron Hirsch Hospital as it stands today in Salonika. Established in 1907 by the famous Jewish philanthropist of the same name, it was one of the finest hospitals in the Balkans, serving the needs of the Jewish community and the city at large. Today it belongs to the Salonika Municipality and has been renamed the Hippocrates General Hospital. (Photo: Timothy DeVinney/Jewish Museum of Greece)

that the Jews began to rebuild their lives immediately. Some emigrated, but those who remained began immediately to reconstruct synagogues, schools, and other communal organizations, including hospitals, and orphanages. As this process began, Greece entered into a renewed period of hostilities with Turkey over the city of Izmir (Smyrna) that led ultimately to a great rout. Then, after the Lausanne agreement in 1923, a mass exchange was carried out between Christians in Anatolia and Muslims in Greece. The emigration of some 100,000 Muslims (including the Ma'min) from Salonika made room for the settlement of over 150,000 Greek Christians from Asia Minor. Almost all of the new Christian arrivals were destitute, bewildered, with little interest in nationalism. Many did not even speak Greek. Here in Salonika they found themselves surrounded by Ladino–speaking Jews. It was a perfect breeding ground for antagonisms on both sides.

The Kapançi mansion, Salonika. The Kapançi were the most assimilated of the Ma'min (Dönme) into Ottoman society. This house is one of the few great urban mansions, along with that of the Alatini family, which give some hint of the prosperity that Salonika enjoyed during the years of transition. (Photo: Timothy DeVinney/Jewish Museum of Greece)

By 1935 there were occasional open conflicts. Riots were fairly common and the Jews were a natural object of abuse. The massive Jewish cemetery that had frustrated even Sabri Pasha in his attempts to expand the city to the east, was desecrated on several occasions. Even the Jewish community itself was divided between progressives, conservatives, activists, and socialists. This year saw the first large emigration to Eretz Israel under the direct influence of David Ben Gurion who organized the departure of 6,000 stevedores and dock-workers to Haifa.

With the opening of hostilities with the Axis forces in 1940, the young Jews of Salonika flocked to the army. By the spring of 1941, the Italian failure in Albania was followed by a German success in Greece, and on the 9th of April the Germans entered Salonika.

Within a week it became obvious that the 60,000 Jews still in the city were marked out for some sort of special treatment. Community offices, the Baron Hirsch Hospital, and several private dwellings were requisitioned, and restrictions were put on the movements of Jews soon afterwards. A new council was created under the Germans, and in the following year, in June of 1942, some 7,000 Jewish males were ordered to appear on a Saturday morning in Freedom Square, the very place where the Young Turk Proclamation of 1904 had been made for Equality, Freedom and Brotherhood. Subjected throughout the course of a day to public humiliations, these Jews were the testing ground for judging public response. There was none. Early in the following week they were all conscripted for public work

The Villa Alatini, Salonika, built in 1888. The Alatini's were one of the most important Jewish families of Salonika at the turn of the 20th century. It was in one of their great town houses that Sultan Abdul Hamid sojourned during his exile after the Young Turk Revolt. (Photo: Timothy DeVinney/Jewish Museum of Greece)

Interior of the Yad Lezikaron Synagogue, Salonika, reconstructed in 1984 in a modern apartment building from the remains of several earlier synagogues, view to the east. The

plaques on the walls list the 32 synagogues of Salonika destroyed in the fire of 1917. (Photo: Timothy DeVinney/Jewish Museum of Greece)

far from Salonika. Later in the year the community was allowed to ransom them back. In this manner the communal wealth of the community was destroyed and its spirit broken. The Jews were now isolated into three ghettos, forced to wear the yellow badge, and to register all of their personal holdings. Finally, on the 14th of March, 1943, the first of 13 transports carried off 2,500 Jews by cattle car to Auschwitz–Birkenau. By mid–August of that year, 56,000 persons had been transported. Nearly all of them perished.

At the termination of the war, 2,000 Jews returned to a city that was all but unrecognizable in terms of any Jewish presence. The community was reorganized and a synagogue reconsecrated. Since that time, a retirement home and two additional synagogues have been built, but the community, which numbers about 1,000 Jews, tries to avoid calling attention to its presence.

Description of the Synagogues

The synagogue now used by the community, that of the Monasteriots, was built in 1927-28 by Jews originally from Monastir (in what for a time was Yugoslavia). It was saved during the war after being requisitioned by the Red Cross. It is a fine building at 35 Syngrou Street. Its interior is laid out in a modified Sephardi form with the *ehal* on the east wall and the bema and *tevah* located in the very center.

Another synagogue, the Ashkenazi Synagogue, is also referred to formally as the Yad Lezikaron Synagogue and informally as the Ke'la Burla Synagogue. ("Burla" is the name of the man who built the original synagogue on this site, in memory of his son who had drowned at sea.) It has been reconstructed at 26 Vas. Herakleios Street in a modern office building in the center of the market area of Salonika (still known as the Modiano Market, after the wealthy Jewish family that owns it). The Yad Lezikaron Synagogue was rebuilt in 1984 out of furniture from two destroyed synagogues: the *ehal* is from the former Ke'la Sarfati Synagogue, and the bema is from the former Baron Hirsch Synagogue.

Exterior of the Monàsterioton Synagogue, Salonika, built in 1925-27, view to the west. (Photo: Timothy DeVinney/Jewish Museum of Greece)

Interior of the Monasterioton Synagogue, Salonika, built in 1925-27, view to the north. The setting of ehal *and bema within a tribune—like area reflects a tradition in Salonika synagogues, about which we know very little. It may have influenced the peculiar*

interior of the Beth Shalom Synagogue in Athens and that of the destroyed synagogue of that name in Hania, Crete. (Photo: Timothy DeVinney/Jewish Museum of Greece)

The Pinhas Institute, which served as a Bikour Holim (out–patient infirmary), one of the many charitable Jewish foundations in Salonika at the turn of the century. This building stood at 31 Alexander Papanastasiou Street, but was recently demolished to make way for a men's sporting–goods store. (Photo: Timothy DeVinney/Jewish Museum of Greece)

A third synagogue, the Avraam Salem, built in 1981, can be found in the Saul Modiano Retirement Home at 83 Kimonos Voga Street (see the map). Its interior is modern and of no particular historical interest.

Other Sites

In light of the history of the Salonika Jewish presence, a stroll through the city can be exciting, as well as sad and evocative. Many of the 19th–century Jewish *konaks*, (town houses), can still be seen. The great mansion of the Modiano family at 65 Megas Alexandros (Alexander the Great) Street, which now houses the Folklore and Ethnography Museum of Macedonia; the Villa Mordoh at 162 Vas. Olgas Avenue, now the home of the Municipal Gallery; the Villa Allatini at 198 Vas. Olgas, now the County Building; and the Villa Bianca at 182 Vas. Olgas Ave., now abandoned; are typical of houses that once graced the 19th–century city. Yeni Cami (New

Mosque), the mosque of the Donme, shorn of its minaret, still stands at 35 Archeological Museum Street, and is being used as a municipal exhibition hall.

The famous cemetery of the city was once located under the present–day precincts of the University of Thessaloniki. This was completely bulldozed by the Germans and nothing remains. Scattered throughout the city, however, bits and pieces of the marble epitaphs can still be seen from tombs that once marked the graves of great rabbis, saints, and sinners—it can be sad to come upon them. The modern, postwar cemetery is in the suburb of Iliopolis, at 31 Karaoli Demetriou Street. It has a collection of some of the stones that have been recovered from the original cemetery. Still other stones can be found at the American Farm School.

How to Visit the Synagogues

The Monastirioton Synagogue, at 35 Syngrou Street (see map), is open for all High Holidays and services on Friday nights and

The Avraam Salem Synagogue in the Saul Modiano Retirement Home, Salonika, built in 1981. (Photo: Timothy DeVinney/Jewish Museum of Greece)

Broken fragments from the great Jewish necropolis of Salonika destroyed during the Second World War, photographed in 1991. (Photo: Timothy DeVinney/Jewish Museum of Greece)

Saturday mornings. It can be visited at other times by contacting the community offices at telephone (031) 275-701. There is a caretaker present at all times, but it may be necessary to get in touch beforehand.

The Ashekanzi (or Yad Lezikaron) Synagogue, at 26 Vas. Herakleios Street (see map) in the market area of Salonika, is open every morning for services at about 8:00 A.M., and for High Holidays. Here again it is best to contact the community beforehand.

The Avraam Salem Synagogue in the Saul Modiano Retirement Home is not normally open to visitors and is of no historical interest. But further information regarding a visit can be obtained from the offices of the community.

Contacts for More Information

For more information on visiting Jewish sites in Salonika, contact the community at (031) 275-701.

Mrs. Sol Shalom, Salonika, ca. 1900. Mrs. Shalom is shown in traditional Salonika costume. (E. Shalom/Jewish Museum of Greece)

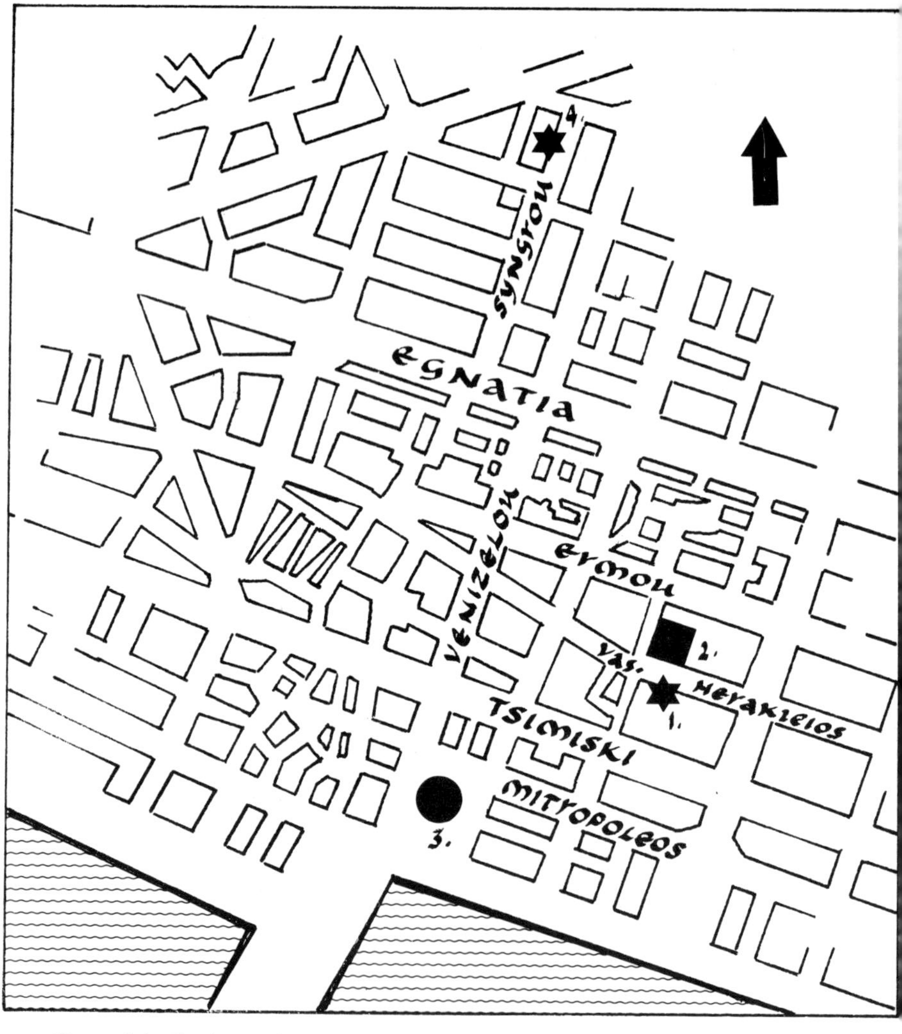

Key to Salonika (central) map: **1.** *Yad Lezikaron* **2.** *Modiano Stoa* **3.** *Freedom Square (Plateia Eleftherias)* **4.** *Monastirioton Synagogue*

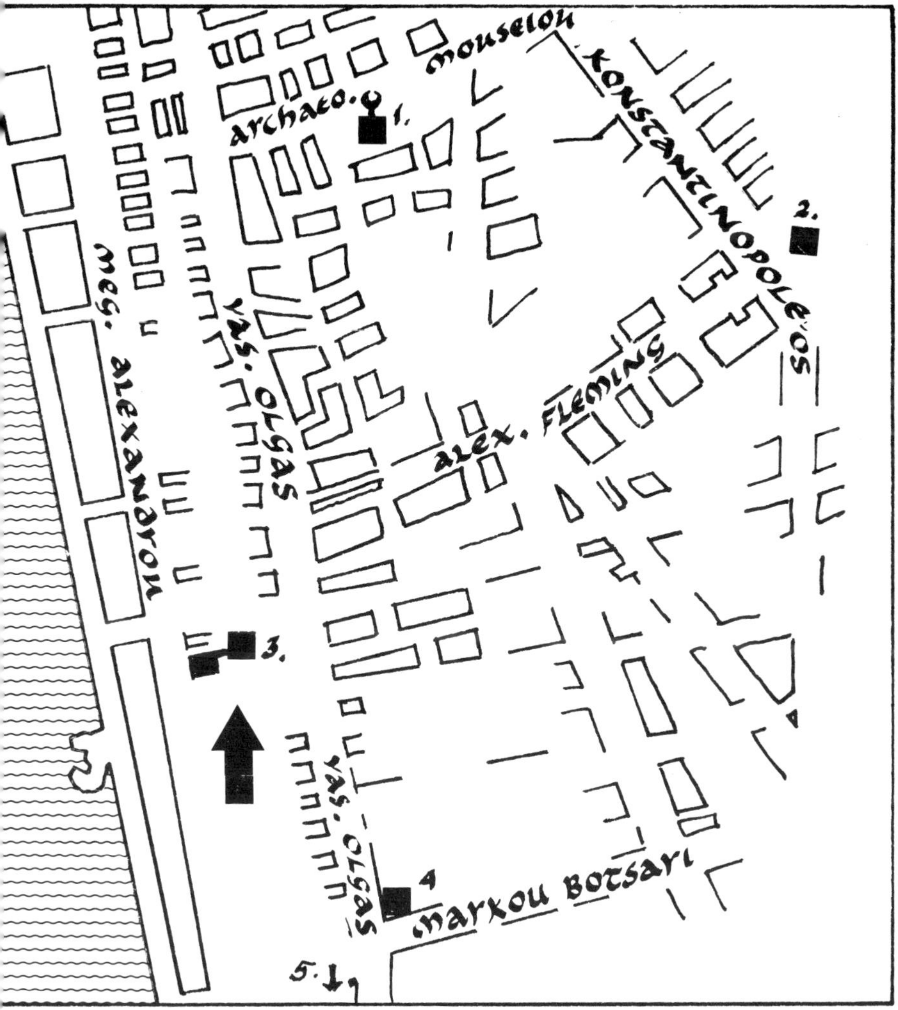

Key to Salonika (south) map: **1.** *Yeni Cami (New Mosque)* **2.** *Baron Hirsch Hospital* **3.** *Villa Modiano (65 M. Alexandrou)* **4.** *Jewish Villa* **5.** *Villa Mordoh (162 Vas. Olgas)* **6.** *Villa Kapanci (108 Vas. Olgas)* **7.** *Villa Bianca (182 Vas. Olgas)* **8.** *Villa Allatini (198 Vas. Olgas)*

Interior of the Yavanim Synagogue of Trikkala, built in the 19th century, reconstructed after 1945, view to the east. Like most Sephardi synagogues it has its bema located in an architecturally defined area in the center facing the ehal. *(Photo: Timothy DeVinney/ Jewish Museum of Greece)*

Trikkala

Trikkala, a modern city in central Thessaly, 330 kilometers (200 miles) north of Athens. Total population: approximately 49,000 (1991), current Jewish population: 68. Extant sites: a functioning synagogue and cemetery.

Historical Background

Trikkala is mentioned by Homer as "Trikke," and was one of several important towns in Thessaly that survived the invasions of Slavs, Bulgarians, and Crusaders who ravaged central Greece during late antiquity and well into medieval times. Trikkala is not mentioned by Benjamin of Tudela in his account of his journey through Greece in the 12th century, but that does not mean there was no Jewish community here. Benjamin's main purpose was neither to make a "grand tour" of Greece nor necessarily to visit all of its Jewish communities. His route very carefully followed the coast and there are a good number of cities and towns that he simply did not reach; Trikkala was undoubtedly one of them.

Until very recent times Trikkala had a Romaniote character that was reflected in the name of the congregation, known as Kahal (Kal) Yavanim (the "Greek congregation"). In the 16th and 17th centuries, a large number of Hungarians, Sepharadim, and Sicilian Jews swelled the community. Quite naturally, the Romaniote Trikkalian Jews tended to maintain their ties to Ioannina (a fellow Romaniote town), while the newcomers associated themselves in trade, marriage, and ritual with Larissa and Salonika (both predominately Sephardi). Both Greek and Spanish were commonly spoken in Trikkala by all three congregations.

We know that tensions between Jews and Christians occasionally broke out in physical violence, and Trikkala's Jews—like those of Ioannina—suffered especially during the revolutionary activities of the fanatic and renegade bishop, Dionysos Skylosophos, in the late 18th century. During the 19th century local antagonisms forced many Jews to emigrate. By 1898 there were only 800 Jews left here, and this number fell to 500 by 1941. At the time of the mass arrest of

Exterior of the Yavanim Synagogue of Trikkala, view to the southwest. Faced as it is

with shops the building is almost hidden from immediate view from the street. (Photo: Timothy DeVinney/Jewish Museum of Greece)

Interior of the Yavanim Synagogue of Trikkala, view to the west toward the bema. (Photo: Timothy DeVinney/Jewish Museum of Greece)

Thessalian Jews by the Nazis in 1943, Trikkala's Jews, like those of Volos and Larissa, had made arrangements beforehand with the partisans and were ready to flee to the mountains or go into hiding. Only a very few were arrested and deported.

At the end of the war the community was immediately reestablished. Over the years, many Jews have left for Athens, Israel, or elsewhere, and today there are only 68 Jews living here. Their community, though small, is active and well integrated into local life.

Description of the Synagogue

Prior to the Second World War, there were three synagogues in Trikkala: the Kal Yavanim (Romaniote), Kal Sepharadi (Sephardi), and Kal Sikiliani (Romaniote–Sicilian). The last two were destroyed entirely during the war, while the oldest, the Kal Yavanim, was gutted by fire. After the war, the Kal Yavanim was quickly reconstructed, but with several interior modifications to accomodate both the Romaniote and Sephardi tradition of synagogue layout in Greece.

A tombstone in the Trikkala Jewish cemetery. The depiction of a hand holding a razor indicates that the deceased, Isaak Solomon, was a barber by profession. He died in 1941. (Photo: Timothy DeVinney/Jewish Museum of Greece)

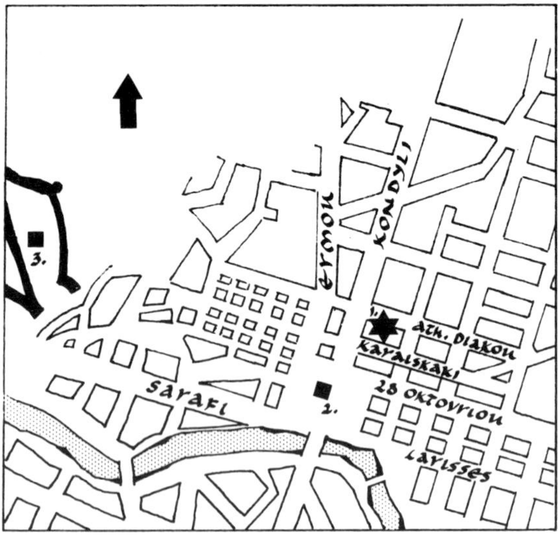

Key to Trikkala map: **1.** *K'K' Yavanim* **2.** *Square* **3.** *Fortress*

The interior of the Kal Yavanim is divided centrally by four equidistant columns in the center of which is a large permanent bema which faces the *ehal* in the east wall. Against the back wall, however, is another bema, conforming to the traditional layout of Romaniote synagogues.

Other Sites

There is a cemetery on the side of a hill to the north of the town. This has some very interesting tombstones with inscriptions depicting the craft or profession of the deceased. Visitors wishing to see the cemetery should first contact the community, since it is normally locked.

How to Visit the Synagogue

The Yavanim synagogue is at 24 Athanasiou Diakou Street (see map). It is open for visitors every weekday morning (but visitors are advised to check with the community first). Services are held on Friday evenings and all High Holidays.

Contacts for More Information

Visitors wishing to see the synagogue or the cemetery should contact the community at (042) 27534.

Verroia

Verroia, a modern town about 70 kilometers (42 miles) south–west of Salonika (Thessaloniki). Total population: approximately 39,000 (1991), current Jewish population: 2. Extant sites: synagogue (not in use), original Jewish quarter with about 50 houses, and a cemetery,

Historical Background

The first mention of Jews in Verroia appears in the Acts of the Apostles (Acts 17:1–13) where they are described as "high minded" in their eager response to Paul of Tarsus and his teaching. It is worth noting that the Jewish community of Salonika, even at this early time, kept close tabs on the community here; the account in Acts also describes a delegation of Salonica rabbis who had come to examine its orthodoxy.

After this brief entry into documented history, the Verroia Jewish community is not mentioned again until quite late: in the period just after the conquest of Constantinople in 1453, when Mehmet II had a conscription of Verroia Jews moved to the Balat quarter of Constantinople. There they constructed a synagogue and maintained close ties with the mother community. It is possible, though unlikely, that there was a continuous Jewish presence in Verroia over the entire period of the intervening 1,300 years. Verroia was attacked and pillaged several times, especially during the Slavic and Bulgarian invasions, and the chances are that Jews fled to Salonika during those periods of stress.

The 15th–century community must have been sufficiently large to provide a "colony" of Jews for Constantinople (Istanbul). It would have been Romaniote, Greek speaking, and it would have maintained the Romaniote *minhag*. During the reign of Sultan Beyazid II, a sizeable number of Spanish and Portuguese Jews settled in Verroia. These most likely came via Salonika and may represent an overflow from the 20,000 Jews that had begun to settle there. Within a very short period of time, Castillian Spanish replaced Greek as the common language, and the Sephardi ritual displaced the Romaniote *minhag*.

South entrance to the Jewish quarter of Verroia (also called the Barbouti quarter), most of which was built in the 18th century, view to the northwest. (Photo: Timothy DeVinney/Jewish Museum of Greece)

After the 16th century, Verroia and Salonika kept close professional ties. The main commercial interests of the Salonika Jews were in the area of textiles, and Verroia was surrounded by springs and running water for washing cloth, especially after dyeing. Verroia also produced very fine kosher cheeses that were in constant demand in Salonika up until modern times. One of the less fortunate stories of the Verroia Jews that have come down to us recounts the death of several merchants who were caught in the mountains by brigands in the 17th century.

The "high mindedness" of the Verroian Jews appears to have been maintained through the late 17th century, as the community was severely shaken and divided very early in the career of Shabbetai Zvi. Nathan of Gaza (the chief apostle of Shabbetai) not only preached here but also founded a school, and for over 40 years the community was divided in its allegiences. In the end, a good number of Verroian Jews converted to Islam and rabbinical provision was made for the immediate divorce of wives who did not follow their husband's example.

In the 18th century a fire destroyed most of the old Jewish *mahallasi* (quarter) and it was quickly rebuilt in quite a grand manner. In keeping with normal Ottoman practice (by contrast to that of the Venetians), the Jews had the right to their own neighborhood within the walls—it was not a "ghetto" in any sense of the word.

The general affluence of the Verroia Jews in the 19th century, as indicated by the rebuilding and in many cases redecorating of their houses at that time, was no doubt caused by better communications between Verroia and its two closely connected fellow Jewish communities in Salonika and Monastir. Those communications were augmented by the new railway lines laid between these cities in 1894.

In the years before the First World War, Verroia was a favorite summer vacation spot for Salonika Jews and many rabbis made visitations here. One of the most notable visitors was R. Jacob Meir, the Chief Rabbi of Salonika, who later moved to Jerusalem and became the Chief Rabbi of the Sepharadim in Eretz Israel.

In 1941 there were 850 Jews in the community. 680 were deported to Auschwitz–Birkenau. At the termination of the war, the community was dissolved and the old Jewish quarter settled by squatters. It is hoped that eventually the importance of the entire quarter will be recognized and it will be reconstructed.

Today there is one Jewish couple left still living in Verroia.

Description of the Synagogue

The synagogue of Verroia is located at almost at the very end of the central corridor of the former Jewish quarter. It is in a very dilapidated state and there are indications that it was considerably

A Hebrew inscription under the eaves of a house in the Jewish quarter of Verroia. Dated 1859, it reads "If I forget thee, O Jerusalem, may my hand wither." (Photo: Timothy DeVinney/Jewish Museum of Greece)

Part of the Jewish quarter of Verroia, built in the 18th century, view to the northwest, with the synagogue at the center of the photograph. (Photo: Timothy DeVinney/Jewish Museum of Greece)

enlarged, probably during the 18th century. In form it resembles many of the former small synagogues of Salonika. It was originally square, though later enlarged to provide greater space for the men and a small interior *mehitza* for the women. At this time the *mehitza* proper was created by incorporating an adjacent house that was built in part against the north wall of the synagogue. Windows, now blocked in, were latticed and provided views of the interior. In layout the synagogue follows the Sephardi alignment. Four columns mark off an area in the center of the synagogue where the bema sits, while the *ehal* is set into the east wall with a small canopy constructed over and before it. The communal *mikveh* (ritual bath) is directly behind the synagogue where descent can be made to the river.

Other Sites

The Jewish *mahalasi* (quarter) consists of a single street running between approximately 50 attached houses bordering it on either side. These multi–storied houses are in fine Macedonian style architecture, and are linked on the ground floor (internally) by connecting doors. Inscriptions in Hebrew appear on many of the

Interior of the synagogue of Verroia, built originally in the 18th century, view to the northeast. The area that is squared off in the center by columns marks the axis of the

interior. Set in the north wall are three plastered rectangles that once held grills behind which was the mehitza. *(Photo: Timothy DeVinney/Jewish Museum of Greece)*

cornices of these houses, with a line from Psalms 137:5: "If I forget thee,O Jerusalem, let my right hand forget its cunning." Most also have a mid–19th century date inscribed on them as well.

The old cemetery of Verroia is directly across the Tripotamos River from the Jewish quarter described above, a bit further down from the synagogue. Stones have been pillaged from here for over the past 30 years and today it looks more like a construction site with hardly anything remaining from the original cemetery.

How to Visit the Synagogue

To reach the synagogue, one first must find the Jewish quarter (also called the Barbouta quarter). This is directly below Konstantinos Raktivan Square (where the courthouse of Verroia is located). To reach that square starting from the archeological museum, drive south to a square called I Elia (the Olive Tree) which is a semi–circular street around a restaurant of the same name. Turn

Interior of the synagogue of Verroia looking south. Under the mehitza *built along the wall is an area that once was used as a school. (Photo: Timothy DeVinney/Jewish Museum of Greece)*

The back of the synagogue of Verroia built against the edge of the ravine that drops down to the Tripotamos River, view to the east. Hidden in the foliage are the remains of the mikveh. *(Photo: Timothy DeVinney/Jewish Museum of Greece)*

right onto Elia Street (mid–way around the semi–circle) and drive up it to where it forks. Take the left fork (Metropoleos Street) straight on to the square where the courthouse is. From there on foot, facing the courthouse, walk to the right on Vas. Konstantinos Street. After a few meters this becomes 10th Merarcheias Street. About 100 meters down 10th Merarcheias Street is an opening on your left in the row of buildings (the only opening in that row). Enter this to reach the Jewish quarter. As you emerge from this covered passage through the houses you will see the synagogue directly across the street and to your right.

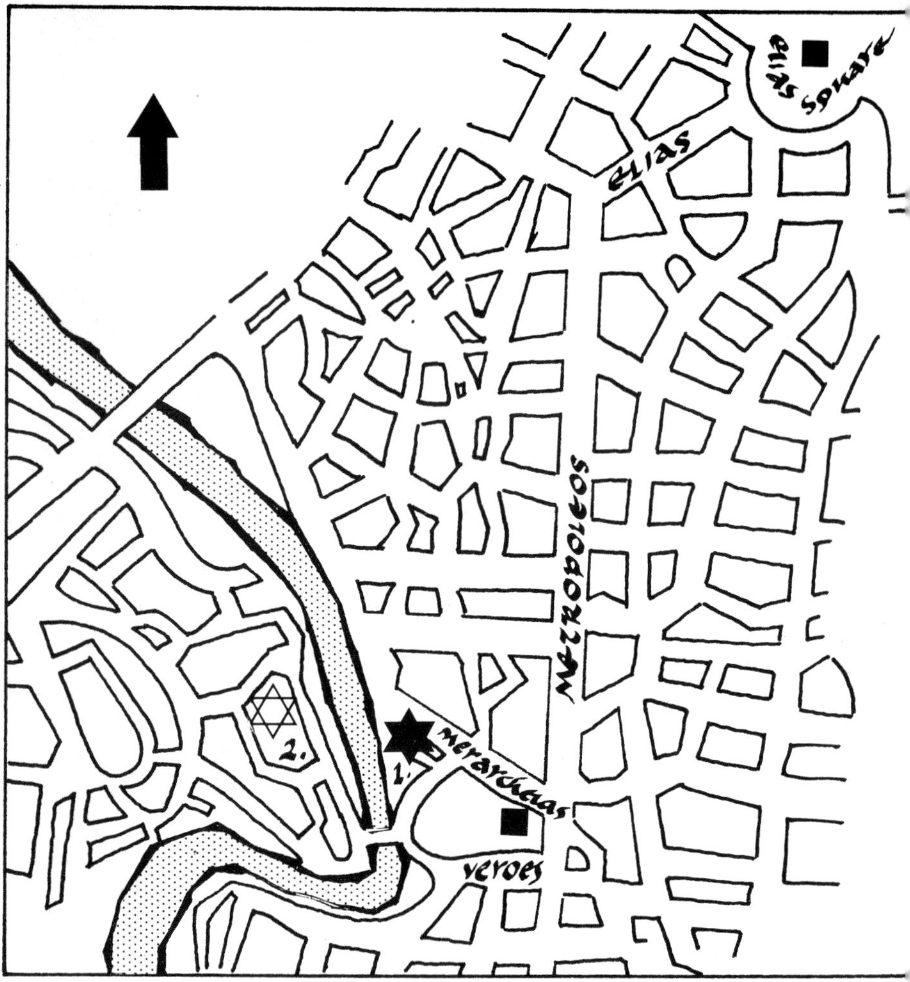

Key to Verroia map: **1.** *Synagogue* **2.** *Cemetery*

The synagogue is not normally open to visitors. But a visit to the old Jewish quarter and a view of the exterior of the synagogue are well worth the trip.

Contacts for More Information

Further information regarding the state of the synagogue of Verroia can be obtained by contacting the Jewish Museum of Greece in Athens (36 Amalias Avenue, Athens 10558, telephone 3231-577 or 3225-582).

Volos

Volos, a port city on the east coast of mainland Greece, 350 kilometers (210 miles) north of Athens. Total population: approximately 116,000 (1991), current Jewish population: 150. Extant sites: functioning synagogue and cemetery.

Historical Background

Volos came into prominence as a port city after the Ottoman conquest of the southern Balkans in the 15th century, and the establishment of peaceful maritime conditions in the upper Aegean Sea. The rich produce of the plain of Thessaly was exported from here (as it still is). Volos competed with Salonika, which played an analogous role for the plain of Macedonia.

There is no evidence of a Jewish presence here prior to the 14th century, though the region surrounding it saw the growth and decline of towns that certainly had quite large Jewish communities at various times, depending on fluctuating economic conditions. Benjamin of Tudela in the 12th century visited and made note of communities in nearby Armylos, Gardiki, and Bissena. These appear to have suffered greatly in the period following the parceling up of the Byzantine Empire under the Fourth Crusade (after 1204). It is likely that the Jews from those other towns had come to settle in Volos by the 15th century.

It is unfortunate that little scholarly work has been done on the Jewish community of Volos, as it appears its members played an important role in trade and maintained close connections with other Romaniote communities in Thessaly as well as the Peloponnese. It does not appear to have attracted Sephardi immigrants in any great numbers, and its predominantly Romaniote character made it a natural haven for Jews fleeing the aftermath of the Greek War of Independence in 1821.

When Volos was made the administrative center for the region in 1840, the town attracted other Jews as well and there were soon sufficient numbers to warrant the creation of a Jewish quarter, located around the Ottoman fortifications in the upper town. By

Interior of the Volos synagogue, view to the east. Though rebuilt after the Second World War, its plan is that of the original 19th–century structure. (Photo: Timothy DeVinney/ Jewish Museum of Greece)

1860 there were at least 35 households. The community swelled rapidly after this date with large numbers of Jews coming from Larissa, Halkis, Ioannina, and Trikkala. In 1865 the Alliance Israelite Universelle, at the request of the community, established one of the first schools of any kind in the Greek peninsula. It attracted Greek Orthodox children as well as those from the Jewish community. At this time a new synagogue was constructed with funds provided by Edmond de Rothschild and Maurice de Hearst. A new cemetery was laid out in 1883. Not long after 1900, the community was legally incorporated under Greek law.

During the Greco–Turkish war of 1897, the Jews of Volos suffered attacks from Christian Greeks and, in the aftermath of riots and threats, many Voliote Jews emigrated to Ottoman Salonika, where conditions were more stable. After the war the community appears to have grown and decreased in size based on the results of the struggles between Greeks and Turks, as well as the final absorption of Salonika and Macedonia into the Greek state in 1913. In 1897 there were approximately 500 Jews in Volos, and by 1913 that number had doubled to 1,000.

Voliote Jews played an active role in nascent Zionism in Greece and in 1919 sent representatives to the peace negotiations following the termination of the First World War, demanding rights for the establishment of a Jewish homeland in Eretz Israel. In 1921, Volos hosted the first pan–Helladic Zionist congress with representatives from all over Greece.

In 1922, the Volos Jews even acquired thespian fame with a performance of Racine's *Esther*. The actors were widely acclaimed and positive critiques appeared in prominent Athenian newspapers. The role of Esther was played by Sarina Mizrahi, a granddaughter of R. David Angel (the chief rabbi of Larissa) and a woman of great energy. Later in her life she was active in promoting WIZO and other Zionist organizations. Mizrahi helped found both the Banot Israel, under the auspices of the Keren Ha–Kayemet in 1923, and the Union of Young Jews, and she worked indefatigably to promote them.

During the decades between the two World Wars, Voliote Jews took a leading role in sponsoring balls, lotteries, celebrations, and

Exterior of the Volos synagogue, view to the southwest. (Photo: Timothy DeVinney/ Jewish Museum of Greece)

similar programs to promote the Zionist movement. It speaks well of the relations between the Greek Christians and Jews of Volos that many of these organizations and events attracted local non–Jewish interest and support as well. Certainly one of the most notable foundations of all was established at the very beginning of the Second World War, called the Fraternity Ozer Dalim. Founded by Frederick Fortes, its aim was to collect and distribute relief to Voliote Jews in need.

It was not until 1943 that the Nazis were in a position to set in motion the machinery of the Final Solution in Volos. Until October of that year, Volos had lain within the jurisdiction of the Italians, who were notoriously unwilling partners in furthering German racial policies. As a consequence, Volos for a time was a haven for Jews fleeing from the north of Greece, especially from Thrace, Macedonia, and Salonika.

As soon as the Italians surrendered in October of 1943, however, the Nazis assumed control of the former Italian– occupied territories. Fortunately, the Jews of Volos were sufficiently well informed by this time of the sinister transfer of Jews which had been occurring especially out of Salonika, and Macedonia, in general, and plans had already been laid for such an eventuality in Volos. Much of the responsibility for this foresight lay with the chief rabbi of Volos, R. Moshe Pessah. Born in Larissa in 1892, he came to Volos at a young age, taught in the Jewish school and was active in both social as well as religious life. He was especially respected by Greek Christians. Pessah was promoted to the position of chief rabbi in 1939, when he was also honored by H.M. King George II and awarded the Phoenix Gilt Cross, one of the highest orders under the Greek monarchy.

At the outbreak of the Second World War, Pessah was very active in encouraging both Jewish and Christian soldiers. His strong connections with the partisans eventually drew him into active involvement in the National Resistance. Through these close contacts with resistance movements, he was able to anticipate some of the Nazi moves. As soon as the signs were clear that an action was being prepared the entire community was warned and its members took flight and either hid in the partisan–held villages of Mount Pelion where they were assisted by the local peasants, or joined the resistance. It is to the credit of both the Voliote Christians and the Orthodox clergy that the escape was so efficiently carried out and that, out of a community of 900, no more than 129 persons perished. These had either been arrested prior to the exodus, or—as in the case of 12 people—they happened to fall into Nazi hands in the following

Miss Sarina Mizrahi of Volos, dressed as Eliza for the Jewish Club production of Racine's Esther *in the Municipal Theater of Volos, 28 February, 1922. In keeping with an ancient tradition in Greece, Volos held annual Purim plays. (Miss Mizrahi was the granddaughter of Chief Rabbi Angel of Larissa.) (Sarina Mizrahi/Jewish Museum of Greece)*

The bema of the Volos synagogue, with the mehitza *above, view to the south. (Photo: Timothy DeVinney/Jewish Museum of Greece)*

year, either in Volos itself or in the nearby villages.

Frustrated in their attempts to seize the Jews themselves, the Nazis destroyed as much as they could of Jewish communal and private property. The synagogue was razed, as well as the school. On the return of the community after the war, JOINT was especially active in assisting its revitalization, and a new synagogue was built within a short period of time. Pessah continued to lead the community and, in recognition of his services to Christians and Jews alike, he was awarded the Cross of George I as well as special honors from the Allied Middle East Military Headquarters. In the aftermath of the first of a series of earthquakes that struck Volos shortly afterwards, his health broke down and he died in 1951 in Salonika. His body was interred for a short time in Volos and then his body was transferred to Jerusalem for final burial.

At the termination of the war, Greece entered into a period of civil war and many Voliote Jews were active in the Leftist cause. At least two Jews from Volos, Chrissoula Fellous and Moshe Yeshoulah, aged 20 and 26, were caught, tried under court martial, and executed for their part in fighting for the leftists.

In 1955-7 Volos was again struck by earthquakes, this time leveling the synagogue and Jewish community buildings. Economic hardships made it difficult for people to reestablish themselves commercially, so many Voliote Jews emigrated to Israel or the U.S., or moved to Athens. Today the community here, while numbering only about 150 Jews, is still active, and justifiably proud of the part it plays in Greek life.

Description of the Synagogue

The present–day synagogue of Volos reproduces to some extent the form and character of that which was erected in 1865 through the assistance of Rothchild and Hearst. As is the custom in many Romaniote communities in Greece, it is referred to locally as simply "the synagogue."

At the time of the original building's construction in 1865, the community numbered 200 people and the building was large enough

Rabbi Moshe Pessah of Volos, with Mr. Michael Cohen, ca. 1950. They are shown entering the church of St. Nicholas in Volos to take part in services marking a national holiday. (Volos Community/Jewish Museum of Greece)

to hold at least all of the men. Built of stone, it stood in the center of a large tile–covered courtyard, which was used for public meetings, as well as providing a place for a communal *sukkah*.

The interior of the synagogue was divided centrally by four columns. Within that central squared–off area was a large elevated bema with two sets of stairs. Facing the bema, on the east wall, was the *ehal. The mehitza* was reached by an exterior staircase and was constructed along the south, north, and west walls. This arrangement is typical of the Romaniote synagogues that we know of from that time.

The entire 19th–century building was razed by the Nazis in 1943. In 1945, through the efforts of the community and JOINT, it was reconstructed almost exactly as it had been, with offices and the school located on the first floor. After the earthquakes of 1955-7, however, the damage was so great that a decision was made to build a new synagogue. By this time the community had been reduced considerably in size. A smaller building was put up in 1960, with no interior divisions, although it maintained the tradition of a centrally located bema and axially aligned *ehal*. The *mehitza* is in the same form as the original.

Other Sites

The Volos cemetery is outside of town in the Nea Ionia district, at 14 Taxiarchon Street. It was established in the 1970's. Its earliest stones, dating from the mid–19th century, were transferred from the other Jewish cemetery of Volos, which was destroyed in the 1970's to make way for a road.

How to Visit the Synagogue

The synagogue (called simply "the synagogue" by the local community) is at the intersection of three streets: Moiseos, Platonos, and Xenofondos (see map). Services are held every Friday evening, Saturday morning, and on High Holidays. Visitors wishing to see the synagogue at other times should contact the community.

Contacts for More Information

For further information regarding access to the synagogue or cemetery, visitors should call the community offices at (0421) 24640 or 25640, between 5:00 P.M. and 8:00 P.M. They do not, however, speak English.

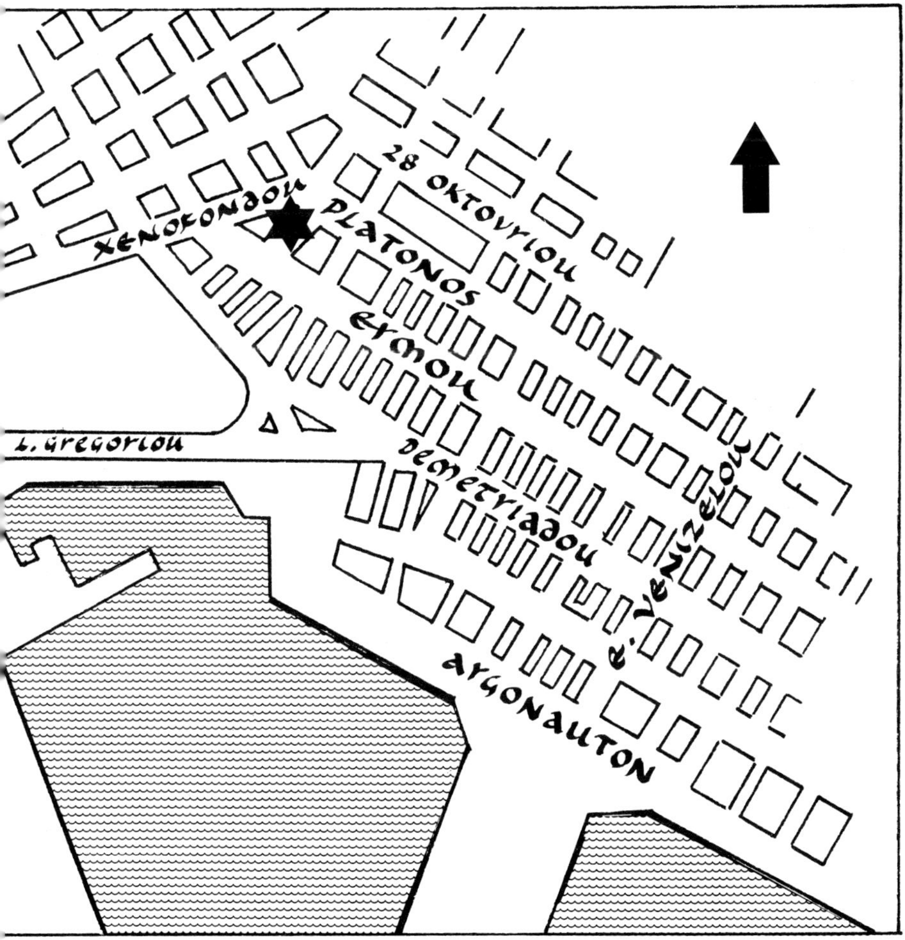

Key to Volos Map: **1.** *Synagogue*

Part Two: Places of Jewish Interest

Andravida

After the partition of the Byzantine Empire under the Fourth Crusade in 1204, Andravida became an important administrative center, as well as a Latin ecclesiastical see. By the mid–13th century it had some 50 Jewish households whose religious needs were served by three rabbis, as noted by the wandering mystic R. Abraham Abulafia. The Jews of Andravida were closely associated with Patras and Corinth, and were actively involved in textile production, both weaving and dyeing. After the 15th century Andravida ceased to have any importance. It is likely that most of the Andravidan Jews moved to Patras, which assumed greater prominence as Andravida itself sank into oblivion.

Aphilon

The exact site of the town referred to as "Aphilon" by Benjamin of Tudela is unknown, but we can deduce from the itinerary of his 12th–century travels that it was south of Arta and across from Ithaka. He mentions thirty families (approximately 150 persons) but provides no other details.

Armylos
(also Harmylos)

Armylos was for many centuries the principal port for Thessaly, especially active in the export of grain. Located on the Pagasitikos Gulf it had a mixed commercial population made up of Jews, Venetians, Pisans, and Genoese. Benjamin of Tudela passed through Armylos in the mid–12th century, and recorded a Jewish community of 400 persons (or perhaps householders). After the Fourth Crusade, Armylos became a bone of contention between the Crusaders until 1308, when it was ravaged and burned by Ferdinand of Majorca and a ferocious band of Catalans. The town never recovered and its Jews, undoubtedly, fled elsewhere. During the Ottoman period, Volos assumed the commercial role that Armylos had once served as the port for Thessaly, and it is likely that many of the members of the early Voliote Jewish community moved there from Armylos.

Arta

Arta was known in antiquity as Ambrakia. It was the capital of King Pyrrhus I of Epirus, whose fame at winning costly battles gave rise to the expression "Pyrrhic victory." On King Pyrrhus's death in 272 B.C.E., Ambrakia lost its short– lived prominence and entered into a long period of obscurity.

Benjamin of Tudela, shortly after leaving Corfu, entered Greece roughly in this area, though it is not clear whether the one hundred Jewish families that he found were at Arta or on the island of Lefkada. The latter seems most likely.

It was not until the period immediately following the Fourth Crusade that Arta once again assumed some importance and well may have attracted Jewish settlement. On the fall of Constantinople to the Crusaders in 1204 a number of Byzantine relatives of the last emperor laid claim to the Latin–occupied throne. Michael I Angelos, a cousin of the last emperor, established himself as despot in Epirus and made Arta his capital, probably due to its proximity to the Peloponnese. Under him and his successors, the city flourished and a Romaniote Jewish community was most likely established.

We know nothing of this community other than that it was well established by the time of the Ottoman conquest in 1449 and appears to have felt its Romaniote identity threatened by the arrival of large numbers of Sephardi, Sicilian, Corfiote, Apuleian, and Calabrian Jews. Until well into the 16th century, there were frequent disputes regarding customs, language, and traditions between the congregations and it often became necessary to appeal to the rabbis of Salonika for mediation. It also became customary for rabbinical aspirants to complete their studies there. In the late 17th century, followers of Shabbetai Zvi added further dissension in the community and a contemporary archbishop of Athens notes wryly that an Artan Jew had fallen to his death from a rooftop after throwing himself heavenward to join the Messiah.

Throughout the 18th century, and especially toward its end, Epirus was quite unsettled. Fought over by Venetians, Ottomans, and then marauding Albanians (Christian and Muslim), Arta did not fare well. There was considerable emigration to Ioannina, Patras, and elsewhere, though some Artan Jews appear to have chosen to assimilate into Ottoman life and, in at least one case, achieved considerable importance and fame. One Artan Jew who converted to Islam, by the name of Ishak, after completing studies in Arta and attracting the attention of the Ottoman authorities here, was sent to Constantinople where he was enrolled in the Imperial School. After his graduation he was appointed professor of mathematics as well as inspector for fortifications in western Anatolia and Greece. In 1821 his proficiency in languages (Greek, Osmanli, Persian, Arabic, Hebrew, French, and Latin) led to his appointment to the Imperial Divan. On his death in 1832 he left many students, a legacy of respect and considerable fame, and several important works on physics, chemistry, and mathematics. Hoca Ishak Effendi is still honored in Turkey as the person responsible for the introduction of Western science into Ottoman intellectual circles.

The Jewish community of Arta continued to exist, though how they fared during the period after 1821 until the end of the 19th century is unknown. Nearby Preveza appears to have attracted a good number of its emigrants. Names common to both Arta and Patras indicate that still others took part in the refounding of the community in Patras. Close links were also maintained with Ioannina and Corfu. For reasons that are unclear, the Artan Jewish community was not recognized under Greek law until 1918-20. By that time it numbered only 150 families. There were two synagogues, one of which was quite ancient, and a school. The community was mainly involved in commerce and had some interests in village produce in the region.

At the time of the Axis partition of Greece, Arta had 384 Jews. In 1944 they were arrested en masse and deported to Auschwitz where almost all of them perished. An attempt was made (as at Patras) to refound a community after the war but it failed, and in 1959 it was officially dissolved under Greek law. All indications of former Jewish life in Arta have since disappeared.

Bissena

Bissena is mentioned by Benjamin of Tudela as being a day's journey from Armylos. It had a small community of 100 Jews, whose religious needs were served by three rabbis. After the Fourth Crusade, Bissena, though not a port, probably suffered a fate similar to that of Armylos. Its economic decline saw the departure of its Jews.

Chios

A 1st–century C.E. Jewish community on Chios is cited by Josephus, though its fortunes until the llth century are unknown. Under the emperor Constantine X Monomachos (1042-1055) there were 15 Jews on the island, who were required to pay additional taxes for the upkeep of the monastery of Nea Moni. It is roughly within the period of the reign of Constantine that the monastery was completely rebuilt and given lavish mosaic decorations, and it is tempting to think that perhaps these funds were directed to that end. The obligation on the Jews continued at least through the reign of Constantine XI Dukas (1059-1067).

A century later, Benjamin of Tudela visited the island and notes a community numbering some 400 Jews, which can only be accounted for by a massive emigration. In 1070, the Seljuq Turks defeated a Byzantine army at Manzikert in eastern Anatolia and thus established the Sultanate of Rum. They then began attacking deep into Byzantine territory, as far as Nicaea and the coast of the

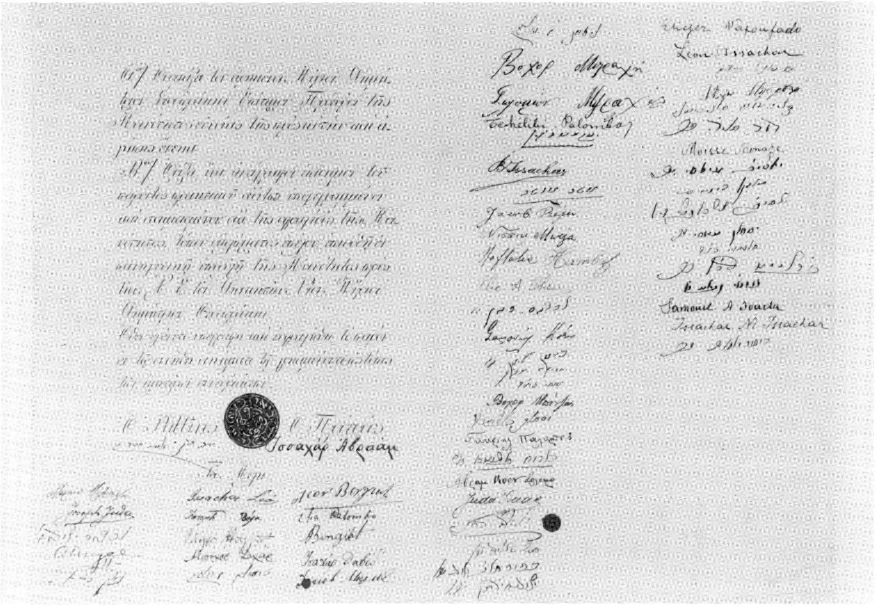

Part of a document signed by the members of the Chios Jewish community issued on 21 May 1913, shortly after the annexation of the island by Greece. It records a decision to name the Christian governor of the island, Dimitrios Theodorakis, as honorary president of the Jewish community. (Jewish Museum of Greece)

Aegean Sea. The exodus of Jews to the islands of the Aegean, including Chios, can certainly be attributed to the very unsettled conditions prevailing in Anatolia.

In 1344 Chios passed into the hands of the Genoese, and Jews were subject to certain restrictions and humiliations. They were required each year to provide the scarlet flag with the cross of St. George that flew from the cathedral church of Chios. They were also obliged to recite formal prayers for the well–being of the pope at Christmas, New Year, and Easter. The main occupations of the Jews of Chios appear to have been in wine–making and petty commerce.

Because of the expansion of the silk–making trade in Chios in the early 16th century, Sephardi Jews began to arrive despite its continued occupation by the Genoese. The Chiote Jewish community remained Romaniote in character, nonetheless, and the new arrivals probably conformed to local practices and *minhag* until after the seizure of Chios by the Ottomans in 1566. At that point a considerable number of Sephardi Jews arrived from nearby Rhodes as well as Salonika. Within a short time, Castillian Spanish and the Sephardi *minhag* drew Chiote Jewry into the complex net of Sephardi communities in the Aegean and on the coast of Anatolia.

The Ottoman conquest of Chios in 1566 occured under conditions that allowed the island a great degree of independance. During the 17th and 18th centuries, Chiote shipping and commerce developed and expanded. Exports of wine, mastic, and olive oil increased the wealth of both the Christian and Jewish communities. The Greek expression "I am Chiote and a Jew" expresses the astute business ability for which both Jews and Christians were not only famous but, at times, notorious.

In the mid–18th century there were about 200 Jews in the community. They and their synagogue occupied an area within the walls of the citadel. The small, wooden synagogue was called the K'K Baal ha–Turim. (It may be that the name of the synagogue is a clue to the origins of the Sephardi Jews of Chios, as the Baal ha–Turim was a famous rabbi of Toledo in the 14th century.)

In the early 19th century the Jewish cemetery of Chios became an important center of pilgrimage for both Jews as well as Muslims, from Rhodes, Bodrum, Izmir and elsewhere. Through an interesting hagiographical invention circulated between 1821-31, it was claimed that one tomb in the cemetery was none other than that of the Baal ha–Turim himself, though it was well known that he had in fact died in Spain in 1343 and been buried in Toledo. The Chiote Jews claimed that, contrary to the accepted biography of the Baal, he'd come to Chios, died of the plague there, and been buried in a tomb that bore no inscription. Visits to his tomb required the removal of shoes, the washing of hands and recitation of certain prescribed psalms, and it was said that miracles occured and petitions were granted, through such pilgrimages.

When the Greek revolt broke out in the Peloponnese in 1821 special envoys were sent to Chios and Samos requesting naval aid in blockading Ottoman sea routes. Both islands enthusiastically responded and were thus drawn into the ensuing war. The initial phase of the revolt did not go well and the Ottoman navy descended on the two islands in full force. Chios bore the brunt of Ottoman retaliation in a wholesale slaughter of some 25,000 people and the enslavement of another 47,000 who glutted the slave markets of Kalamata, Libya, and Algeria. The Jews played a passive role during the entire affair. Enclosed as they were within the Ottoman citadel they took no part in the fighting, and the Christians, understandably perhaps, never really forgave them. There may well have been an initial overt reaction against the Jews (even prior to the massacre). The famous Purim of Chios which, toward the end of the 19th century was said to commemorate the survival of the community during the earthquake of 1881, in fact dates back to 1821.

In 1875 a fire destroyed a large portion of the commercial center of Chios, to be followed in 1881 by an earthquake which all but destroyed the Jewish quarter. The old synagogue of Chios was destroyed by fire in 1888. It was rebuilt in stone outside the walls. Funds for this purpose were provided in part by a Greek Christian Chiote named G. Horemis, who also obtained funds to this end from the Rothschilds in Paris.

Relations between Jews and Christians, which had always been tense became increasingly strained toward the end of the 19th century. The first case of blood libel directed against Jews on Chios come in 1892, and it was followed by yet another in 1897 at the moment when Greco–Turkish hostilities broke out. In Crete the Christians set upon Muslim Cretans as well as Jews, and large numbers of the latter fled to Chios where a special organization, the Chica Alianza, was established to assist them. At this time the entire population of Chios consisted of 73,800 Christians (Greeks and Armenians), 6,000 Muslims, and 200 Jews. It is of interest that, despite the tensions in that same year (1897),a new quai was to be inaugurated and the chief mufti of the island was to deliver the prayers. Because he was ill the honor was passed on to the metropolitan of the island who also happened to be ill. In the end the Turkish governor requested that the chief rabbi deliver the prayers, which were duly recited in Hebrew in the presence of the Ottoman authorities, Greek Christian notables, and the Jewish community.

In 1912 Chios was ceded to Greece and many Jews left shortly after to settle in either Izmir, Alexandria, or Istanbul. There is an interesting document in the Jewish Museum of Greece in which the entire Jewish community of 47 members (males) unanimously voted, with their chief rabbi, to appoint the new Greek governor of the island, Mr Dimitri Theodorakis, as their president.

By the time the Axis occupation started, hardly any Jews remained on Chios. With the exception of those holding Turkish papers, those who had remained on the island were arrested in 1944 and sent to Auschwitz–Birkenau. There are no Jews on Chios today.

It is worth visiting the citadel and looking through the various Jewish tombstones from the old cemetery that have been collected there—there are, undoubtedly, others still to be found.

Corinth

There is little if any doubt that Corinth had a sizeable Jewish community in antiquity. Located on one of the main trade arteries connecting the Aegean Sea and the Gulf of Corinth, it had a quite cosmopolitan character. After the founding of Alexandria, it also maintained close commercial ties with Egypt. These factors would have made Jewish settlement inevitable, though the community that Paul visited may well have been one that had been refounded after the destruction of Corinth by the Romans in the 2nd century B.C.E.

Paul's Letters to the Corinthians and references to the Jews here, might be taken to indicate that they were quite an exotic group and heavily infested with Gnosticism. There were a large number of Jewish–oriented gentiles as well and these elements formed the nucleus of the first Christian community here.

Under the emperor Claudius, the Jews were expelled for a period of time. After the destruction of Jerusalem in 71 C.E., over 6,000 Jewish slaves were brought to dig the proposed canal that was to provide direct access to the Gulf of Corinth from the Aegean Sea. After the failure of this attempt it may well be that many of these Jews settled in Corinth, for archeological remains show that there was at least one synagogue here that dated from the 3rd century. In

Stone plinth with menoroth, lulavs, *and* ethrogim, *Corinth, ca. 3rd century* C.E., *found during the excavations at ancient Corinth. (Corinth Archeological Excavations)*

395, Corinth's Jews fled to the island of Aegina in the face of attacks by the Goths. They later returned, but nothing is known of the community until the 12th century. At that time they were involved in silk production and dyeing. Together with the Jews of Thebes, they figured in the booty that was carried off to Sicily by George of Antioch to enrich the Norman kingdom there. Later in that same century Benjamin of Tudela remarks on the presence of 300 Jews in Corinth.

Unlike the Jews of Thebes, Corinthian Jews do not appear to have fared well after the Crusader conquest of Greece and the Peloponnese. There are references to individual Corinthian Jews in the 14th century, but nothing is known of the community and it may well have died out even prior to the Ottoman conquest.

Today there are several inscribed stones in the storerooms of the archeological museum of Corinth. One of these appears to have been a capital, inscribed with a *menorah*. Another that appears to have been a lintel has an inscription with the Greek letters "——goge Evr——," suggesting the words: "(Syna)goge Evr(aion)" (Synagogue of the Jews). These could well have come from two different buildings, but the locations of those original buildings have not yet been discovered.

Corone

Corone is a small town that dominates the broad entrance to the Gulf of Messenia and was, with Methone, so important to Venice that the two were called the "Eyes of the Empire." Jews had been living there from the 12th century, even before the arrival of the Venetians. As in the case of many Jewish communities in the Peloponnese, their main occupations were textile manufacturing, dyeing and, probably, commerce. In 1501 the Ottomans seized the fortress after an especially bloody seige and the Venetian garrison of some 7,000 men was slaughtered. By 1520, Spanish Jews began to settle in Corone, though we have no record of their numbers. In 1646 the town suffered under the same raid that ravaged Methone and many Muslim and Jewish slaves were taken. The Venetians retook Corone in 1685. The Jewish community, undoubtedly still mindful of the heavy taxes imposed on them by the Venetians in the past, left the city and moved elsewhere. There are no identifiably Jewish sites here today.

Didimoticho

Didimoticho, along with many cities in Thrace and Macedonia, has an erratically documented history. On the basis of the antiquity of the town, its strategic location and proximity to Adrianoupolis (Edirne), it has been claimed that Didimoticho had a Jewish community prior to the Ottoman conquest in the early 14th century. In particular this seems likely for the time when John VI Cantacuzenos was proclaimed Byzantine emperor in 1347.

Later, under Sultan Murad I, Didimoticho was the capitol of the Ottoman Empire for a time, until the seizure of Adrianoupolis in 1361. Its importance during those years may well have attracted Jews. There was a considerable immigration of Ashkenazi Jews into Thrace following their expulsion from Hungary in 1376 and France in 1394. The existence of Ashkenazi names among Didimoticho Jews prior to 1943 would seem to support the possibility of a community dating from that time. It should be mentioned, however, that the

Interior of the former Didimoticho synagogue. The columned and arched central area marks the site of the bema, set axially in front of the ehal. *(Photo: Timothy DeVinney/Jewish Museum of Greece)*

Exterior of the former synagogue of Didimoticho, built in 1924, photographed here in

August, 1980, view to the east, showing forecourt as well. (Photo: Timothy DeVinney/ Jewish Museum of Greece)

A snapshot taken by an unidentified person, showing the transfer of the Jews of Didimoticho to Alexandroupolis in 1943 in preparation for their deportation to Treblinka by the Nazis and the Bulgarians. (Jewish Museum of Greece)

earliest tombstone found in the Jewish cemetery of Didimoticho bears the date 1456.

We have little information regarding the community after the 14th century, other than that it was expanded at some point by an influx of Sephardi Jews, and that Spanish became the common language. It appears that its fortunes were dominated by those of the great Jewish communities in Edirne, Salonika, and Sophia. The Jewish quarter during the mid–19th century was southeast of the Mosque of Beyazid I, near the town center. There were 30 households here at that time.

By the end of the 19th century there were some 485 Jews here. The energy and growing needs of the community are indicated by the foundation of an Alliance Israelite School. French, Hebrew, and Ladino were taught and to a degree mastered by the youth of the community. Especially after the absorption of Thrace into Greece in 1913, the Jewish community continued to grow. In 1924 a new community center was constructed, incorporating a synagogue, school and community offices. The handsome brick building reflected a moderately wealthy and certainly active community.

The interior of the synagogue proper was characterized by a squared–off area with columns on each corner, enclosing the bema. The *ehal* was directly in front of this central structure, set in the east wall. The women's section was on an upper balcony, extending from the west wall. This plan is typical of most Sephardi synagogues in Thrace, Macedonia, and Thessaly.

On the eve of the Second World War, there were some 1,000 Jews in Didimoticho. With the outbreak of hostilities, many fled. Those who remained fell within a special zone occupied by the Germans (the remainder of Thrace was given to the Bulgarians). As a consequence, the impact of German racial laws was immediate and in 1943 some 900 Jews were sent to Auschwitz with the convoys from Salonika. There were only 33 survivors.

Today there are only 3 Jews living in Didimoticho. The synagogue complex was sold in 1985 and the building razed. The Jewish cemetery can still be seen, but its location on the west bank of the Evros River, marking the border between Turkey and Greece, is a military zone and cannot be visited.

Drama

Drama has a history going back to antiquity. It's mentioned by Thucydides as "Drabeskos," and was one of several Thracian towns inhabited by a somewhat exotic people known as the Edonians who worshipped the god Dionysios in notoriously frenzied rites and ceremonies. It's not mentioned as having a Jewish community until the late 12th century, when Benjamin of Tudela visited Drama and found 140 householders.

Drama fared badly during the 14th century with the decline of the Byzantine Empire and yet, like Kavala, it may well have attracted the resettlement of Jews from Hungary after the fall of Budapest in 1529. After the 17th century, like most towns in Thrace, Drama was active in the cultivation and production of both tobacco and silk and its Jews took a leading role in its commerce. The community here was closely linked with Serres, Kavala, Salonika, and Sophia both by marriage and trade.

In 1940 the Jewish community here was one of the largest in Thrace, with some 1,200 Jews. Immediately after the Bulgarians occupied Thrace, the Jews were offered special consideration in return for accepting "Bulgarization" (taking Bulgarian citizenship and speaking Bulgarian). On refusing this they were stripped of almost all social amenities and their means of carrying out normal business. Like their compatriots, the Greek Christians, they were harassed constantly. In 1943 they were arrested en masse and sent first to Kavala and then to the city of Lom on the Danube River, and finally by boat to Vienna where they were handed to the Nazis for subsequent execution at Treblinka. In 1948 there were only 40 Jews left in Drama, and today there are but a few individuals.

Florina

Florina had a Sephardi Jewish community by the 17th century. During this period, the commercial activities radiating from Salonika linked Florina, Kastoria, and Karditsa. Little is known of the community until the 20th century, when Florina and the surrounding area were annexed by Greece. The community underwent a religious crisis when the Christian Sabbath was imposed under Greek Law, requiring that Jewish shops remain open on Saturday. Large numbers of Jews emigrated as a result, and only the poorer remained behind.

In 1940 there were some 400 Jews left in the community. Almost all of them were involved in petty trades (as pedlars, for example). The Jews of Florina were arrested by the Nazis in 1943, sent by convoy to Salonika, and from there to Auschwitz. Only 65 persons survived. There is no Jewish community at present and nothing remains from former times.

Herakleion

The Jewish quarter in Herakleion is barely discernible today. From at least the early 13th century, it was located on the waterfront within the Venetian walls. Today this corresponds to an area roughly delineated by Venizelou Street (along the waterfront), Makariou Street (along the walls to the west), and Giamalaki Street (to the east). An extension of the quarter existed between Gazi and Theotokopoulou streets, bordered to the north by the waterfront. The Venetian church of St. Peter, now in ruins, was between the two quarters. When its bells rang for vespers, they also signaled to Jews that it was time to cease all work for Shabbat. In this area there were originally four synagogues, though during the Ottoman period only two are ever mentioned.

By 1941 only one of these synagogues was still in use and it was bombed and destroyed during the war. Because it was set within a deeply excavated area, however, its floor plan and substructure were still visible as late as 1963, when the site was filled in, leveled, and the present day Xenia Hotel constructed on top of it. The custom of constructing a building below ground level was a means whereby a structure of some height could be erected, without violating the law forbidding Jews to build houses of worship (synagogues) that were as high, or higher, than neighboring churches.

Fortunately, from some simple sketches made of the foundations prior to their being filled in, it is clear that the building was in the form of a traditional basilica. It was oriented on an east–west axis with three aisles formed by two parallel rows of columns, three columns to each row. Over these sprang pointed arches parallel to the axis. The main entrance was on the long south wall. Adjacent to it was a smaller entrance that may have given access to the *mehitza*, which would have been located on a balcony along the west wall, supported by the first pair of columns. The bema was constructed within the area marked by those same two columns to the west and the two in the center. The *ehal* was on the east wall within an apse that projected externally. The pointed arches make it clear that this building was erected during the Venetian period and probably in the

16th century, when the Jewish quarter expanded to the east. In form, however, it may have kept conservatively to a very ancient and native type of synagogue.

The area between the Xenia Hotel and the Ethnographic Museum across the street, corresponds to the heart of the Jewish quarter, and the oldest Venetian house fronts here were once owned by Jews. The building housing the Ethnographic Museum itself was formerly a Jewish residence. Two sculptures in its collection of heraldic inscriptions are of particular interest to us. These are carved with crowned lions bearing swords and belonged to the She'altiel and Franco families. The first of these may well have been the subject of a rabbinical debate we know about in the 16th century. At that time a member of the She'altiel family by the name of Grazziano Hen decorated the synagogue and demanded in return that his name and escutcheon be displayed above the *ehal*, along with a marble tablet inscribed with the names of members of his family. It appears that what especially upset the rabbis was that he also wanted the title "Gaon" placed before his own name. (The title "Gaon," meaning "honorable" in Hebrew, is generally reserved for rabbis.) After a serious rabbinical debate it was decided that the tablet could be put over the entrance to the synagogue, but not inside it. Unfortunately, neither of these sculptures can be related accurately to a specific building, although it is likely that the museum acquired them in 1963, when the synagogue substructure was filled in.

In an area behind the museum, there are 5 small stones with inscriptions in Hebrew, which probably come from the now–destroyed cemetery.

(For a historical background to the Herakleion community, see the historical introduction to HANIA.)

Jabustrissa

Jabustrissa is of the towns visited by Benjamin of Tudela in the 12th century which are today unknown. According to his itinerary he apparently reached it after leaving Halkis on his journey north. He notes that it had some 500 Jews (100 families).

Kastoria

The city of Kastoria was founded by the emperor Diocletian in the 3rd century C.E., and Jews probably settled here not long afterwards. During the reign of the Emperor Justinian I (517-65) and despite his restrictive legislation, the community grew considerably and was given permission to construct its quarter within the fortifications. The Slavic invasions into the Greek peninsula were just beginning at this time, and they probably were the reason for Byzantine authorities extending protection to the community. Until well into the 10th century nothing is known of the community. They would, certainly, have fared little better than most of the inhabitants of towns that lay in the path of invaders such as the Bulgarians, Avars, Petchenegs, and, finally, the Normans. Later evidence attests to the fact that the Kastoria Jews were Romaniote, Greek speaking and in close contact with other communities that shared the Romaniote *minhag*. By the early 12th century the Jewish community was quite large and numbered between 2,500 and 3,000 persons, out of a total population of some 20,000. It had an important rabbinical academy and one of its foremost rabbis, Tobias ben Elizar, was greatly admired by Rashi.

In the wake of the break–up of the Byzantine Empire in the early 13th century, Kastoria became a somewhat neglected corner until Byzantine authority was reestablished. Some important Jewish writers are known from this period in Kastoria's history, such as R. Meir, and another rabbi, Leon Judah (b. Moshe Moskoni), who was also an avid collector of Hebrew manuscripts. Though little remains of their work, there were at least two other rabbinical figures who contributed to the further evolution of the Romaniote *minhag*: R. David b. Eliezar and R. Eli b. Abraham. The former, a composer of liturgical hymns, was active in the 14th century. In 1453, just a short time before the fall of Constantinople, R. Abraham was responsible for setting down in a definitive manner the Romaniote *minhag* according to its contemporary usage.

Kastoria had fallen to the Turks in 1385, and from the evidence afforded by the activity of these writers it appears that the Jews were creative and productive under the secure religious and social conditions. After the fall of Constantinople in 1453, Mehmet's policy of revitalizing the city by conscripting minority groups saw a good number of Kastriote Jews uprooted and sent there under the leadership of R. Mathathias Tamar. They constructed a synagogue in the Balat quarter of Istanbul which stands to this day, and maintained close relations with the Kastoria community until the Second World War. Despite this association between Kastoria and Istanbul, however, Monastir exerted the greatest influence on the Kastoria community, and through it on other Romaniote communities in the lower Balkans.

Exactly when the first Sephardi Jews arrived is unknown. It is likely that they came in relatively small numbers at the beginning. The Romaniote *minhag* was maintained certainly until well after 1537 when Jews arrived from Apuleia, Italy. This emigration from Italy was substantial and resulted in expanding the size of Jewish communities in Ioannina, Corfu, Larissa, Monastir, as well as Kastoria. Diluted by dispersion, the Apuleian Jews had little immediate influence, until shortly afterwards, when Sephardi Jews from Salonika also began to arrive and settle in the city. Kastoria's principal attraction was its very lucrative fur trade. With these new arrivals, matters changed considerably as the linguistic proximity of Italian and Spanish, plus their more or less common rite, gave the Sephardi newcomers an upper hand. Added to this was a certain attitude of cultural superiority that always marked the Sephardi involvement with a Romaniote. Within a very short period of time, Ladino replaced Greek as the common language of the Jews in Kastoria. The Romaniotes were forced to accept the Spanish *minhag* and the entire community was Hispanicized.

Certain Romaniote customs were stubbornly adhered to, however. As late as 1567 it was still the custom to recognize as legal a marriage that had been performed in the presence of two witnesses with the offering of any gift to a woman accompanied by the words "with this I consecrate you to myself." Apparently there were serious enough disagreements over this to prompt an appeal by the Sephardi

Jews to the Beth Din of Salonika. The custom was condemned in favor of the more accepted Sephardi ritual requiring both a *minyan* and a *ketubbah*. Despite this, as late as 1710, the Salonika decision was generally ignored. In that year, a young man of no means, by the name of Jacob Cohen, managed to thrust into the hands of the only daughter of the wealthiest Jew in Kastoria a bouquet of flowers and shout out loud in the middle of the street, "I take thee after the manner of *kidouchia*." Needless to say, the girl's father, Abraham Abalag, raised an enormous storm of protest, and in the end the marriage was annulled and the *hascama* of Salonika made absolutely binding on the entire community regardless of origin.

After the 18th century, Kastoriote Jews appear frequently in prominent positions in other Jewish communities. One of the most notable was Isaac de Mayo, also known as Isaac ha–Sar. Shortly after setting in Larissa, at the beginning of the 18th century, his astute financial abilities came to the attention of the Osman Pasha, who appointed him financial advisor with the title of Saraf Bashi, or Tafsar. In this capacity Isaac proved successful and shared much of his rise to fame with other Jewish communities both in Greece and in Turkey proper. He provided endowments to synagogues and at least one of these is preserved in a stone inscription now located in the external wall of the Halkis synagogue where he is mentioned by title. In Istanbul, Izmir, and Salonika he gave considerable sums of money for the printing of Hebrew books.

In the early 18th century there were four synagogues in Kastoria. It is most likely that one was the Romaniote, another the Apuleian, and the other two Spanish and Portuguese. In 1719 three of these (we don't know for certain which ones) were destroyed in a fire that swept through the Jewish quarter, and it was not until 1750 that a new synagogue was built to replace those that had been burned down. From the name of the donor, Jacob Bahor Benveniste, it can be assumed that at least one of the Sephardi synagogues had perished in the fire. In 1828 this new synagogue was also burned down. Two years later, it was rebuilt, after the model of the Kal Shalom in Salonika, and given the name Aragon.

From the descriptions we have of the Aragon synagogue, it appears to have been somewhat similar to the synagogue of Komotini (which still stands) and possibly to that of Serres (now destroyed). It was very large and had a dome or rotunda. It was, however, unique in having the *ehal* on the west wall. The bema was located not under the dome but against the east wall, reached by 18 steps located on either side. This axial layout is peculiar and bears more in common to Romaniote synagogue plans. Unfortunately, the synagogue did not survive the Second World War nor, for that matter, did the Jewish quarter.

Despite attempts to paint an idyllic picture of Jewish–Christian relations in Kastoria it is known that there were serious commercial rivalries. Kastoria was famous for its furs. Furs were collected and processed here according to techniques involving slicing the skins and re–sewing them in a process that extended their length. Beaver, fox, and other commercially important furs were shipped not only to Salonika and Istanbul, but—via Monastir—up into Western Europe. The inevitable rivalry at times took on serious dimensions, including blood libels, of which one outstanding case occured 1879. It is of interest that even after the absorption of Kastoria into the modern Greek state at the beginning of this century, this rivalry was carried to New York, where both Kastoriote Jews and Christians had immigrated and set up fur businesses.

We have little accurate data on the community during the early part of this century. By 1928 there were only some 900 Jews still living in the city out a total population of 10,308. In 1943 under the German occupation the Jews of Kastoria were arrested and shipped to Salonika where they were sent by cattle car to Auschwitz–Birkenau. There were only 35 survivors.

Today nothing worthy of note remains of the community. The cemetery, from which a few stones have been found, was bulldozed some years ago. The quarter itself is roughly distinguishable within the walls of the old city but nothing specifically identifiable remains.

Kavala

Nothing is known of either an ancient or medieval Jewish community in Kavala. In antiquity the town was known as "Neapolis," and it was the usual port of debarkation for persons arriving by sea from the east. Paul of Tarsus passed through Kavala on his way to Philippi and the fact that he did not spend time here would indicate the absence of a Jewish community.

In the ensuing centuries, Kavala, either as "Neapolis" or,as it was later known,"Christoupolis," fared badly. On several occasions it was raided both from the land and the sea, and in 1185 it was burned to the ground by the Normans. In the 14th century, it was burned again under the Catalans and afterwards was caught in the chaos of the final years of the Byzantine Empire.

Stable conditions were only established after the Pax Ottomanica. Kavala appears to have been given its first Jewish community (at least in recorded history) when large numbers of Hungarian Jews were brought here after the fall of Budapest in 1529. Later, Sephardi Jews from Salonika and Adrianoupolis (Edirne) arrived to enlarge the community. We know little of the process of "Hispanization" of the Ashkenazi Jews of Kavala other than that it was effective: by the 19th century, the community was Spanish speaking and conformed to the Sephardi rite.

Kavala became a very important town and port after the introduction of tobacco cultivation and processing in Thrace. Its warehouses were famous and the Jewish community was active in both the production of tobacco and its export. A new and quite spacious synagogue was built in 1885. By 1900 the community numbered over 2,500 persons.

During the Balkan Wars, Kavala suffered two horrendous periods of Bulgarian occupation to be followed by a third in 1942-44. During the last, the Bulgarians attempted to force Jews in Thrace, and in Kavala, in particular, to accept Bulgarian identity (official Bulgarian citizenship) in their attempt to "Bulgarize" the region. The Jews adamantly refused. As a community, they considered themselves to be Greek. As a result, together with the other Jews of Thrace, they

The interior of the oratory of Kavala, photographed in August, 1980. (Photo: Timothy DeVinney/Jewish Museum of Greece)

were severely restricted in their movements and activities as early as 1941. They were arrested in 1943, and sent by convoy to the city of Lom on the Danube River and placed on boats for the journey north. Their fate is still a matter of some contention. Many are known to have drowned when the overloaded boats sank. The majority, however, were handed over to the Nazis in Vienna and from there sent to Treblinka for extermination. This particular "action" involved some 5,000 Jews, from Kavala, Komotini, and Drama.

At the end of the war, the surviving Kavalan Jews succeeded in reestablishing a semblance of a community. The old synagogue had been destroyed, but a small oratory served the community's needs. Today the community has faded and, after the recent death of its last president, appears to have ceased to be active as such.

A Jewish cemetery still exists here. It is some distance from the town to the east and is not easy to find. But some local taxi drivers know the area and, as the surrounding wall has been breached once found it can be entered easily. The burials are mostly from the 19th and 20th centuries and are of no particular interest.

Krissa

Krissa and its Jews have been the subject of interesting speculation into modern times. Benjamin of Tudela cites this town in his travels made during the 12th–century, noting that it had 200 families. It is described as not far from Nafpactos, and on the route that would took him to Itea where he ferried across the Corinthian Gulf to the Peloponnese. This must refer to the modern village of Krissa, on the road from Delphi to the gulf. What is especially intriguing about his record is that he takes pains to note that the Jews lived in isolation from other Jews, possessed their own farmlands, and reaped and sowed their own fields. It is known that such communities existed in medieval times on the island of Crete and that they provided kosher products for sale and export, including wine, cheese and wheat. The fate of the Krissa community of farming Jews is unknown, though there is a possibility that living "alone" resulted in their eventual assimilation.

Kyparissia

Kyparissia is a port on the Ionian Gulf and was a major port and fortress during the Venetian period (13th–18th centuries). Along with Modon (Methone) and Corone, also in Messinia, it attracted a Jewish settlement about which we know next to nothing. During the dramatic events of the Greek War of Independance (1821-1831) the community appears to have been assimilated through conversion. A few Jewish names were still to be found among the Christian population until the Second World War.

Lamia

Lamia did not play a notable role in ancient history. In fact, little is know of its history until quite well into the Byzantine period, when its Jewish community is mentioned by Benjamin of Tudela as numbering some 200 individuals. In one of the few asides in Benjamin's account of his travels he alludes to the Vlachs of the region as especially friendly to Jews, even going so far as to adopt Jewish names. This peculiar attraction of the Vlachs to Jews continued well into the Ottoman period. It was noted several times that whereas Vlachs would rob and then murder the Christian merchants they came upon in the mountains, Jews were only robbed!

Not long after Benjamin's passage through Greece, Lamia fell to the Franks with the dismemberment of the Byzantine Empire. It was known for a while as "Gipton," and then, under the Catalan Company, as "El Cito," and finally by the Ottomans after 1450 as "Zitouni." It appears the Jews of Lamia weathered those troubled years reasonably well, because in the re–populating of Constantinople by Mehmet II in 1455, some 42 Jewish families were brought in from Lamia. By the end of the 16th century, Lamia was left with only 42 Jews. In modern times what remained of the community appears to have been absorbed by either Larissa or Trikkala or both.

Lefkada

(also Santa Maura)

Lefkada is one of the Ionian Islands, near Corfu. There is some contention among scholars today concerning where Benjamin of Tudela actually arrived in Greece after leaving Corfu. Arta is one possibility and Lefkada is another. In either case, he mentions the presence of 100 families (approximately 500 persons) at his point of arrival.

By 1682, Lefkada had certainly attracted a large Jewish community, as an English traveler of that time was given the impression that it was inhabited only by Jews. This was only two years before the Venetians retook the island from the Ottomans, and perhaps reflects a massive incursion of Sephardi Jews that may have taken place in the 16th century. Today, nothing of this Jewish community remains.

Lemnos

The island of Lemnos has a position that must have attracted Jewish settlement, especially after its take–over by Venice in the 13th century. The island is quite large and situated before the entrance to the Dardenelles, roughly mid–way between Constantinople and Salonika by sea. There was a network of Jewish communities on both sides of the Dardenelles at that time and, while not mentioned specifically until the 19th century, it seems highly improbable that there was not a community here from much earlier than that. It may have ceased to exist for a period of time because of the Russian occupation of the island in 1770.

In the mid–19th century there were approximately 30 Jewish families on Lemnos. They appear to have been of mixed Romaniote–Sephardi background, as they were unable to agree on either community structure, a synagogue, or even a cemetery. They did, however, have a rabbi who acted as *shohet*, *hazan*, and *mohel*, and they possessed one Sepher Torah. Services were held in a private house.

In 1904 there were only 10 Jewish families left here, and, when Lemnos fell to Greece in 1912, these left the island.

Lesbos

(also Mytilene)

Lesbos is mentioned by Benjamin of Tudela as having some 1,500 Jews scattered in ten villages throughout the island. When he came through Byzantine territory in the late 12th century most of Anatolia was being absorbed into the growing Seljuq Turkish Sultanate. Both Christians and Jews were leaving Anatolia at that time to avoid being caught in the midst of vicious wars. Many fled to Crete, still others to Italy, and certainly many settled on the islands of the Aegean, including Lesbos. This is also why Benjamin's itinerary follows the coastal islands rather than the coast itself. The Jewish presence on

Lesbos was most likely mixed (from various towns on the mainland) and for that reason divided into ten congregations.

After the Ottoman conquest of Constantinople in 1453 Lesbos was frequented by Jews who specialized in the production of the fine kosher cheeses that were exported to the capital.

In the 19th century, there was still a Jewish community of some 200 on Lesbos, most having close connections with either Smyrna or Gallipoli. But by 1912 only 30 were left and these emigrated after 1912 when the island was ceded to Greece.

Modon

(also Methone)

Modon is south of Pylos on the shore of the Ionian Gulf. There appears to have been a Jewish community here during the 12th century, but it was not until the Venetians took control of it in the early 13th century that Jews are recorded as having a sizeable presence. In the late 15th century, there were 300 families here, all living in a ghetto outside the city walls. They were actively involved in commerce, the dyeing of textiles, and leather tanning.

In 1501 Modon fell to the Ottomans and the ghetto was demolished, permitting the Jews to reside within the city. The community grew with the arrival of Sephardi immigrants. Thirty years later, Modon was dealt a death blow by the Knights of Malta when they attacked it and carried off large numbers of Muslim and Jewish slaves. A century later, during the Veneto– Turkish war of 1646, Modon again suffered badly and it appears that its remaining Jewish community moved elsewhere. Today there are no recognizeably Jewish remnants.

Nafpactos

(also Lepanto)

There is neither documentary nor archeological evidence to verify a Jewish presence in Nafpactos in antiquity. Nonetheless, it is most probable that there was a Jewish community here, due to its dominant location on the Gulf of Corinth as a major port for Aetolia, as well as its close association with Patras, located opposite on the Peloponnese. The presence of sizeable Jewish communities in Corinth and Sikyon, also on the gulf, lends additional credibility to this view.

Benjamin of Tudela is our earliest source of information on the existence of an organized community here. He noted 100 Jews, though most likely he was referring to householders, so that the total Jewish population was approximately 500. Adjacent Patras had only 250 Jews, which can be attributed to the chaos caused by Norman attacks on the Peloponnese. The opportunity for more secure commercial and domestic conditions in Nafpactos came to an end in the aftermath of the Fourth Crusade. The port was caught up in the rivalries between the Byzantine despot of Epirus and the Crusader principate in the Morea (Peloponnese), until in 1294 it passed into the hands of Philip of Anjou through his marriage with Tamar of Arta. During the next 100 years, the Jews may have enjoyed some economic advancement due to reduced pressure from Epirus, but in 1380 Nafpactos was seized by Albanians. In 1407 it was sold to the Venetians.

We can only assume that in general the Jews of the town fared well or badly according to the whims of the dominant power. There was undoubtedly a sizeable increase in the community when Patras was taken by Constantine Palaeologos in 1429 and it is recorded that most of the Patras Jews crossed over to Nafpactos. The Jews were certainly Romaniote, Greek speaking and mostly involved in commerce, though it is possible that they were landholders as well. Olives, oil, wine, and iron exports, as well as some dealings in slavery, appear to have been the basis of their economic life here.

From what little we know, Venetian control was never especially tight. The continued presence of Albanians was a source of many problems until 1499. Then the Albanians surrendered the town to the Ottomans, who by this time controlled most of the Peloponnese. Patras and Nafpactos once again became cooperative entrepots dominating what in Turkish was called "Kucuk Canakkale" (the "Little Dardenelles"), though neither escaped further attempts on the part of Venetians to reestablish their dominance over the Gulf of Corinth. By 1521, there were only 84 Jewish families in Nafpactos, and in 1571 the famous Battle of Lepanto took place not far away, with the Ottomans suffering their first major naval defeat against a Christian armada.

Despite their defeat, the Ottomans recovered sufficiently to consolidate their holdings in Greece. Evlivye Celebi visited Nafpactos in 1670. He appears to have enjoyed his visit but does not mention the Jews, though they must have already had quite a large community, because in 1700 there were 850 Jews here, out of a total population of 5,000 (2,500 Christians and 1,670 Muslims). By this time the Romaniote character of the community must also have undergone certain changes with the arrival of Jews from Spain, Sicily, and Apuleia (Italy). The fact that there were two synagogues would tend to support the conclusion that there were two congregations.

That there were frictions and even commercial rivalry between Jews and Christians is shown in an interesting event that took place not long after the Venetians managed to seize the town in 1701. A young Christian shepherd and itinerant preacher from Kalavrita appeared in Nafpactos and caused considerable commotion by denouncing the Jewish practice of closing their shops on Saturdays for Shabbat. In itself this implies that the Jews had for a time been in a position of economic strength sufficient to enable them to assert their own customs. The fact that they were now forced to comply with Christian practices seems to indicate that they had, at some earlier time, lost that position.

During the 18th century, Nafpactos suffered greatly with the extension of Ali Pasha's control into southern Greece. Albanian raids, plus the consequences of restored Ottoman rule, resulted in a general decline. By 1806 there were only 30 Jewish families (approximately 150 persons) here, out of a total population of 2,650. During the Greek Revolution the community and its synagogues vanished.

Five gravestones dating from the 16th century are all that remains of the former cemetery and these, unfortunately, are in private hands.

Naxos

Naxos is not mentioned anywhere as having had a Jewish community prior to the 13th century. After the dismemberment of the Byzantine Empire under the Fourth Crusade, Naxos fell under the sway of Venice and appears to have attracted Jews: either Venetian or, possibly, Romaniote. Nothing is known of that community.

In the middle of the 16th century, Naxos fell to the Ottomans, and in 1566 Joseph Nasi, the son–in–law and nephew of Dona Grazia Mendes, was appointed Duke of Naxos by Selim II. Joseph Nasi (or, as he is also known, Don Jose Mendes) is an elusive character in contemporary historical accounts. Quite apart from his decided interest in furthering Jewish settlement in Eretz Israel, especially in Tiberias, he was also a shrewd opportunist and his influence on Selim II was not entirely positive. The great vizier Sokullu Mehmet was justifiably quite wary of Don Jose and especially of his self–aggrandizing influence on Selim. After Selim's death in 1575, Don Jose's star began to wane until he appears to have been discredited after the Battle of Lepanto. It is not surprising that someone like Sokullu Mehmet, who was aristocratic, learned, and committed to the public welfare, did not get along with Don Jose. After all, the latter, like many of the Marranos, was considered outrageous even by Jews, because of his behaviour and his dandy habits in dress and manners. Don Jose never visited Naxos, which was ruled in absentia by his representative, Franciso Coronello, a descendant of the famous Castillian Seneor family. It is most likely that the Jewish community was enlarged at about that time by the arrival of Sephardi Jews. After 1570 the Jewish quarter was re–located north of the present "Bourgo."

The early synagogue (for which we have no date) was in the immediate vicinity of where the church of Hagia Sophia still stands. The church had been constructed in 1545 within the synagogue's courtyard. Later, a new synagogue was built just behind the present Fontanna Fountain. Since by the late 16th century, the arrival of Marranos. or, at best, Spanish Jews into a Romaniote community usually meant inner–communal crises, the new synagogue undoubtedly represents a separate congregation. This building apparently collapsed in 1758.

Statistics regarding the size of the community are scarce. In 1579 there were 500 members, but by 1621 this figure had fallen to 283, with three rabbis serving their needs. Silk production and weaving appear to have been their main occupations.

During the Russo–Turkish War of 1770-74, the Russian fleet occupied Naxos for a short period. The Jews were harassed and the majority fled. By the beginning of the 20th century only three families. By 1941 there were none.

Nothing remains of either synagogue. The cemetery, which was once at the base of the Aplomata Hill just behind where the Travis Fountain is today, is also gone.

Parga

Parga is a port town in Epirus, just south of the port of Igoumenitsa. Little mention is made of it in antiquity, though it figures as a footnote in the accounts of the Battle of Actium in 31 B.C.E. Augustus brought his fleet together here just prior to setting out to defeat Mark Anthony.

In the 14th century, Greek–speaking Albanians descended from the mountains and settled most of the surrounding promontory. In 1401 they requested that Venice take control. Under the Venetians, Parga prospered and attracted not only Rabbinical Jews but a Karaite community as well. We know little if anything about either community other than the that they raised especially fine citrons (*ethrogim* in Hebrew), which were highly sought after in European and North African Jewish communities for use as one of the necessary liturgical plants during the celebration of Sukkoth (the Feast of Tabernacles). Vast quantities of these were packed and shipped directly from Parga.

Ali Pasha's revolt, which had a great effect on commerce in Epirus and in northern Greece in general, caused considerable consternation to Jews throughout the Diaspora, concerning the continued availability of citrons. There was some rivalry between the Jews of Parga and those of Corfu over the commerce in *etrogim* and, after the turn of the 19th century, Parga lost its dominance of the market.

Today there is nothing to bear witness to the Jews of Parga save the fine groves of citrons, descendants of those they planted and cared for.

Patras

A Jewish presence in Patras dates back to Roman times but, as in the case of most Jewish communities in Greece, it was not continuous. There is reliable information regarding the existence of a community during early Byzantine times until the 12th century, when Benjamin of Tudela visited the city and found 50 Jews living here with two resident rabbis.

After the Latin conquest of the Peloponnese in the 13th century, Patras was governed by its Catholic archbishop and Jews were allowed to retain many of the rights they'd had under Roman–Byzantine law, including the right to own property and till the land. At that time the community would have been Romaniote. From names found on surviving epitaphs in Mistra (Sparta), it appears that there was close contact between the two towns. Unfortunately, almost nothing is known of the Jews of Patras during the following two centuries, other than the fact that the community continued to exist. Shortly after the Ottoman conquest in the late 15th century, Jews from Spain, Sicily, and Apuleia (Italy) settled here and substantially enlarged the Jewish presence. It has been suggested that there were four congregations here at that time, each maintaining its own *minhag* and traditions.

In the mid–17th century, Patras had a total population of 5,000 (Muslims, Christians, and Jews). One third of this total were Jews and they played an important role in the economic life of the town. As a significant port, Patras had sea links with Corinth to the east and, via the Ionian Islands to the west, to Venice and Crete. Opposite Patras, the Jewish community at Nafpactos maintained close relations. Undoubtedly the Jews here, as elsewhere, were primarily involved in textiles (mainly silk), as well as dyeing. At that time it is likely that there was an Ashkenazi congregation in Patras possibly made up of German Jews, because we know that the father of Shabbetai Zvi, Mordocai, was born here and later moved to Izmir. The name "Sevi" or "Zvi" is not a Sephardi name and it is known that Shabbetai knew some German.

During the 17th century this time Jews were active in a number of professions including medicine, textile manufacture and trade. It is also likely that the Jews were involved in the very lucrative slave market and may thus have had close contacts with Kalamata, which was its regional center.

The Jewish quarter at that time was located to northeast of the citadel and the cemetery was not far away, across the valley that drops from its walls. Nothing remains of either.

During the 18th century, Patras in general and the Jews in particular fared badly. A plague raged through the city in 1756. There were several attacks by the Venetians and a general economic shift resulted in reducing the importance of the city. To these calamities must be added the confusion wrought by Ali Pasa in his attempt to create an independant state out of Epirus. By 1805 Patras could boast of only a few Jewish families. With the Greek revolt of 1821, the Jews everywhere in the Peloponnese were either slaughtered, forced to convert to Christianity, or moved north. By 1829 there were no Jews in the Peloponnese, much less Patras.

With the creation of a Greek state in 1832 and the cessation of hostilities with the Ottomans, Patras once again became an important entrepot and individual Jews were attracted to the town. Many of these appear to have come from Zakynthos, Arta, and Preveza, and certainly Corfu. By 1905 a community was incorporated under law, and a cemetery had been acquired. In 1921 a synagogue was built.

The new synagogue resembled those constructed in Greece under direct Venetian influence. The ground floor contained offices as well as the rabbi's quarters, while the first floor was occupied by the

Exterior of the synagogue of Patras, built in 1926, photographed in November of 1978, two years prior to its demolition. The entrance proper is to the right. The door on the left led to the rabbi's offices and home. (Photo: Timothy DeVinney/Jewish Museum of Greece)

The bema of the former Patras synagogue in November of 1978. In keeping with the Romaniote tradition this was set against the west wall. (Photo: Timothy DeVinney/ Jewish Museum of Greece)

synagogue proper, and the school. The interior furnishings of the synagogue were constructed by Christian carpenters from Corfu in neo–classic style. The interior layout followed that of the Scuola Greca also of Corfu, with the *ehal* against the east wall and, axially opposite to it, an elevated bema with two sets of stairs. The benches for the congregants were arranged facing each other along the axis. Additional benches were arranged along the walls and a *mehitza* (women's section) was separated from the sanctuary by a latticed screen. From surviving *tikkim* (Torah cases), *me'ilim*, (Torah coverings), and silver dedications, it appears that gifts were given to the synagogue at its dedication by the Herakleion Jewish community (which was in the process of being dissolved), as well as by the Scuola Greca in Corfu.

By 1941 the community had grown considerably and numbered some 240 members. Greek–speaking, they were fully integrated into the economic and social life of Patras and were on good terms with their fellow citizens. The community was connected by marriage with the communities at Arta, Preveza, Corfu, and Zakynthos. From

The bema of the Patras synagogue as reconstructed in the Jewish Museum of Greece, Athens. (Photo: Timothy DeVinney/Jewish Museum of Greece)

books, posters, and ravaged documents found under the *ehal*, it seems that there was an active Zionist youth group, as well as a progressive program in Hebrew for the children.

Shortly before March of 1944, most of the community fled Patras and went into hiding, in either nearby villages or the mountains with the partisans. A dozen or so families remained and were arrested, transported to Athens and subsequently to Auschwitz Birkenau, where they perished.

At the termination of the Second World War, attempts were made to revive the community. The synagogue and its contents had all been saved, though many surviving members chose to move to Athens, or to emigrate to either Israel or the US. By 1979 an official decision was made to dissolve the community. The contents of the synagogue were removed for safe–keeping to the Jewish Museum of

The ehal *of the former Patras synagogue in November of 1978, two years before the building was demolished. To the right in the background is the grill that separated the* mehitza *from the main body of the synagogue. (Photo: Timothy DeVinney/Jewish Museum of Greece)*

The ehal *of the Patras synagogue as it is today in the Jewish Museum of Greece, Athens. (Photo: Timothy DeVinney/Jewish Museum of Greece)*

Greece in Athens and the building was razed. The synagogue interior has been reconstructed in the museum and was re–dedicated with the name K'K Alkabetz by the Chief Rabbi of France, S. Sirat in 1984. Many of *ketubbot* (wedding contracts), liturgical silver, and textiles and *tikkim*, (Torah cases) are on display in the museum as well.

In Patras itself there is nothing now to indicate the passing of its Jewish community, other than 30 inscriptions dating back to the 16th century, which are in the storehouse of the Archeological Museum.

Preveza

Modern Preveza rests on the site of one of several cities founded by King Pyrrhus of Epirus—in this case, the city of Berenikia, named after his mother–in–law. From the time it was founded in 290 B.C.E,

Preveza has had a tumultuous history, because the western coast of Greece in general was open to piracy in antiquity, and raiding Normans and others in the early Middle Ages.

Benjamin of Tudela passed near Preveza, but makes no mention of any Jews, and it is therefore likely that there were few if any residing here. After the 15th century, Preveza changed hands frequently: to Venice in 1499, to Ottoman Turkey in 1699, again to Venice in 1717, to the French in 1797, and in the following year Ali Pasha claimed it again for the Ottomans. In the 16th century, we know that Preveza had an active Jewish community of some importance, involved in trade in the Adriatic. It appears, however, to have died out, perhaps due to the unsettled times at the end of the century. In any case, little is known of it.

In general, Jews are seldom if ever mentioned in connection with Preveza until after the middle part of the 19th century. Then Jews from Arta and Ioannina and a few from Corfu began to set up businesses here, but their numbers were not sufficient to form a community until 1903. At that time a synagogue was built, and formal recognition obtained for legalization under R. Moshe of Ioannina.

In 1912, the town of Preveza was incorporated into the modern Greek state. By 1920 the community numbered 85 households (about 450 persons), most of them originally from Arta. There was a school with 105 children in attendance and at least one teacher from the Alliance Israelite Universelle.

By 1940 the Jewish community had shrunk to 250. Many had emigrated to Athens, Patras, or even the US. In March of 1943, almost the entire community was arrested by the Nazis and sent with the first convoy of Jews from Athens to Auschwitz. Out of the Preveza Jews, 172 were immediately chosen for the sonderkommandos. From the entire community there were only 15 survivors. The community is now extinct and nothing remains to mark its brief existence.

Rethymnon

There are no surviving remains from Jewish life in Rethymnon. The exact location of the Jewish quarter is only a matter of conjecture though it appears to have been located roughly in the area bordered by Melesinou, Smyrnis, and Koroneou streets. The location of the cemetery is unknown and an inscription noted by Gerola in the beginning of this century has been lost. In the back of the Archeological Museum is a stele with a Magen David and an inscription in Russian. It marked the grave of an unknown Russian Jewish sailor, who apparently died during the Allied occupation of Crete, before its declaration as a republic in 1909.
(For a historical account of the Rethymnon Jewish community, see the historical introduction under HANIA).

Samos

Samos, like Lesbos, may have received large Jewish immigration during the late llth and early 12th centuries as a consequence of the Seljuq expansion into Anatolia. Samos was visited by Benjamin of Tudela toward the end of the 12th century and he mentions "300 Jews" on the island. If that number refers only to households, it would mean some 1,500 Jews were resident here at that time.

Samos was depopulated after the Ottoman conquest in 1453, and remained so until the 17th century. After that its fortunes were such that it would not have been attractive for Jewish settlement. It was ruled by an archbishop for a time, then suffered heavy damage during the Greek revolt, and finally in 1834 became almost autonomous under a Greek prince. It was united formally to Greece in 1912.

Serres

(also Siris, Serrai, and Siroz)

Serres is one of the most important cities in Macedonia. It was known as Siris in antiquity, Serrai by the Byzantines, and Siroz by the Ottomans. It has had a very turbulent history, which may account for the lack of any reliable information regarding its Jewish community until well into the 14th century. From the 4th century it bore the brunt of Visigothic, Hunnic, Alanic, Bulgarian Avaric, Slavic and Catalan invasions.

Finally, in 1368, it was seized by the Ottomans and after that date it entered into a period of relative tranquility and prosperity until it was burned and ravaged by the Bulgarians during the period of the First and Second Balkan Wars of our century.

We know there were Jews living in the city for part, if not all, of its history, because there was a Romaniote host community here to receive the Sephardi Jews who arrived in the early 16th century. There also appears to have been a small Ashkenazi community and, to judge by family names, still other Jews who had come from North Africa as well as Apuleia in Italy.

There is some evidence that there was a good deal of tension within the community, which would only be natural considering the diverse origins of its original members, who were in turn numerically swamped by Spanish Jewish arrivals. An early communal law, ratified by the Ottomans, forbade the creation of a new congregation or the building of a second synagogue.

The Great Synagogue of Serres was quite imposing. Although it was burned in the late 18th century, rebuilt, burnt again in the early 19th century, and then rebuilt a last time, it kept to its original form. It is said to have been able to hold over 2,000 persons and we are fortunate to have a description of it. The Kal Gadol, as it was known, had an imposing exterior with a great lantered dome that had the notoriety of being higher than that of the nearby Christian church. The structure itself was roughly square and the interior was dominated by the dome under which stood the bema on an elevated platfrom, with two sets of 15 steps. The lower areas of the bema were decorated with pastoral paintings and the upper portion inscribed with the names of donors. There must have been columns supporting a baldequin over the bema as silver and glass lamps hung all about it. The rim of the dome was also hung with lamps. The interior was well lit during the day by 26 large windows (according to a tradition, this was the numerical equivalent of the Holy Name). The *ehal* was in a niche in the east wall. The *mehitza* (women's section—also known as the *snoga*) was located in several upper galleries. Attached to the synagogue were a rabbinical library, a yeshivah, a hall of studies, a *heder* (primary school), as well as a hospice. A small oratory or *midrash* was used for weekly prayers, or by latecomers.

Attempts to build a second synagogue (implying a second congregation) were apparently common in the 16th century during what must have been the process of Hispanization of local indigenous Jews. During that time, under the pressure of new arrivals, the Jews began to settle in other neighborhoods and some of them took this opportunity to demand their own synagogue. They were especially numerous in an area known as the Arapcilar or Dogarby Mahalessi, which was at an inconvenient distance for walking to the Kal Gadol on Shabbat (as required by Jewish law). In the end a small *midrash* was built, against the rulings of the rabbis of Kal Gadol, though a major problem remained in the absence of any Sepher Torah scrolls. Thus it was that late on a Friday night, several young men broke into the Great Synagogue through the *meldar* (toilet) to acquire some. They were discovered in the course of the attempted theft, and a fight ensued in which one of the young men was stabbed to death and several of the others seriously wounded. This incident remained for centuries as a point of contention in the community, the members of which were always quite cantankerous, it appears.

Serres boasted a number of important rabbis, most of whom came from Salonika. In the 16th century, R. Salomon ha–Hironi (the "Cedar of Lebanon," as he was known), as well as a student of his, R. Salomon ha Cohen, were active here. Both were well known for their Talmudic studies. The latter traveled widely, was a collector of manuscripts, and eventually settled in Nafpactos, where he died in 1579. A rabbinical dynasty was also established by the Miranda family in the 16th century, and many commentaries and *responsa* by rabbis of this family were widely circulated throughout the Near East in various yeshivoth.

Serres was also noted for its mystics and kabbalists. There were three societies that carried out kabbalistic studies according to the discipline of the Zohar. As late as 1870, two prominent families, the Amon and Ovadia, were well known for their secret teachings.

The decline of Serres as a commercial center began in 1865 when new railway lines were laid that tended to isolate the town. As if to underline the traditional inner turmoil of the Jews of Serres, commercial rivalry flared up anew with the arrival of Salonika Jewish brokers and entrepreneurs. Not to be left behind, a number of very prominent Ma'min settled here at this time as well and, bizarrely, the indigenous Serres Jews began to move to Kavala, Xanthi, Drama, and even Salonika.

Located as it was in Macedonia, Serres was caught in the intense nationalist aspirations of Young Turks, Bulgarians, Serbs and Greeks. In the two Balkan wars of 1912-13 it suffered greatly during a short Bulgarian occupation prior to its being absorbed into Greece.

By 1941 the community of Serres numbered only 600 persons. In the division of Greece by the Axis Powers, Serres fell to the Bulgarians, who arrested the entire Jewish community in 1943. Shortly after the arrest they were taken to Kavala and from there to the city of Lom on the Danube where they were given over to the Germans to be shipped to Treblinka. Only 3 Jews survived.

Since the Second World War, Serres has seen great economic and urban growth and it is almost impossible to distinguish the old town from the new. Jewish remains in the old quarter have been leveled, though the former Jewish school of Serres now functions as the 16th Demotic School and can be found on Athanasiou Argyrou Street. A few old Jewish houses still stand in the vicinity.

Sparta/Mistra

Attempts have been made to interpret the famous letter from the Spartan king Areus to the High Priest Onias I, mentioned in 1 Macc. 12: 20-23 and referred to by Josephus (Ant. 12:22-26), as evidence that there was a Jewish presence in Sparta as early as the 3rd century B.C.E. Furthermore, Philo, writing shortly before Josephus, mentions Jews living in the Peloponnese and it seems unlikely that they would have avoided Sparta. However, there is no archeological evidence to support such a view.

In the course of the later 4th century, Sparta was ravaged by the Visigoths under Alaric and after this never fully recovered its fortunes. By the 6th century, Slavs were penetrating deep into Greece and by the 9th century most of the coastal areas were suffering periodic raids by Muslims from Crete.

The first dependable reference to Jews in Sparta appears in the period just after the beginning of Byzantine recovery in the 10th century, when St. Nikon was active in missionary work both in the southern Peloponnese and in Crete. Two of the great problems facing the Byzantines were the re–Christianization of Crete after its nearly complete conversion to Islam and the conversion of the many Slavs who had settled in the Peloponnese. Jews were not excluded from Nikon's endeavors. At some unspecified date in the late 10th century, Sparta was struck by plague and Nikon claimed it was caused by the Jews. At his instigation, they were driven out. Shortly afterwards, John Aratos brought back several Jews to assist in building a church and was himself beaten by Nikon for his action. It was not until Nikon died that Jews returned returned to Sparta.

Shortly after the dismemberment of the Byzantine Empire under the Fourth Crusade, William Villhardouin established himself at Sparta. Because the site of the ancient city had few natural defenses, he chose a hill located some 4 miles (7 kilometers) distant as the site of his citadel. That citadel resembles a certain type of cheese known as *mezithra* in Greek, and in time the name was corrupted into *Mistra*. Within a few years, a small town grew up around the citadel and a sufficient number of Jews were attracted to it to form a community.

In 1262 Mistra passed back into the hands of the Byzantines and its Jews probably fared well enough. They were involved in the manufacture of silk and other textiles, as well as trade. In the 14th and early 15th centuries, the town assumed a new administrative importance as the second most important city in the Byzantine Empire, and a great number of intellectuals, craftsmen, artists and artisans were drawn to it. Unfortunately, we have no documents regarding what must have been a very interesting Jewish presence here during that time.

In 1460 the town fell to the Ottomans. For the following two centuries, Jews continued to prosper and we have several references to individuals, the economic and social organization of the community, as well as several epitaphs. By the early 16th century the original Romaniote community was swelled by the arrival of Sephardi, North African, and Italian Jews. It appears that there were four synagogues and that Jews took a leading, if not dominant role in the economic life of Mistra, especially in the very lucrative silk trade.

In 1687 Mistra fell to the Venetians and suffered economically as a result. Many Jews undoubtedly left, but there are extant tombstones indicating that the community continued to exist. In 1715 when the Ottoman Turks retook Mistra, the community burst once again into activity. The French invested a great deal of capital buying raw materials, and both Jews and Turks from Tripoli and Mistra acted as middlemen.

A Greek revolt occured in 1770 in the Peloponnese, and supported by the Russians, the Greeks beseiged Mistra. The town fell and was held for a short time by the Greeks, but was then retaken and the Ottomans allowed roaming bands of Albanians to plunder at will throughout the Peloponnese. By 1780, Mistra had been reduced to an insignificant town of 8,000. (In1687, at the time of the Venetian conquest, it had numbered 50,000.) In1821, when the Greek Revolution broke out, the remaining Jews of Mistra fled to Tripoli where they were killed.

Nothing remains in Mistra to mark the passing of this community.

The old Jewish quarter was called the "Evraiki" and was located north from the upper bastion about a quarter of a mile (half a kilometer). During the Venetian occupation, Jews had lived within the walls, as well as in an outer suburb called the "Marac" or "Exohorion". There are 14 Jewish gravestones in the museum of Mistra, all dating from the 16-17th centuries, as well as an additional 37 that were deposited in the Athens Archeological Museum storerooms shortly after their removal in 1916.

Thebes

After its eclipse in late antiquity, Thebes emerged again in the 10th century as an administrative center, as well as one of the most important producers of silk. It appears that Jews very quickly became active in both the production and dyeing of silk, most of which was destined for the imperial monopoly in Constantinople. In 1147 the rich warehouses of Thebes were the target of an attack by George of Antioch, the Greek renegade admiral of King Roger I of Sicily. As one writer puts it, Thebes was "coldy and expertly looted." Not only was the silk carried off, but so were a great number of silk workers, many of whom were Jews. But Thebes was quick to recover. Twenty years later Benjamin of Tudela stayed here, and he mentions a large community of 2,000 Jews, without making any reference to the pillage of 1147. It is interesting to note that at that time there were as many Jews in Thebes—a comparatively small town—as there were in Constantinople.

In 1218 Thebes was visited by Judah al-Harizi, the medieval traveler. He was impressed by the size of the Jewish community as well as by some of its literary achievements. He is slightly critical of local poetry but highly appreciative of both the wines and conversation he enjoyed. Of all of the Jewish communities he visited in the Balkans, Thebes is the only one he mentions by name.

During the 13th and well into the 14th century, Theban Jews maintained close relations with other Romaniote Jewish communities in Corinth, Nafpactos, Patras, and, undoubtedly, Halkis. After the Ottoman conquest, however, Thebes fell on hard times. By the mid part of the 16th century there were only 100 households here, though it was still sufficiently important to attract the attention of R. Elijah Mizrahi, the second chief rabbi of the Ottoman Empire. He mentions Thebes in a *responsa* of 1525.

There appears to have been an influx of Sephardi Jews into the town at some point, because there are a number of *responsa* by R. Samuel of Medina (d. 1589) directed to Thebes from Constantinople. These seem to reflect *halakhic* (legal) problems between Romaniote and Sephardi Jews. Like most Jewish communities in the 17th century, Thebes was shaken by the messianic movement of Shabbetai Zvi and was apparently visited by a number of his folllowers.

During the 18th century, Thebes and the surrounding territories were ravaged on several occasions by Albanians. Tensions also arose within Thebes between Greeks and Jews. These are reflected in sumptuary laws regarding Jewish dress that were enacted by the rabbis to avoid provoking envy on the part of the Christians.

By 1740 the community had shrunk to 50 households. Throughout the period after 1770, the Jews found themselves caught up in the worsening conficts between Greeks, Albanians, and Ottomans. By 1821 the community had ceased to exist altogether.

The ancient Jewish quarter of Thebes was located in the southern section of the modern town at the summit of the Cadmaea, not far from the cathedral. Within living memory, the area was still known as the "Evraiki" ("Jewish"). The Jewish cemetery was on a small hill known as the "Evraiomnemata" (the "Jewish memorials") was just above the Dirke River to the west of town. Thebes has not been systematically excavated and it is likely that remains are yet to be found. In the museum of Thebes there are six epitaphs in Hebrew, dating from the 14th to 16th centuries.

Tripolis

Tripolis, in the central Peloponnese, only rose to importance after the Ottoman conquest, when was made the administrative center of the Peloponnese. Nothing is known, however, of the Jewish community here, other than that it did exist and was most likely made up of Romaniote as well as Sephardi Jews.

After 1770 Tripolis was heavily fortified, and it quite naturally became a refugee center for both Turks and Jews from throughout the Peloponnese, when the Greek revolution broke out in 1821. On the fall of Tripolis, almost all of its several thousand inhabitants, both Turkish and Jewish, were massacred.

Xanthi

We have no documentation on the Jewish community of Xanthi, aside from the fact that before the Second World War it numbered 550 Jews and after the War there were 6 Jews left here. Today there are none. The synagogue of Xanthi still stands but is no longer in use.

Exterior of the synagogue of Xanthi, photographed in 1980. (Photo: Timothy DeVinney/Jewish Museum of Greece)

Interior of the synagogue of Xanthi, built in early 20th century, view toward where the ehal once was, photographed in 1980. (Photo: Timothy DeVinney/Jewish Museum of Greece)

Zakynthos
(also Zante)

There is no documentary evidence of a Jewish presence on Zakynthos prior to the 16th century C.E. The fact that Spanish Jews began to settle here after the Expulsion, however, would seem to hint at the existence of a prior community. This community would doubtless have been Romaniote and within the Venetian economic hegemony over the Ionian and Cretan seas which it had established in the 13th century. With the arrival of Sephardi Jews, and in keeping with common Venetian practice, the Jews were restricted to a ghetto or *zudeccha* and obliged to wear the yellow badge.

Shortly after the fall of Crete to the Ottomans in 1669, a large number of Veneto–Cretan Jews settled on Zakynthos and established their own congregation. It was located outside the old *zudeccha* and was called the "Candia" ("Cretan"). In the course of the 18th century, both the Candiote and Sephardi synagogues were expanded, indicating a substantial increase in the size of both congregations. Mention should also be made of the fact that the alternative name of the Etz Hayyim synagogue in Hania, Crete, was "Zakynthinote," indicating close ties between the two Jewish communities.

Several Zakynthinote Jews achieved prominence, including a branch of the Del Medigo family and Avraham ben Shabetai ha Kohen (1670-1729) both from Crete. The later was noted for his poetical works as well as his commentaries on biblical subjects.

The lintel of the Candiote synagogue of Zakynthos as it was just after the earthquake of 1952. (Jewish Museum of Greece)

The main street in the Jewish quarter of Zakynthos as it was in 1948, before the earthquake of 1952. The second large structure from the left is one of two Zakynthos synagogues (not the Candiote). Like the synagogues of Corfu and Patras, it was built on the first floor—in the Venetian manner. (Jewish Museum of Greece)

During the 18th and early 19th centuries, more Jews arrived to enlarge the Jewish presence here. For the most part these new arrivals were Romaniotes fleeing the havoc that raged in the Peloponnese during the rebellion of Ali Pasa and then the Greek revolution of 1821. As Greek–speaking Jews, they very quickly asserted their predominance and Ladino was made obsolete. By the end of the 19th century both synagogues continued to function and the total Jewish population numbered 310 persons. Jewish economic interests on Zakynthos were overshadowed by those of nearby Corfu, and for the most part Jews were involved in modest trade, and small crafts.

In 1941 Zakynthos and the Ionian Islands fell to the Italians, who

The main street in the Jewish quarter of Zakynthos as it was immediately following the earthquake of 1952. Compare with photograph on facing page where the palm tree can be seen standing in both. (Jewish Museum of Greece)

had little sympathy for German racism. On the surrender of the Italians to the Allies in 1943, however, all of this changed radically. In the spring of 1944 an order was issued under General Stroop for the arrest and transportation of the Ionian Jews. Greek–speaking and commercially insignificant, the Jews were dramatically protected by the mayor of Zakynthos as well as by its archbishop, Chrysostomos. Almost all of them fled to the mountains or went into hiding. At the termination of hostilities virtually the entire community could be accounted for.

In 1947 a large number of Zakynthinote Jews made *aliya* (emigrated) to Israel and still others moved to Athens. In 1952 the island was struck by a severe earthquake and the entire Jewish quarter and its two synagogues were destroyed. Not long afterwards, the remaining Jews moved to Athens.

All that remains of the Jewish presence in Zakynthos are the cemetery, not far from the town, and a memorial plaque marking the site of the former Candiote Synagogue.

Glossary

The following terms used in this guide may be unfamiliar.

Aedicule. A small room or niche for containing a statue or giving prominence to it.

Alliance Israelite school. See Alliance Israelite Universelle.

Alliance Israelite Universelle. An international organization founded in Paris in 1860 for the purpose of furthering Jewish education. After 1890 it was especially active in Jewish communities in the Ottoman Empire, the Balkans in general, and in Greece. Its schools furthered secular education and classes were taught in French. Its central archives in Paris are still one of the main sources of information regarding the conditions in Jewish communities in Greece during the late 19th and early 20th centuries.

apse. An apse is a concave projection usually found in basilicas. In Hellenistic and Roman civic buildings this could contain a throne or image of the emperor. In Christian buildings it provided room for the sanctuary and in Jewish synagogues it quite often provided space for the Throne of Moses or for the *ehal*.

Arvit. Evening prayer service, one of three periods of prayer that are recited daily by observant Jews. They correspond roughly to the periods of the day during which special offerings were made in the Temple. (See also Ma'ariv and Shahrit).

Ashkenazi (Pl. Ashkenazim). A Jew from central or eastern Europe. Traditionally they followed the Babylonian Talmud and had a ritual or *minhag* of their own. Today the term is used to quite loosely to characterize non–Sephardi Jews, though this use is not entirely accurate.

Atrium. An atrium is a courtyard, usually in front of a basilica.

b. Abbreviation for "ben" ("son" in Hebrew). In a name "b." indicates the son of the person named.

Babylonian Captivity. The period between 587 and 534 B.C.E. after the destruction of the First Temple. It is sometimes known simply as the Exile.

Babylonian Talmud. The written version of the Oral Law, as it was developed and codified in the Persian Academies. It is more comprehensive and inclusive than the shorter Palestinian Talmud, which eventually it replaced. Today it is universal, but in the early Middle Ages it was especially important in the formation of Ashkenazi and Sephardi Jews and those within the Islamic world. Byzantine Jewry tended to use the Palestinian Talmud until quite a late date.

Balkan Wars. A period of conflict in the southern Balkans that lasted from 1912 to 1913. The First Balkan War saw an alliance of Serbia, Bulgaria, and Greece against the Ottoman Empire. Greece acquired Epirus, several of the Aegean Islands and also was recently established Cretan Republic. In the following year, with the Second Balkan War, the former allies went to war with each other and Greece managed to acquire Salonika as well as a large portion of Macedonia.

basilica. Originally, a term used for royal audience halls under the Hellenistic monarchs of the Near East. In time it was adopted by Romans to refer to civic buildings, and later by both Christians and Jews for religious structures. The term is used loosely for buildings that are long and more often than not divided internally by rows of columns. In layout it was preceded by an atrium and terminated in a apse.

B.C.E./C.E. ('Before the Common Era" and "Common Era") Equivalent to B.C./A.D. and in general less awkward for Muslims, Jews, Buddhists, and other non–Christians.

bema. (Gr. "step") A raised platform or pulpit in a synagogue, from which the Torah is elevated and read. It appears to have been inspired in synagogues by the bema that was erected in the Temple of Jerusalem by Ezra after the Babylonian Captivity and from which he publicly read and instructed the newly returned Judaeans. It symbolizes Mt. Sinai and the "Giving of the Law to Israel." Its position in a synagogue varies.

Benjamin of Tudela. A Spanish Jewish gem merchant who travelled through Byzantine territories in the late 12th century. He entered Greece at Corfu and eventually made his way through many Byzantine towns, noting the Jewish communities, economic activities, and leadership. His work the *Book of Travel (Sepher ha–Massa'ot)* is one of the main sources of over–all information on the Jews of the 12th century in Greece.

Beth Din. A rabbinical court made up of three rabbis. Questions of marriage, divorce, and other decisions regulating Jewish religious as well as social life are under the jurisdiction of the Beth Din.

blood libel. Accusations against Jews claiming that they have committed ritual murder. An unknown Greek writer from Alexandria, by the name of Democritus, was the first to make the accusation in the 1st century C.E., claiming that Jews would sacrifice a Greek boy every seven years. The story was embellished by Apion and appears to be the root of all later accusations. In Greece such slanders against Jewish communities and individuals became very virulent in the 19th century, especially in Corfu, Rhodes, Chios, and Crete.

C.E. Common Era. See B.C.E.

chief rabbi. A title given to rabbis who have either jurisdiction or authority over a Jewish community or over other rabbis. See also hahambasi.

Diaspora. A somewhat loose term that characterizes Jewish life and fortunes outside Eretz Israel. There have been several "diasporas," in which Jews have been forced to leave Eretz Israel, as in the periods after the Babylonian destructuion of Jersualem and the First Temple in 587 B.C.E. or in 71 C.E. after the destruction of the Second Temple and again in the 2nd century with the disaster of the Barkochba rebellion. The attraction of Hellenism and its international character led to a peaceful dispersion of Jews into great cities of the Greek world such as Alexandria, Antioch and, of course, the many towns and cities mentioned in this book. The Sephardi Jews at times referred to the expulsion from Spain as a Second Exile (the first being the Babylonian).

Dönme. From the Turkish root "to turn." The Dönme are the followers of Shabbetai Zvi, who either entered into Islam on his conversion or after his death. The term "Dönme" is slightly derogatory and they are more properly called "Ma'min." (See Ma'min.)

ehal. Sometimes referred to as the "Aron ha–Kodesh." The *ehal* is the place in which the Scrolls of the Law (Hb. Sepher Torah) are stored and protected in a synagogue. It can be either a small room constructed in an apse, or a large armoire–like edifice. It is, as a rule, to be found at the eastern end of the synagogue.

Eretz Israel or Eretz. The "Land of Israel" is the territory specifically promised to Abraham and his descendants, and to Moses and the Israelites at the time of the making of the Covenant. It is this "land" in which all of the halakic demands of the Law must be observed.

Etz Hayyim. Literally "Tree of Life." At times the Sepher Torah is referred to as the Etz Hayyim and among Romaniote Jews it was common to give this as a name to synagogues.

ex voto. Dedications, either in the form of silver tablets or other small ornaments inscribed with names, dates and prayers. Among Romaniote Jews they are often called "Shaddayoth" as they usually have the Holy Name "Shaddai" on them.

firman (or ferman). An Ottoman term for an official or legal writ.

Gaon. A title of honor meaning "eminence" that was given to the deans of rabbinical schools, especially in Islamic lands.

Gothic Invasions. A general term used to cover the period from the late 4th century until the middle of the 5th when Germanic or Gothic tribes penetrated and broke up the unity of the Roman Empire and established themselves as nation states in the West.

Gnostic. Religious initiates into secret teachings. These teachings usually claimed to provide the initiate, or Gnostic, with arcane wisdom. In the early Common Era, there were Jewish, pagan, and even Christian Gnostics, and it is still not clear if and how they influenced each other.

hahambaşi. The Ottoman term for a chief rabbi. It has a general meaning for any important rabbi but a specific meaning as well. A somewhat late attempt to authenticate the authority of the *hahambaşi* of Istanbul in 1834 claimed that Mehmet II, shortly after the taking of Constantinople, appointed the Byzantine chief rabbi of the city, a Cretan named Moses Kapsalis, as the chief rabbi of the Ottoman Empire with the title *hahambaşi*. By 1526, when the successor of Kapsali, R. Eliahu Mizrahi died, there were so many difficulties between the Romaniotes and the newly arrived Sepharadim that the office was not filled there after until 1834, when it was "revived." The chief rabbi of Istanbul is still called the *hahambaşi*.

Halaka. A binding legal decision derived either from the Torah or from tradition.

hazan. A cantor. Among Greek Jews the title is usually given to a secondary rabbi in a community.

herem. (Heb. "excommunication'') A formal injunction against either an individual or even a community for the commission of an offence. Punishment varies according to the seriousness of the matter; for an individual it can mean banishment from the community and for a community it can mean that it is not allowed to perform certain halakically required obligations such as circumcision, ritual slaughter, etc.

High Holidays. These are the three Pilgrim Festivals of Pesah (Passover), Shavuoth (Pentecost or Weeks) and Sukkot (Tabernacles), plus Rosh Ha–Shannah (New Year) and Yom Kippour (the Day of Atonement). The dates for these are based on the lunar calendar and thus their Julian calendar equivalents change every year.

JOINT. The American Joint Distribution Committee, which, along with HIAS (the Hebrew Immigration Aid Society), was founded in 1945 to assist in the rehabilitation of Jewish communities and to foster emigration to Eretz.

Kal. (Kehal). Congregation. i.e. Synagogue.

Karaite. A sect of Jews who maintain a literal observance of the Law of Moses (Torah) and do not accept rabbinical interpretations as contained in either the Talmud or later commentaries. They were especially active in the Byzantine and Ottoman Empires and were at odds with Rabbinical or Talmudic Jews.

kettubah. A marriage contract making clear certain obligations and responsibilities for both groom and bride. A *kettubah*, is written in Aramaic and according to a formula found in the Talmud. The handing of a *kettubah* in the presence of a *minyan* legally constitutes a wedding. Romaniote *kettubot* have some peculiarites, one of which is a small postscript signed and witnessd on the day after the marriage, in which the bride's virginity is attested to (or lack thereof, as the case might have been).

kosher (or kashrut). Food that is considered to be halakically fit for consumption. This determines not only what kind of animal can be eaten but how it is killed, examined, prepared for cooking, and may or may not be eaten with it. Fish without scales, for example, are forbidden, as are mammals without a cloven hoof and a split lip. (See also Shohet.)

Ladino (also Judezmo). A Castilian Spanish dialect spoken by the Sepharadim. It evolved after the expulsion from Spain in 1492, and includes heavy accretions of Turkish, Arabic, Greek, and Slav.

Luah ha Brith. The Ten Commandments or Tables of the Law.

lulav. A palm branch. The *lulav*, in conjunction with an *etrog* and a *menorah*, can often be seen in Hellenistic Jewish symbolism and is often found in Jewish catacombs and decorative arts. *Lulav* and *etrog* are the most important plants (along with myrtle and willow) used in the performance of rituals during the Feast of Sukkot (Tabernacles).

Ma'ariv. One of the three recitations of daily prayer. Ma'ariv is said in the afternoon. (Cf. Arvit and Shahrit)

Magen David. The Shield of David. A six pointed star made up of two triangles. It was not, until very recent times, a specifically Jewish symbol and can be found in Greece, Turkey, and the Near East in use by Muslims, Christians, as well as Jews, in a variety of decorative devices.

mahallasi. Ottoman term for a neighborhood. A "Yahudi Mahallasi" was a Jewish quarter but was not, in any sense of the word, a ghetto.

Mahzor. Festival prayer book. (See also High Holidays)

Marrano. A term of derogation used to refer to Portuguese and Spanish Jews who had converted to Christianity. Sometimes they are referred to as "conversos." Especially after their arrival in the Ottoman Empire, the Marranos had difficulties in orthodox Jewish communities and usually established their own congregations.

megillah. A scroll from which is read one of the texts of the Scriptures. Five prescribed *meggilot* must be read each year. The one most often heard is that of Esther used at Purim. Ioannina was especially famous for its very beautiful *megillah* cases.

mehitza. The women's section in a synagogue, which is set off by being located on an upper floor or segregated by means of a grill or *eben* curtain.

menorah. A seven branched candelabra. In antiquity it symbolized the Temple and was, along with the *lulav* and *etrog*, one of the most common images of Jewish identity.

Midrash. A formal system of the study of the Law.

millet. A semi–autonomous ethno–religous minority recognized under Shari'a (Islamic) Law. The rights of a *millet* were traditionally given to People of the Book, i.e., Jews and Christians, though it was also extended to include Zoroastrians and some others.

mikveh. A ritual bath consisting of 40 cubits of "un–contained" (i.e. running) water. The laws governing the use of a *mikveh* are quite complex and require total emersion three times. For women it is necessary to perform a *mikveh* after menstruation and birth, and for both men and women after sexual intercourse. For persons who write the Torah or even *mezzuzot (shoferim)*, it is also required that they perform a *mikveh*, before starting to work. Christian baptism is a form of the *mikveh*.

minhag. Custom or rite. In Greece there were traditionally two main *minhagim*: that of the Romaniotes and that of the Sepharadim.

These both differed in some respects from the rite of Ashkenazi Jews but not in essence.

minyan. A quorum of ten Jewish males, the presence of which is required to perform or make legal certain rites of passage or prayers. (See also oratory)

mohel. A person qualified to perform circumcisions.

Ma'min (Pl. Ma'minler). Also known as the "Dönme" (from the Turkish root "to turn"). The Ma'min are the followers of Shabbetai Zvi who either entered into Islam on his conversion or after his death. The term "Dönme" is slightly derogatory and they are more properly called "Ma'min." The Ma'min are sometimes erroneously called "crypto–Jews" . In fact they have an identity and eschatology distinctly their own and the few Jewish practices they observe are well integrated into an autonomous system of thought and practice. It is estimated that 10 to 13 % of the population of Salonika were Ma'minler before 1922. Well before this date they were active in trade, commerce, the Ottoman civil service, banking, and the military. As Muslims they were forced to emigrate to Turkey during the exchange of populations between Greece and Turkey in 1922. Today there are perhaps as many as 30,000 Ma'minler living in Turkey.

Nasi. "prince " A title once born by the chief officer of the Senhedrin (Great Assembly) in Jerusalem. It was later used by the patriarch until the dissolution of the office under Emperor Theodosios II. (See also Patriarch)

ner tamid. A lamp kept burning before the *ehal*. It is meant to symbolize the ever–burning lamp that once stood in the Temple.

oratory. A room used for ordinary prayers, especially during weekdays. These were normally called *minyans* by Romaniote Jews in Greece.

Patriarch. As a formal title amongst Jews this refers to the nasi or "prince" of the Jews who was the official head of the Jewish people in exile under Roman law from the 2nd century until the early 5th century C.E. when the office was abolished. Not to be confused with the five Christian patriarchs.

pergola. An arbor or covered walkway. In the courtyards of Greek synagogues, pergolas were normally used to support grape–arbors and as communal *sukkahs* (huts) for the celebration of Sukkot.

Pesah (Passover). The celebration of the departure of the Israelites from Egypt into Sinai. The Feast lasts for eight days, during which no leavened bread (or other food subject to fermentation by yeast) may be eaten.

Pilgrim Festivals. The three festivals of Pesah, Shavuot and Sukkot. These were celebrated where possible by going "up" to Jerusalem (hence "pilgrim"). Each has a historical as well as agricultural significance. They mark turning points in the creation of the Israelite people as well as changes in the season (planting and harvesting).

piyyutim. Special hymns added to the liturgy. These can be of great beauty and in the case of Romaniote Jews were often written in Greek using Hebrew characters.

Purim. A festival held in the spring celebrating the saving of the Jews of Babylonia by Queen Esther. In Greece, especially among Romaniote Jews, it was a time for masquerades and theater performances of the story. Some communities had "special" Purims commemorating crises in their communal existence when they were saved from destruction. Of special interest is the "Sicilian Purim," observed by descendants of Sicilian Jews in Ioannina and central Greece. There were other special Purims celebrated in Crete, Chios, Corfu, and Komotini. These also had specially written *meggilot* that were read for the occasion. (See also *megillah*)

R. Abbreviation for "rabbi" (or "teacher").

Rabbinical Jews. Jews who recognize Talmudic and hence rabbinical interpretations of the Torah.

responsa. An exchange of letters between rabbis concerning halakic problems and decisions.

Romaniote. A Greek or Balkan Jew whose origins can be traced back to Byzantine Jewry. At one time they had their own quite distinct *minhag* and followed the the Palestinian Talmud.

Sephardi (or Sepharad). A Portuguese or Spanish Jew. Amongst the Jews in Greece, the Balkans, and Turkey, the term is used only for those Jews whose origins are in Spain or Portugal.

Sepher Torah. The Torah or Five Books of Moses (Genesis, Exodus, Leviticus, Numbers, and Deuteronomy) written on a scroll. The Law or Torah can only be read publicly from a Sepher.

Septuagint. The first translation into Greek of the Hebrew Scriptures, made in the 3rd century B.C.E. in Alexandria. In the 6th century C.E., a law was enacted under the emperor Justinian I, that forbade Jews from reading the Torah in any language other than Greek, and, specifically, they were required to use either the Septuagint translation or that of Aquila (a 2nd–century CE Greek convert to Judaism). Romaniote Jews were especially proud of maintaining this tradition well into modern times.

Shabbetai Zvi. A 17th–century rabbi from Smyrna who was proclaimed the Messiah in 1669. He was a man of considerable influence and his charismatic quality drew to him great numbers of not only Jews, but also Muslims and Christians. He eventually converted to Islam. His followers in Europe were known as Shabbeteans and were quite heterodox in their Judaism. Those who followed him into Islam became known as the Ma'min and developed a much more coherant theology and eschatology. (See also Ma'min)

Shahrit. The morning prayer recited by observant Jews. During Shahrit it is obligatory to wear a *talleth* and, on weekdays, *tephilin*. (See also Arvit and Ma'ariv.)

shofar. A ram's horn that is used as a ritual trumpet and blown on certain occasions, during Rosh Ha–Shanna and Yom Kippur.

shohet. A ritual slaughterer, whose duty is to provide kosher meat for a community.

Siddur. The book containing weekly prayers, those used on Sabbath and at the celebration of the New Moon.

sukkah. A small hut or booth that is covered with branches and is eaten in during the period of the celebration of Sukkot. It is meant to recall the days when Israel lived in such dwellings in the Sinai prior to entering Canaa. Usually in Greece there were (and still are) communal *sukkoth* built under pergolas near the synagogue.

Sukkot. The Feast of Tabernacles (or Booths). One of the three Pilgrim Festivals. (See also Pilgrim Festival and *sukkah*)

synthronos. A curved bench built around the base of an apse.

talleth. A rectangular shawl set with ritual fringes (*tsitsiot*) at its four corners, worn by Jewish men for morning prayer, on the eve of the Day of Atonement (eve of Yom Kippour), as well as during the Day of Atonement itself. The *talleth* may have been derived from the ancient Hellenistic *chlamys* and the fringes added to set Jews apart. The fringes are tied in a special manner with symbolic connotations and are intended to remind the wearer of certain commandments from Scripture.

Talmud Torah. A primary school intended to give children a basic knowledge of the Torah.

Tanah. The Holy Scriptures made up of T(Torah), N(eviim) and K(etuvim): the Law, the Prophets and Writings.

tevah. A reader's desk. In Romaniote synagogues in Greece a *tevah* is usually located in front of the *ehal* and is used during the week. In some synagogues the bema is fitted with a *tevah*.

tefillin. Two small leather boxes set with leather thongs. The Shema (the injunction: "Hear, O Israel, the Lord is thy God, the Lord is One....") is written out in its entirety on parchment and enclosed in each of the boxes. They are worn by men during morning prayers and not on Shabbat or on the major Jewish holidays. One is bound around the left arm with the box resting near the heart. The other fits on the head so that it touches the hairline (or where the hairline once was, as the case may be).

tik. A wooden or metal case holding the Sepher Torah. The custom is unique to Romaniote Jews in Greece. (The Sepharadim wrap their Sepher Torah in cloth coverings called *me'ilim*.)

Torah. The Five Books of Moses and as such the most authoritative part of Scripture. (See also Sepher Torah)

WIZO. Women's International Zionist Organization, founded in London in 1920.

yeshivah. A school or academy for the study of the Torah.

Bibliography for Further Reading

The following books have been selected to provide additional material on the Jews of Greece and the Ottoman Empire. There are a number of quite excellent bibliographies, which are complete up to the year 1989. It is anticipated that they will be updated soon.

Bibliographies

Attal, R. *Les Juifs de Grece: Bibliographie*. Jerusalem, 1984.

Kitroeff, A. *Bibliography of the Jews of Modern Greece*. New York, 1986.

Mor, M., and U. Rapaport. *Bibliography of the Works on Jewish History in the Hellenistic and Roman Periods: 1976-1980*. Jerusalem, 1984.

The *Bulletin of Judaeo Greek Studies* is quarterly published by the Faculty of Oriental Studies at Cambridge University in Great Britain. This contains recent articles, books, and notices on research in the field.

General Books of Interest

Angel, M. *The Jews of Rhodes*. New York, 1978.

Argenti, M. *The Jews of Chios*. Cambridge, 1955.

Bowman S. *The Jews of Byzantium*. Alabama, 1985.

Dalven, R. *The Jews of Ioannina*. New York, 1990.

Franco, M. *Essai sur L'Histoire des Israelites de L'Empire Ottoman*. Paris, 1980.

Galante, A. *Histoire des Juifs de Turquie*. 9 vols. Istanbul, 1990.

Lewis, B. *The Jews of Islam*. Princeton, 1984.

Levy, I. *The Jews of Rhodes*. San Francisco, 1990.

Nehama, J. *Histoire des Israelites de Salonique*. 6 vols. Thessaloniki, 1935.

Roth, C. *The House of Nasi*. Philadelphia, 1948.

——. *Dona Gracia of the House of Nasi*. Philadelphia, 1977.

Sharf, A. *Byzantine Jewry*. London, 1971.

Sephiha, H. *L'Agonie des Judeo–Espagnols*. Paris, 1990.

Stavroulakis, N. *Cookbook of the Jews of Greece*. Athens, 1988.

——. *The Jews of Greece*. Athens, 1990.

Tcherikover, V. *Hellenistic Civilization and the Jews*. New York, 1982.

Tudela, B. *The Itinerary of Benjamin of Tudela*. Miami, 1987.

Index

Notes